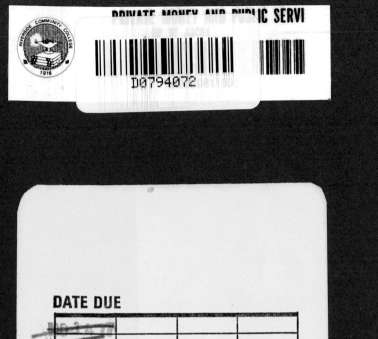

PRIVATE MONEY AND PUBLIC SERVICE

PRIVATE MONEY AND PUBLIC SERVICE

The Role of Foundations in American Society

by MERRIMON CUNINGGIM

McGRAW-HILL BOOK COMPANY

New York   St. Louis   San Francisco   Düsseldorf
London   Mexico   Sydney   Toronto

123456789BPBP798765432

Library of Congress Cataloging in Publication Data

Cuninggim, Merrimon.
    Private money and public service.

    1. Endowments—United States. I. Title.
HV97.A3C84   361.7′6′0973   72-3820
ISBN 0-07-073774-6

FIRST EDITION

To

THE FIVE IN OUR FAMILY WHO KNOW ALL ABOUT
THE JOY OF GIVING, AND HAVE TRIED TO TEACH
ME—WHITTY, LEE, PENNY, TERRY AND BUNNY.

Preface

" . . . foundations have freed large parts of the world from the curse of diseases such as malaria and yellow fever; have brought enjoyment of the arts to millions of people; have created and helped support universities and research institutes; have clarified and otherwise served the law; have in many practical ways promoted international understanding and have encouraged the cause of peace; have shown how population can be controlled and people fed; have helped develop broadly trained leadership for business and government; have significantly aided the emerging nations; have importantly contributed to our growing knowledge of physical and living nature; have been alert in aiding new fields of activity; have helped to clarify the goals of present-day humanistic scholarship; have made possible the development of important new scientific instruments for studying the atom, the cell, and the star; have, in language and area studies, anticipated and provided for some of the pressing needs of our country in its new worldwide responsibility; have created multi-million-dollar free funds for basic research; have recently developed and supported several projects to extend the opportunities of higher education to qualified Negroes; and have liberated thousands of gifted individuals from the limitations of inadequate education, thus freeing them for greater service to society." (Warren Weaver, *U. S. Philanthropic Foundations: Their History, Structure, Management, and Record,* New York, Harper & Row, 1967, p. 448.)

As a college president my father often had to call upon foundations. His batting average was not very good: he must have had ten No's for every Yes he collected, or maybe even more. But back in the twenties and thirties this was what he expected, and very few college presidents did any better.

Part of the game was to pepper foundations with so many requests that the law of averages, at least, if not their overwhelming good sense or some special inside track, would take care of you. There were fewer foundations in those days, and Ivy had the preferred position then as well as now. Dad's college wasn't Ivy; it was a small denominational institution, offending many of its own churchmen because it wasn't fundamentalist, yet specializing in training missionaries, which was hardly a major interest of foundations. As I look back on it, I think he did right well.

In spite of his being turned down over and over again, I don't remember that he was ever critical or cynical about foundations. That they could have had better sense was something the family accepted without rancor; but Mother felt this way about most of the people that Dad had to deal with—students, faculty, churchmen, tradesmen—who didn't always see eye to eye with him. Foundations did the best they could, probably; and even when they didn't, one had to take a charitable attitude. So I grew up with a healthy disrespect for the wisdom of foundations, coupled with appreciation for those occasions when they saw the light; with neither awe nor malice for them.

It is a useful point of view for one who works for a foundation. It has stood me in good stead in these recent days when charges against foundations have come to be loud, sharp, insistent and often unsound. The thing most often lacking is discrimination, between those charges that are valid and those that are not.

Thus the idea of this book was born. Having now been with the Danforth Foundation for over ten years, I have had a chance to see this and a number of other foundations in close operation. As a result I have come to feel that foundation people themselves need to be more aware of how the general public looks upon their work, and the public itself needs to be better informed about the behavior of foundations. What is America's present attitude toward philanthropy? What are the main charges being leveled against those engaged in large-scale benevolence? To what extent are these criticisms supported by the facts, and to what extent are they based on serious misunderstandings? Apart from the particular headline achievements of some of the larger and better known foundations, what is the overall record of accomplishment that foundations of all sorts and sizes have written? Does the present state of government regulation of foundations help or hinder in their performance of philanthropic purposes? What ought foundations themselves do in order to repair their public image?

For many years my colleagues and I on the Staff of the Danforth Foundation, together with members of our Board of Trustees, have addressed ourselves to such questions as they apply specifically to our operation. As time has passed I have come to think more and more about the application of such questions to other foundations and to the foundation field in general. The chance to put some of these thoughts in writing was made available to me by the Board of the Foundation in the form of a partial leave, or semi-sabbatical, which I appreciated greatly.

It will be clear enough from even a cursory reading that I write from the bias of admiration for the work of foundations in this country and an abiding belief in their value to society. My attitude is obviously affirmative, and a negative or even neutral point of view would have been impossible to sustain. In recent writings about foundations such a positive attitude has been stated less often, I believe, than the facts justify, and the exaggerated charges of critics have too seldom been questioned and examined.

A second bias, I hope, will be equally clear to the careful reader. My own experience in foundation work has made me aware that some of the charges are true, and some others have at least partial truth to them. This means that foundations have a job to do in setting their own house in order and in giving the public a better understanding of their purposes, and programs. To this end as much as to the end of affirming the value and achievements of foundations is this book written.

Yet no one can presume to speak for the foundation field as a whole, of course. Fortunately I have had lots of help, though the inadequacies of what follows are altogether my own. Out of an embarrassingly large company of staff colleagues, fellow philanthropoids of other foundations and laymen friends who have counseled me, often when they may not have been aware of it, I must mention by name two persons for whose aid I am especially indebted and deeply grateful. They are Whitty, my wife, and Kay Putnam, who works with me at the Foundation. Without them there would have been no book.

MERRIMON CUNINGGIM

Contents

PRIVATE MONEY AND PUBLIC SERVICE

I

Caught in the Act of Helping

A. INTRODUCTION

FOUNDATIONS are in serious trouble.

To whatever extent it may once have existed, the era of good feeling seems to be over. Foundations are said to be "under fire," and the loss in public confidence, either hailed or deplored, is generally proclaimed. Whether they deserve to have a poor reputation or their faults are as bad as alleged or their accomplishments have been fully appreciated are matters for careful examination in the body of this book. But the point of beginning must be the recognition that foundations are suspect.

Of all the kinds of benevolence practiced in our society, the sort that seems to be in most disrepute is the activity of the large foundations. The giving of individual donors and the work of small foundations, company and community funds and charitable trusts may also be criticized from time to time. But these agencies are less visible, whereas the large foundations are inescapably in the public eye.

The Local Family Fund of Anytown, U.S.A., may do something to displease the good citizens of the town and its environs, but very few others ever hear of it. Let the big foundations seem to misbehave, however, and the press is bound to pick it up. The news travels across the country, and the outraged reaction is registered with the foundations themselves and with congressmen. Even the local merchant, going about his innocent busi-

1

ness, may feel the pinch when he tries to sell Ford's cars, Kellogg's corn flakes, Lilly's pills or Purina's Dog Chow.

This essay is intended to examine the phenomenon of attack and defense: of widespread criticism on the one hand, and on the other, something less than widespread rejoinder. Why are the foundations in such bad odor? What, specifically, are the charges? Are they justified? Why have the foundations not made systematic, persuasive answer?

Other questions must be faced: Shorn of all boasting and glory language, what is the record of foundation achievement? Does the Tax Reform Act of 1969 help or hinder the foundations from performing their legitimate tasks? Foundations profess the support of humane values, and join with other such institutions—churches, universities, hospitals, courts of justice— in attempting to serve mankind. When their legitimate efforts are encumbered, or even proscribed, then by that much the effectiveness of the values they affirm is lessened. Do the regulations that Congress has imposed, or the attitudes that critics have expressed, prevent foundations from accomplishing their proper purpose?

Finally, what *are* their proper functions? What is the basic rationale for foundations? For philanthropy as a whole?

Before proceeding to a discussion of these questions in turn, we should pause to recognize some of the inherent difficulties. Hardly any agency in society is as poorly prepared to defend itself against attack as is a philanthropic foundation. This grows partly out of its history and partly out of its essential nature.

As for history, foundations have never been accustomed to think or act as a group, and only lately has it appeared that they need to do so. In the past it was generally felt that philanthropy was a private act, and even when one's philanthropy had come to be organized into a foundation, it had until recently been thought to be the donor's personal exercise of benevolence. If on rare occasion some other foundation were to receive unfavorable publicity, then this was obviously that other foundation's concern. Up until fairly recent times, foundations as a group simply did not recognize that their common activity of philanthropy was under more general suspicion, for the individual good name that each of them thought it possessed was felt to be sufficient protection against any possibility of public clamor.

The essential nature of foundations has also made it hard to fend off or reply to charges leveled against them. Other types of tax-exempt institutions have their built-in defenders and protagonists, usually in considerable numbers. When, say, a church or a university incurs the displeasure of some segment of the public, its parishioners or alumni, as the case may be, are ready at hand to do battle. For a church or a university the battle may turn out to be, of course, a civil war, for attack as well as defense may come from inside the institution. But the point is, such organizations have their own well-defined and numerous constituencies, whereas a foundation, even one of the very large ones, is composed of a quite small group of people.

Moreover, the very nature of the foundation's work makes it extremely awkward for the institution to call upon the support of those who have received benefit from it. None of us as children ever liked our parents' reminder, "Now say thank you." Furthermore, if recipients were to be mindful of the need for coming to the support of their benefactors without having their memory jogged, they would still feel a certain awkwardness in doing so. Wouldn't it inevitably be interpreted as an effort to ingratiate oneself further into the good graces of the foundation?

So it is that because of the very nature of a foundation's activity it has no automatic cheering section, no easy occasion for celebration, no ritual of thanksgiving or praise. When a foundation is attacked, it is all alone. Tears are not called for. All that is of moment here is to note the fact that when foundations are criticized, they often find it hard, by history and nature, to reply.

B. Definition and Diversity

Before we begin to examine the nature of the trouble in which foundations find themselves, a brief word should be said about the kind of organization we are considering. All sorts of things are called foundations, and no one type of institution has exclusive use of the word. If some agency of government or some program of community action, or some point of beginning, or some article of clothing, or some building stone, calls itself a foundation, each is within its linguistic rights.

For the purposes of this essay, however, the term "foundation" is being used to denote a non-governmental agency existing to serve the public good. Usually it is an endowed agency, its resources having been set aside as an endowment by some original donor or group of donors. But on occasion it may receive as well as disburse regular contributions, and may possess little or no endowment. Usually its way of serving the public is through the making of grants or subventions to recipients of various sorts and sizes, either individuals or organizations. On occasion, however, a foundation may support an action program of its own design, administered by its own staff. Rarely will a foundation be able to tackle anything as grandiose as "the general welfare"; it will normally choose some particular segment for its special area of concern. But most foundation charters are written in language sufficiently expansive to give room for change in direction.

Foundations of the sort that this essay considers are often modified by the adjective "private," but it is something of a misnomer and one ought to be chary about using the word. Their funds are not private, for the money no longer belongs to the original donor, whoever he is. Rather, it is public money, set aside to be so by an uncommon act of stewardship on the part of the donor. Correspondingly, the activities of foundations are not private, for a catalogue of them must be reported to the government as the representative of the people, and anyone is privileged to have a look. Their field of operation is not limited to the so-called private sector, for grants of many foundations have traditionally been made to a wide variety of governmental units and programs, large and small.

The only sense in which "private" applies is that the decisions of foundations are not in the hands of the general public or of Government. This is, of course, an immensely important

4

distinction; and the trouble is, we simply do not have a suitable word to describe the peculiar mixture of public and private that characterizes a foundation—a combination of public interest and public service with private judgment. It is for this reason that in the simplified definition above, the modifier is "non-governmental." To say it in that way may be more illuminating than simply to call foundations unmodifiedly "private." A fuller definition might run to such a complicated, jawbreaking sentence as the following: Foundations are non-governmental agencies, privately established and managed, but in which the public has a stake and which are answerable to Government, possessing financial resources, usually in the form of endowment, and existing to serve the general welfare or some chosen segment of it, usually in the form of grants.

Even this grab bag of a definition, with hedges and possibilities for exceptions, may give the impression that foundations as a group are pretty much of a piece, each member of the group having a great deal in common with all its fellows, more in common than in contrast. The actual fact, however, is that the diversity among foundations is immense, and one of the first things that the general public needs to know about them is that they are not all alike. Their diversity is stretched across a broader spectrum than is perhaps the case for any other category of charitable or humane institution. All churches, no matter what their great differences, exist for the common purpose of worshipping God or some God-substitute. All colleges, again no matter what their great differences, engage in the common function of teaching and learning. But for foundations there is no overarching goal or program, stated in even the most general terms, that is accepted or practiced by all. It is the outside observer trying to compose a normative description, who says foundations exist, or at least should, to "serve the general welfare. . . ." Unfortunately, many foundations own to no such aim.

Size is one mark of their diversity. The range runs all the way from the colossus of the group, the Ford Foundation, with the market value of its holdings over $3 billion, down to funds whose assets are literally zero, or maybe even a few that have liabilities and nothing else. From time to time commentators have set various categories of size, so that the total mass can be divided into manageable and describable groups. Among the common dividing lines are the figures ten million and one hundred million, those falling below the ten million being "small" foundations, those between the two figures being "medium-sized," and those above the one-hundred-million mark being "large." In this essay, those will be the meanings given to those adjectives.

It must be noted, however, that such a pattern is quite unsatisfactory. A foundation whose assets are $15 million is likely to be an entirely different kind of philanthropic agency from one whose assets are $90 million; yet both are in the medium category.

Moreover, the two ends of the scale are unusually imprecise. In respect to the large foundations there are probably somewhere around thirty-five whose assets are over the line of $100 million. Figures fluctuate, up-to-date information is often not available, and thus no one can say for sure at any particular time. The chief trouble with the category, however, is the size of Ford, for it is over three times larger than the next largest, which is either Rockefeller or Lilly or the recently aggrandized Robert Wood Johnson Foundation. Ford's comparative immensity poses problems and opens up opportunities of which other foundations, even other large ones, are only dimly aware. Perhaps there ought to be another dividing line at this end of the scale, $1 billion, with only the Ford Foundation above that line in solitary splendor.[1]

Certainly there needs to be another dividing line, perhaps two, at the other end of the scale. Foundations of $8-, $6-, or $4-million are able to undertake programs and make grants on a systematic basis, in pursuit of some well-defined aim, whereas foundations of less than a million in size may be tempted to disburse their income in less thoughtful ways. Foundations of less than $100,000 in size may be simply instruments for personal

1. For information on individual foundations, see Marianna O. Lewis and Patricia Bowers, eds., *The Foundation Directory*, Edition 4, New York, Columbia University Press, 1971. (Hereafter referred to as FD-4.) For news about the Robert Wood Johnson Foundation, see *Foundation News*, January–February, 1972, p. 39.

6

benevolence, though the recipients could be equally as worthy as those of the large foundations. One million and $100,000, therefore, might be further dividing lines in trying to set up reasonable categories of foundations. Size is no determinant of quality of work, of course, but some understanding of the wide disparity in size among foundations is important in the consideration of problems that face the field.

This question is complicated by the fact that market value of assets is not the only way, perhaps not the most accurate way, of measuring the relative size of foundations. Surely what a foundation does is a better indicator than how much its resources add up to, especially when its resources are measured in the imprecise terms of an ever-changing market value of its portfolio. If the criterion is the annual dollar activity of the foundation, then the breakdown of the group would be quite different. We shall return to this matter in other connections having to do with policy on annual expenditures and requirements as to pay-out. Suffice it now to say that the scale in this regard would be equally extensive with, though quite different from, the spectrum based on market value of assets. The two ends, however, might look much the same, for at one end would be the Ford Foundation, with annual dollar activity something over $200 million, and at the other some few foundations whose annual "activity" is zero.

Size is only the beginning of the various factors that make up the huge diversity among foundations. Take, for example, the tremendous differences in respect to ways in which foundations make decisions on their grants and other activities. At one end of this workload scale would be a considerable number of foundations, most of them large, that are able to make affirmative response to less than 5 percent, in a few cases considerably less, of the multitude of requests that come their way. At the other end of the scale are foundations, most of them small, that don't receive any requests at all. Some foundations, large and small, work at their job of philanthropy throughout the entire year, and try to space their work so as to be able to deal with program and grant possibilities in a conscientious and evenhanded way. Other foundations, not all of them small, are whimsical and

7

sometimes frantic operations, and may end up the year in a flurry of December grant-making, to be sure that they have spent all that the law requires.

Size, however measured, is necessarily a chief factor in professional staffing, but even among the large foundations there are great differences in the number, experience and overall quality of the staff members. Size is not a reliable guideline in regard to the extent to which a foundation calls upon competent experts for advice in the chosen field of activity, but the use of wise counsel is itself another important factor in the determination of differences among foundations.

Still other factors are relevant. For example, sponsorship differs greatly: most foundations were established by an individual or a family, but they may retain for only a few years, or for a generation, or forever, the prevailing traits of a family fund. Those traits themselves will differ hugely in their effect on the foundation's activity. Though being a family fund will mean in general that one person or a small group of people will set the guidelines and dominate the decisions of the foundation, those guidelines and decisions can be narrow or broad, selfish or selfless, poorly or well conceived and executed.

Foundations are often sponsored by companies and corporations, as extensions of their regular programs of benevolence, and by communities—groups of like-minded people from various families and businesses, by towns, cities, regions. Again, geography is a factor of large disparity. In few other areas of activity does New York bestride the world to the extent it does in organized philanthropy. A majority of the large foundations have their offices there, and an immense number of the smaller ones as well. The latest edition of the *Foundation Directory* shows that out of the 5,454 listed for the country as a whole (according to special size eligibilities for inclusion, to be noted hereafter), 1,161 are in New York City. This has its effect on the activity of foundations in other parts of the country, for it tends to increase the temptation to become parochial in interest and activity. It is not pertinent to the point at issue to explore the pros and cons of this problem now. All that is intended is to point out that one further mark of difference among foundations grows out of the geography of the field, for the locations of foundations explain some part of the huge diversity in outlook and program.

Almost nothing has been said about the diversity in program itself, which may be the largest single factor in explaining the differences among foundations and the most difficult one in arriving at a precise definition of the field. Hardly an area that man has ever explored, certainly none that is legal and moral, has been omitted from the catalogue of foundations' concerns. In succeeding pages, and especially in Chapter IV, illustrations of the tremendous variety of foundation activities will be given, but they will be necessarily selective, and thus only barely suggestive of the cornucopia of philanthropic work.

The marks of difference are so numerous and broadly applicable that, once realized, they tend to obscure a couple of characteristics that nearly all foundations possess in common. Foundations do not hold sole ownership of the purpose to serve the general welfare. They share their humane intentions with many other kinds of tax-exempt and charitable organizations. But two things do indeed separate them from these other institutions. First, foundations do not have to raise money for their operating budgets or for the support of their various activities By definition, they have the money to start with. Second, their money is relatively uncommitted. That is, a church must use its income to be a church, a school to be a school, whereas a foundation can exercise a considerable amount of freedom in determining what it will do. It possesses the capacity to change its mind about what it shall do without changing its essential nature as a foundation. These marks of distinctiveness are of considerable importance in enabling us to separate foundations from other types of non-profit institutions, and as far as they go, they are useful descriptives of the field of our inquiry.[2]

In light of their diversity how can one presume to throw all foundations into a single pot? The result is indigestible. In any

2. See *Foundations, Private Giving and Public Policy: Report and Recommendations of the Commission on Foundations and Private Philanthropy* (Peter G. Peterson, Chairman), Chicago, University of Chicago Press, 1970, pp. 39–41. (Hereafter referred to as Report of Peterson Commission.)

effort to understand foundations the first thing to say is that everybody, supporters and critics alike, must learn to discriminate among the various kinds and types of foundations. The achievement of one doesn't tell anything at all about the record of another. By the same token, the misbehavior of one should not be allowed to throw suspicion on another. The American public has learned to discriminate between Harvard and Podunk —and this is not to say that Podunk may not also have its achievements or its problems. All of us know the difference between General Motors and the local repair shop, between the Library of Congress and the book collection of the junior high school, between the Metropolitan Opera and the benefit musicale. No disparagement of either end of any of those pairings is intended. In days of cynicism toward prestigious institutions, perhaps special assurance should be given that no finger of scorn is being pointed at Harvard, General Motors, the Library of Congress or the Metropolitan Opera. It is needful to look at foundations for what they are, in much the way that the public has already begun to learn to discriminate among individual specimens in other fields of activity.

In this essay I shall focus upon the large foundations. The first thing to be said about them, therefore, is that not even all the large ones are alike. They differ greatly among themselves as well as from foundations of other sizes.

C. A Note on History and Motivation

Foundations are largely a creation of the twentieth century. Historians of organized philanthropy put its beginnings in the post–Civil War period of the nineteenth century, and even into earlier times; and the history of benevolence, of course, goes back for centuries. Foundations as we know them today, however, are a relatively new development.

This is not the place for a detailed record of the history of American foundations. Such information is readily available,[3]

3. See F. Emerson Andrews, *Philanthropic Foundations*, New York, Russell Sage Foundation, 1956; Warren Weaver, *U.S. Philanthropic Foundations: Their History, Structure, Management, and Record*, New

and all we need to do is to note a few facts as background for the present scene. Yet even the most cursory reference to the past must take note of the two big names in the establishment of philanthropic funds in this country, Andrew Carnegie and John D. Rockefeller. Their central agencies of benevolence were the Carnegie Corporation, established in 1911, and the Rockefeller Foundation, established in 1913. Each man set up a constellation of other funds for special purposes, such as the Carnegie Endowment for International Peace and the General Education Board, and other men of large wealth followed suit around the same time. In the first two decades of this century such foundations as Commonwealth, Milbank Memorial, Julius Rosenwald, Russell Sage and Surdna were started.

The twenties and thirties saw a considerable extension of the practice whereby families of means set aside assets in charitable trusts. Among the funds established during these decades were the Danforth, Duke, John Simon Guggenheim, Hartford, Hazen, Hill, Juilliard, Kellogg, Kettering, Kresge, Markle, Rosenberg and Woodruff foundations.

A new surge of development took place after World War II and has only now begun to subside. Many of today's largest foundations, even though some may have been established at an earlier time, have received the greatest proportion of their funds in these recent decades. Among this number are Ford, Robert Wood Johnson, Kaiser, Lilly, A. W. Mellon, R. K. Mellon, Moody, Mott, Pew, Sid Richardson, Rockefeller Brothers, Scaife and Sloan.

From the beginning the growth in number and resources of foundations has been hard to document. The first listing made in 1915, had twenty-seven names. It is likely that as late as 1930 the number was still less than two hundred. Thereafter a series of volumes entitled *American Foundations and Their Fields* slowly built up a body of fairly reliable data. Volume VI in 1948 contained information about 899 foundations; Volume VII, 1955, the last of the series, listed 4,162. Raw growth was

York, Harper and Row, 1967; Abraham Flexner, *Funds and Foundations*, New York, Harper & Brothers, 1952.

not the sole explanation. The most important event was the opening of tax returns to public inspection in 1950. From then on statistics became somewhat more reliable.[4]

The first *Foundation Directory* was published in 1960. It proposed to include only those foundations above $50,000 in assets or $10,000 in annual grants, and found 5,202 foundations that qualified for inclusion. Its estimate as to the total number of foundations in existence at that time was 12,000.[5]

Four years later the second edition of the *Foundation Directory* adjusted its standard of eligibility to $100,000 in assets, and the number that then qualified was 6,007. The overall estimate of foundations in existence was thought to be 15,000.[6]

The criterion for inclusion was again changed for the third edition of the *Directory,* published in 1967. Foundations at that time had to be $200,000 in size of assets, and 6,803 were listed, with the estimate for the overall number being 18,000.[7]

The fourth edition of the *Foundation Directory* came off the press late in 1971. Once again changes were made in the eligibilities for inclusion, so as to keep the compilation from getting too large. The minimum standards were set at $500,000 in assets and/or $25,000 in annual grants, and 5,454 foundations qualified for inclusion on this basis.[8]

Such figures tell us that the number of foundations is large, is probably still growing and is unknown. The latter fact is at least as important as the other two, for the embarrassing truth about the field is that nobody, not even the Internal Revenue Service,

4. F. Emerson Andrews, "Introduction," in Ann D. Walton and Marianna O. Lewis, eds., *The Foundation Directory,* Edition 2, New York, Russell Sage Foundation, 1964, pp. 11–16. (Hereafter referred to as FD-2.) See also periodic volumes of *American Foundations and Their Fields,* with various editors and publishers, from 1931 to 1955.

5. Ann D. Walton, *et. al.,* eds., "Introduction," *The Foundation Directory,* Edition 1, New York, Russell Sage Foundation, 1960. (Hereafter referred to as FD-1.)

6. FD-2, pp. 9–16.

7. Marianna O. Lewis, ed., *The Foundation Directory,* Edition 3, New York, Russell Sage Foundation, 1967, pp. 7–13. (Hereafter referred to as FD-3.)

8. FD-4, pp. vii–x.

knows how many foundations there are. The IRS published its first list, containing 30,262 entries, in 1968; but since it had no sound definition as to what a foundation is, its list is not fully acceptable. Even higher estimates, such as Representative Patman's oft-repeated figure of 45,124[9] are made by those not directly connected with the field who have some critical axe to grind. The Foundation Center, whose only axe is the furnishing of reliable information, estimates that there may have been somewhere around 26,000 in 1971, over 95 percent of which have been established since World War II.[10]

Figures in some of the categories of size are a little easier to come by. It was noted above that probably only one foundation is larger than one billion in assets and that around thirty-five are larger than one hundred million. Even here, however, the numbers are subject to guesswork and shifting fortunes. In categories of smaller size the Foundation Center estimates that there are approximately 300 foundations between ten and one hundred million, and around 1,850 between one and ten million. This leaves somewhere between thirty-two and thirty-three hundred of less than a million in assets but still large enough to be included in the latest *Directory*. Those of even smaller size amount to over twenty thousand.[11]

The overall size of the assets held by foundations is subject to similar uncertainty. This should not be a matter of large surprise when one remembers that any individual foundation is likely not to know from day to day what the size of its own portfolio happens to be. Sums, therefore, are bound to be rough. The best guess as to the aggregate of foundation assets is that the figure is somewhere over twenty-six billion. It is reliably known that assets of all foundations larger than one million each in size total just about twenty-four billion. Thus the imbalance in the field becomes clear even though precise figures cannot be se-

9. Weaver, *op. cit.*, p. 57; F. Emerson Andrews, *Patman and Foundations: Review and Assessment,* New York, The Foundation Center, 1968, p. 8.

10. FD-4, p. viii.

11. *Ibid.*, pp. viii–x.

13

cured: less than 10 percent of the foundations hold over 90 percent of the assets.[12]

Trouble is, on the 990-A forms that foundations use in reporting to the Internal Revenue Service, some list assets at cost or at book value rather than at current market value. The lack of uniform reporting and of thorough governmental auditing means that totals taken from 990-A's are not reliable. The Commission on Foundations and Private Philanthropy (hereafter to be referred to as the Peterson Commission, for its chairman Peter Peterson) reported the example of the Irvine Foundation, "which until 1969 carried its assets at approximately $6 million. In 1969 it filed a form 990-A which reflected assets in excess of $100 million, and there have been estimates that the market value of that foundation's property is considerably higher."[13]

Though the large foundations, those over one hundred million in size, constitute less than 2 percent of the total number of philanthropic funds in this country, justification for centering attention on them in this essay grows out of the fact that they possess a disproportionate share of all foundation assets. The thirty-five or so in the large category hold something over $10 billion in assets, perhaps around two-fifths of the total, and all the thousands of smaller foundations share the remaining approximately three-fifths. The disproportion carries over into grant-making. Of the estimated $1.8 billion in annual grant-making by all foundations, something around one-third comes from the large foundations, and as small a number as "the hundred largest foundations account for roughly half of the total annual grants of all foundations."[14]

Lest these figures throw the full picture out of balance, however, it should be noted that the $1.8 billion in grants of all foundations represents less than 10 percent of the $18.3 billion total for American philanthropic giving in 1969, as estimated by

12. *Ibid.*, pp. viii–xii. In April, 1972, the Editor of FD-4 estimated the current assets at $28 billion, because of recent advances in the stock market and the new money received by the Robert Wood Johnson Foundation.

13. Report of Peterson Commission, *op. cit.*, p. 49.

14. *Ibid.*, p. 51. Figure of $1.8 billion comes from FD-4, p. xiv.

14

the American Association of Fund-Raising Council.[15] Foundation resources and activity are concentrated in the large foundations, but even their comparatively sizeable annual benevolences account for probably less than 3 percent of the amount expended in philanthropy each year.

How did people of wealth come to use the instrument of the foundation as the expression for their philanthropic activity? What are the motives that account for the tremendous proliferation in numbers and the remarkable increase in assets of foundations during this century, especially since World War II? If in areas susceptible of statistical analysis we are ultimately reduced to guesswork, even more so in the area of motivation must we rely on opinion, inference and hunch. This has not kept people, both admirers and critics, from expressing themselves, and like everything else connected with foundations, variety is the rule.[16]

All sorts of reasons are given by donors for establishing foundations. Perhaps other reasons that donors would rather not have publicized were also present. Many of these unsavory motivations have been charged against donors by critics, both mild and muckraking. To some of these we shall return in later chapters, when we deal with the criticisms that have been levelled against foundations and with their response.

But let it be recorded now as one man's opinion that the most widely prevalent reason for the establishment of foundations has been the decent philanthropic urge on the part of the donor. Many people of means, including some of very great wealth, have been sensitive to the preferred economic status they have achieved or inherited, sensitive also to the needs of people of less privilege all around them, and have thus wanted to share their good fortune (double-entendre, if you wish) with others.

15. *Giving USA,* New York, American Association of Fund-Raising Council, Inc., 1971, p. 7. (Incidentally, the AAFRC's estimate for foundation grants in 1970 is only $1.7 billion; pp. 8, 21.)

16. For discussion of motives in establishing foundations, see Weaver, *op. cit.,* chap. 8; Andrews, *Philanthropic Foundations, op. cit.,* chap. 2; Report of the Peterson Commission, *op. cit.,* pp. 45–47; Joseph C. Kiger, *Operating Principles of the Larger Foundations,* New York, Russell Sage Foundation, 1954, chap. 1.

15

These same people, of course, have often been subject to selfish as well as to selfless motives. The gamut runs from relatively innocent expressions of ego all the way to criminal acts of self-dealing. A donor may simply want to see his name in lights, at least the dignified lights of an incorporated foundation. He may want to escape the annoyance of answering hosts of personal appeals himself. He may wish to get appropriate tax deductions. He may want to retain some continuing control over the way in which his charitable donations will be used. He may take advantage of whatever loopholes continue to exist. He may skirt the edges of the law, or even transgress it. In other words, various degrees of selfishness have undoubtedly been present in the establishment of foundations through the years.

This is about what one would have to say in respect to the motivations of almost any person going into almost any line of activity. For the doctor or the businessman, for the minister or the lawyer, or for that matter, for the housewife, he or she could be expected to pursue the self-chosen task with a combination of selflessness and selfishness. From person to person high-minded idealism and personal advantage are mixed together in varying proportions—and so it undoubtedly is with philanthropists. Only the gullible will adopt the positions at either extreme, that the motive for establishing a foundation is either pure, unsullied benevolence, calling for unqualified approbation, or unrelieved venality, calling for complete condemnation. To the extent to which evidence of motivation is available in the life stories of donors and the histories of foundations, the self-denying and self-asserting reasons are mixed in ways that reflect accurately the ambivalent human condition of all of us.

D. Appreciation of Foundations

In a day when attacks on foundations are rife, one must go out of his way to register the conviction that a genuine philanthropic urge has existed and continues to exist. Criticism is not the only attitude toward foundations that the public displays. Other feelings prevail. To put censure into its proper perspective,

16

we should take note of some of the other attitudes current in our society.

First is ignorance. The American public knows very little about foundations. Not even Ford is a household word, at least when it applies to philanthropy. To the great mass of citizens, foundations are vague, fuzzy entities that go about doing, or thinking they do, good. But what, how, when and where are generally unknown.

Moreover, most Americans don't particularly care. Apathy is the oft-paired partner of ignorance. Those somewhat mysterious agencies, the foundations, may affect the lives of a chosen few, but their benefactions seldom touch, at least directly, the everyday existence of the faceless many. Foundations would do well to realize, and might sometimes be delighted, that the public views them with considerable indifference.

But more positive attitudes also exist. Next is awe. Foundation officials often have to put up with the embarrassment of unearned respect. Their offices are thought to be distant, thickly carpeted and hushed. They themselves are the next thing to God Almighty, and are either about to accept a high, nonelective post in Government or planning to turn it down because the job isn't good enough—unless, of course, they've just come from Washington. When a foundation official takes such reverence seriously, his shirt does indeed get stuffed. Even if he escapes this unjustified self-esteem, he can't escape the absurdity that laymen sometimes look upon him and his institution as Olympian. It is a notion as ridiculous as Mt. Olympus of old, and as much a psychological fact.

If there is any logic at all to such an attitude, it grows out of another which is occasionally forgotten by foundation people themselves when pressed by unfavorable circumstance. I refer to the feeling of admiration with which foundations are often viewed. Awe can be associated with fear, of course, or dread, but it can also be partner to honor and appreciation. The latter attitudes, in fact, are widely current among that portion of the American public not characterized by ignorance or apathy toward foundations. In other words, among those who know and those who

17

care, a considerable host seem genuinely to admire the work of the large philanthropic funds. Praise and approbation are generously expressed, not alone to individual foundations themselves but to the world around.[17]

Here one must be on guard. *God Bless You, Mr. Rosewater* is more than the inspired and satirical title of a Kurt Vonnegut novel.[18] It is also the actual pose of the sycophant whom every foundation runs into now and again. In my experience, small family funds are more likely to be fooled by servile flattery than are large foundations, and trustees are more susceptible than staff members—but this judgment may mean no more than that I am a staff member of a large foundation. In any event, small or large, trustee or staff, most foundation people learn to tell the difference between artful compliments and sincere, disinterested commendation. The latter exists in encouraging measure, and constitutes one of the major reactions of the public toward organized philanthropy.

But everybody wants something. Even the truly disinterested may want something for someone else. To the extent to which this is an accurate appraisal of the human condition, it suggests a third positive attitude taken by the public toward foundations. Alongside awe and admiration is expectancy.

The lower level is well represented by the mendicant, hat in hand. It might be of interest to others to know that foundation people occasionally play this game with each other. An officer of Foundation A may approach Foundation B for some cause of personal concern, especially if his own organization is not supporting that cause. Like his non-foundation friends he will look

17. See, for example, Whitney M. Young, Jr., "Foundations Under Attack," in Thomas C. Reeves, ed., *Foundations Under Fire*, Ithaca, Cornell University Press, 1970; Robert D. Calkins, *The Role of the Philanthropic Foundation*, Washington, Cosmos Club, 1969; Irwin Ross, "Let's Not Fence in the Foundations," in *Fortune*, June 1969; statements of Herman Wells, Theodore M. Hesburgh, Frank C. Erwin, Jr., John Cooper, Felix Robb, W. Russell Arrington, Carl Kaysen, O. Meredith Wilson, Kermit Gordon, and others in *Foundations and the Tax Bill*, New York, The Foundation Center, 1969; and various authors, Part II, "Judgments Concerning the Value of Foundation Aid," in Weaver, *op. cit.*, pp. 221–457.

18. Kurt Vonnegut, Jr., *God Bless You, Mr. Rosewater*, New York, Dell Publishing Co., 1965.

expectantly to other foundations for support of some institution or project in which he believes; he may even look to his own, often in vain. By definition, a foundation is the place to which one goes for cash-lined succor. It is the American adult's Santa Claus. We all make out our lists and live in hope.

But this is not the kind of expectancy of which I speak. There is a higher form, with less of self and self-interest in it. It comes from knowing a person or an institution quite well over a period of time. Such knowledge gives one a feel for that person's or institution's character and a confidence that future actions will be consistent with it. The confidence may be misplaced, of course, for men and institutions change character from time to time. But that is ex post facto thinking. The point is, at any one time in the life of a person or an institution, the observer comes to expect a continuation of activity consistent with the known past.

Most people who are knowledgeable about foundations seem to have a generous expectation of them of this sort. They know that foundations have addressed themselves to serious social problems; they expect that such social concerns will continue. They know that foundations have done a lot of good; they assume that such work will be carried on. They credit foundations with substantial accomplishments in the past; they anticipate further achievements. The world of foundations is often the beneficiary of this kind of affirmative attitude, something more than backward-looking admiration, a happy antidote for all the criticism that comes their way.

E. The Attack on Foundations

Criticism, however, is the newsworthy attitude. Ignorance and perhaps apathy are understandable. Awe, admiration and a generous expectation of continuing good works should occasion no surprise. What catches the eye is the suspicion now visited upon foundations by a considerable segment of the public. The current attack has made foundations more visible than their good works ever managed to do, more visible than at any time in the history of organized philanthropy in this country.

19

But attacks on foundations are not a new phenomenon. Ever since some of the titans of industry began to organize their philanthropies in the early years of this century, critics have been present to raise questions about the sincerity of their efforts, the benefits that were likely to accrue to the public and the disinterestedness of those who praised the development.[19]

The first hullabaloo to catch the attention of the public was the effort to secure a Federal charter for the Rockefeller Foundation in 1910–1912. Objections arose in Congress and elsewhere, for this was the Progressive Era, when trust-busting and the fear of big business were wide concerns. Since the Rockefeller Foundation's initial resources consisted in $50 million worth of Jersey Standard stock, cries of "tainted money" and "creeping capitalism" were raised to prevent the Foundation's receiving a Federal charter, though it easily secured one from the state of New York in 1913.[20] A first congressional investigation, that of the Walsh Commission, followed soon thereafter. Though it warned the public about foundations because they were tied up with big business, Congress gave scant heed to the Walsh report in 1915.[21]

This early criticism made little impression on the public mind, for foundations were few in number and most people were delighted to think that some of the fortunes of big industrialists might be put to the benefit of the general public. For the next thirty-five years or so, foundations grew substantially in numbers and resources, and their uncontroversial good deeds began to be more widely known and generally applauded. Occasionally the chronicler of the business career of some tycoon or, closer home, the executive of some foundation would raise the question about whether the finances or programs of the foundations were as

19. See Ferdinand Lundberg, *The Rich and the Super-Rich*, New York, Bantam Books, 1968, chap. 10; Eduard C. Lindeman, *Wealth and Culture*, New York, Harcourt Brace, 1936; Joseph C. Goulden, *The Money Givers*, New York, Random House, 1971, chap. 2.

20. See Report of Peterson Commission, *op. cit.*, p. 63; Goulden, *op. cit.*, pp. 32–37.

21. See Weaver, *op. cit.*, pp. 170–171; Kiger, *op. cit.*, pp. 85–88; Harold M. Keele, *Unpublished Proceedings of New York University's Ninth Biennial Conference on Charitable Foundations: An Exercise in Censorship*, Chicago, 1970, pp. 7–9.

20

beneficial as they ought to be to American society.[22] But until about 1950, few serious criticisms of foundations were voiced, and foundations themselves were lulled into an easy acceptance of the approbation that the general public seemed to give.

With the coming of Senator Joseph McCarthy, foundations along with universities, churches and other organizations for the service of society found themselves under suspicion and attack. An article in the *American Legion Magazine* charged that foundations were supporting "outright communists, fellow travelers, socialists, do-gooders, one-worlders, wild-eyed Utopians and well-meaning dupes."[23] Obviously a Congressional investigation was in order, and accordingly in 1952 the House of Representatives set up the Cox Committee to track down the subversion. Rare for those excitable times, the Committee failed to find substantiation of the wild charges being made and, with suggestions for some improvements here and there, gave the foundations a generally clean report.[24]

The final statement of the Cox Committee was published in 1953, but Representative Reece, a nominal member who had attended only one committee meeting, was not satisfied. He persuaded Congress to embark upon the same investigation again, only this time he meant for it to reach a different conclusion. Both the content and the method of the Reece Committee's investigation were roundly condemned, and the result would have been laughable if the country had not been caught in the grip of the McCarthy hysteria. Only one foundation representative appeared before the Committee, and the whole sorry show, involving public discord among its members and staff, was called off before it had run its appointed course. In its final report, issued in 1954, the majority asserted but did not substantiate the "diabolical conspiracy" that foundations were said to be engaged

22. See Kiger, *op. cit.,* pp. 88–91.
23. Quoted in Report of Peterson Commission, *op. cit.,* p. 65.
24. See *Final Report of the Select Committee to Investigate Foundations and Other Organizations,* U.S. House, 82d Congress, 2d Session, House Report No. 2514, Washington, D.C., Government Printing Office, 1953; Kiger, *op. cit.,* pp. 91–97; Keele, *op. cit.,* pp. 9–14; Helen Hill Miller, "Investigating the Foundations," *The Reporter,* November 24, 1953, pp. 37–40

in, and the minority accused the majority of having made an "unseemly effort to reach a predetermined conclusion."[25]

Needless to say, no legislation resulted, and some commentators felt that little harm was done. But even when an investigation turns out to be a farce, the impression is left that there must be something there to investigate. With the Reece Committee's following so soon on the heels of the Cox Committee, foundations occupied the center stage of public attention, and the legitimacy of criticism seemed upheld.

The last of the four Congressional investigations to date is the sporadic inquiry by Representative Wright Patman, begun in 1961 and seemingly not yet concluded. Whereas the Walsh Committee thought that foundation programs might be reactionary and the Cox Committee questioned whether they were engaged in subversive activities, with the Reece Committee doing a delirious repeat of the same line, the focus of attention for Patman has been the alleged financial misbehavior of foundations. As Chairman of the House Select Committee on Small Business he has used the device of issuing published reports to the members of his own committee as a way of calling attention to a number of abuses that he and his staff have uncovered. In his various reports he has made sweeping charges about the business activities and fiscal policies of foundations; he has castigated the Internal Revenue Service for not having policed the situation adequately; and he has recommended drastic changes in the law for the closer regulation of foundation behavior.[26]

It is not easy to arrive at a fair summary of such a broad and unsystematic investigation. On the one hand, Patman has performed a public service by calling attention to some misdeeds and naming a few names, and by raising the issue as to whether

25. See Weaver, *op. cit.*, pp. 174–179; Report of Peterson Commission, *op. cit.*, pp. 66–67; Robert M. Hutchins, *Freedom, Education and the Fund*, New York, Meridian, 1956, pp. 201–207, quoted in Reeves, *op. cit.*, pp. 112–120.

26. See various Installments of *Tax-Exempt Foundations and Charitable Trusts: Their Impact on Our Economy*, Washington, D.C., Government Printing Office, beginning in 1962, the widely publicized series of Reports, six to date, of Mr. Patman, to his own Subcommittee. (Hereafter referred to as Patman Reports, with number and date.)

foundations are observing proper standards in their financial affairs and whether legislation to require them to do so is adequate. On the other hand, sloppy staff work, scarehead publicity, the technique of taking the minute part for the massive whole, the unwillingness to confess to or retract patent error—all these things have been flaws in the Patman story and have undoubtedly hurt the reputation of foundations in general. Whatever the balance to be drawn between benefit and harm, the Patman investigation, together with numerous other treatments that it provoked, succeeded in keeping the spotlight on foundations during the sixties.[27]

Building on the interest that Patman had aroused, the Treasury Department appointed a special committee to have a careful look at foundations and their behavior, and to make recommendations as to desirable legislative or executive action. The Treasury Department Report on Private Foundations came out in 1965 with a group of balanced judgments and constructive proposals. The work of this committee does not really belong under the heading of an attack of foundations, but its existence was undoubtedly due to the fact that Patman's and other attacks were widespread, and its report laid solid groundwork for the deliberations leading up to the Tax Reform Act of 1969.[28] Ever since the Cox and Reece committees, and especially since Patman's outbursts, foundations have received an immense amount of public attention, much of it critical, some of it hostile. Numerous books and magazine articles have taken foundations to task. Politicians such as Governor Wallace have discovered that their supporters are prepared to cheer when foundations

27. For a variety of points of view on the Patman investigations, see Lundberg, *op. cit.,* pp. 470–497; Weaver, *op. cit.,* pp. 179–185; Keele, *op. cit.,* pp. 17–20; Goulden, *op. cit.,* pp. 229–237; Wright Patman, "The Free-Wheeling Foundations," *The Progressive,* June, 1967, pp. 27–31; Andrews, *Patman and Foundations: Review and Assessment, op. cit.*

28. See *Treasury Department Report on Private Foundations,* Committee on Finance, United States Senate, Washington, D.C., Government Printing Office, 1965. (Hereafter referred to as Treasury Department Report.) See also Weaver, *op. cit.,* pp. 185–186; Staff of the Russell Sage Foundation, "Views of the Treasury Report," in *Foundation News,* March, 1968, pp. 29–33.

are attacked.[29] The time when the American public blandly assumed their virtues, or ignored them, or when they could afford to ignore the public, is done, and foundations are having to get used to the new experience of being highly visible, distrusted and condemned.

Criticism is of varying degrees, of course. It can be mild in tone and constructive in spirit. It can be virulent and destructive. It can be anything in between. Today's attack on foundations is not a uniform assault, with an inner consistency of vigor or passion. Nor does it possess a harmony of content, as we shall see in Chapters II and III. Postponing to those chapters a discussion of the specific charges that are made and the answers that foundations give to them, we simply take note at this point that the attack is widespread and real.[30]

F. THE DISREPUTE OF GIVING

It is not foundations alone, however, that feel the opprobrium of the critic. Suspicion has come to be visited upon the individual donor, especially if he has the capacity and inclination to make large gifts. Suspicion is directed also at both profit-making and non-profit institutions—industries or universities, corporations or churches—especially if their contributions seem to be at the expense of the self-interest of shareholders, parishioners or other members of the institutions' immediate constituencies.

The attack on foundations is only one aspect of the general disrepute into which benevolence of any sort and size seems to have fallen. This attitude toward giving is sufficiently pervasive to require a special look, for even if foundations were to be completely successful in fending off the attacks directed at them,

29. See Stephan Lesher, "Who knows what frustrations lurk in the hearts of X million Americans? George Wallace knows—and he's off and running," *New York Times Magazine,* January 2, 1972; Richard Fitzgerald, "In Re: Gov. Wallace vs. Foundations," *Non-Profit Report,* December, 1971, pp. 7–8, and "Governor Wallace's Foundation Targets," *Ibid.,* January, 1972, p. 15.

30. See, for example, Lundberg, *op. cit.,* chap. 10; Goulden, *op. cit.*; Reeves, *op. cit.,* pp. 1–35; quotations in *Ibid.* from Fred J. Cook, pp. 127–133 and Burton Raffel, pp. 86–93; Taylor Branch, "The Case Against Foundations," *The Washington Monthly,* July, 1971, pp. 3–18.

the problem in its deeper form of the suspicion of benevolence in general might make the foundations' efforts of little account.

Once there was a time when benevolence was listed high in the catalogue of American virtues.[31] The early American aphorism "Earn all you can, save all you can, give all you can" was a neat and widely accepted summary of the Puritan and capitalist ethic. For an earlier day Ben Franklin was its promulgator and embodiment. At a later time Andrew Carnegie, among many other hard-driving philanthropists, preached the doctrine most persuasively.[32]

The ethic of work was related, of course, to the ethic for everything else. Life was seamless, and if in one sense Sunday was set aside, in another sense its temper was consistent with the rest of the week. Work hard. Get ahead. This is, of course, a vale of tears, but God helps those who help themselves. For most of its citizens America was the Promised Land.

So, earn all you can. Nothing wrong with that. Nobody is suggesting that one cheat in order to do so. Fundamental to any such advice is the acceptance of the basic moral principles of honesty and fair play. The maxim is shorthand, of course. A more complete version would read: Earn all you can as long as you don't gouge or swindle; play the game straight but play it hard.

To this day the proposition has the seal of much public approval. In Western society those at either end of the economic spectrum are looked at askance—the fellow who won't work because he doesn't want to ("lazy, shiftless, no-good"), and the fellow who won't work because he doesn't have to ("pampered darling, silver spoon in his mouth"). The great mass in the middle get on with it. Even those who, like the housewife, are once removed from the pay-window know that life is not meant to be either pecunious or impecunious leisure. All may not earn in the precise sense, but nearly all submit to the spirit of the

31. See Herbert W. Schneider, *A History of American Philosophy*, New York, Columbia University Press, 1946, chap. IV, "Benevolence"; Robert H. Bremner, *American Philanthropy*, Chicago, University of Chicago Press, 1960.
32. See Andrew Carnegie, *The Gospel of Wealth*, New York, Century Company, 1900.

advice. All of them may not earn all they can, but most of them have a grudging admiration for the big earners. Even envy is inverted admiration. Today's frantic scramble of human effort, in which all but the drop- and cop-outs are engaged, is proof that at least this part of the old ethic has survived.

But left to itself alone the saying is clearly incomplete. Earn, and that's an end to it? What for? The doctrine of work for work's sake may have a hard splendor about it, but it is never going to win any popularity prize.

So, save all you can. Rainy day. Waste is sinful. Who knows what the future will bring? You may need it, or somebody close to you. Be prepared.

The aphorism now begins to sound moral. For most people there is an inevitability to earning, or at least working; and to pretend that it has much of an ethical quality is to give it unjustified airs. One has no choice. But saving is something else. It has an oughtness and a rightness about it. However often one disobeys, one knows it to be disobedience. Less practiced than its predecessor maxim, it is more enjoined as a moral imperative. Down to the present time it has kept its high standing as a folkway involving some measure of ethical sensitivity. The opprobrium still visited upon its opposites—squandering, dissipating one's resources, wasting one's substance in riotous living—is sufficient sign that putting some part of one's earnings aside is the right and righteous thing to do, however much one dislikes it.

But the nagging bite of personal dissatisfaction begins almost at once. Saving, too, is incomplete. Less fun because it is more high-minded, it is still not high-minded enough to save it from its own exaggerations of hoarding and downright parsimony. Nobody can live to himself alone. At least, nobody ought to try it. Every great ethical system has admonished man to recognize his human relatedness; and even those who have no God to love, as well as those who do, give lip-service to loving one's neighbor.

So, give all you can. Give time. Give consideration. Not least, give money. Stop and have a look at the poor traveller. Bind up his wounds. Send him on his way with a purse. It is not he

26

who is good. It is you who must be Good to the Samaritan. The challenging scriptural question, Who is my neighbor? received a testing answer, as if the question had been, What is neighborly behavior? It is the act of giving.

And so nobility entered the economic commandment. Earning points inward, toward self. Saving stays inward, with self. Giving turns outward, toward somebody else or something other. The third is the maxim that redeems the other two, purging them of selfishness, putting them in a social perspective.

To stop short with the first, or even with the first and second, is to be crass and, perhaps worse, aimless—or at least to appear to be aimless. Even one who gives nary a damn about anybody else somehow hates to say so. If he cares anything at all about his fellows' opinions of him, he needs some sort of justification for piling asset on asset and stashing it all away. To give all one can—that's the ticket. He may not do so, of course, but that's another story. What matters is that he has latched on to a noble purpose that somehow sanctifies his acquisitiveness. He has a reason for his earning and saving, one that enhances his own self-esteem and casts an aura of unctuous rectitude around his daily routine. Give—or at least express the intent.

It is easy to be snide. Yet I do not mean to suggest that only the first two were taken seriously and the third was always a cynical addendum. On the contrary, in the economic ethic of an earlier day the three went together. That is, all three were well thought of, and probably in ascending order. He who earned all he could was commended. If he managed to hang onto it, the admiration increased. And if he took the third step and used his earnings and savings for the benefit of those around him, then the community responded with its highest accolades. For it was within the understanding of even the ethically obtuse that free-will, selfless giving was the most demanding of the approved disciplines; according to the Bible, "more blessed" than always to be on the receiving end. It took stamina to earn all one could. It took self-denial to save. But giving required on top of those virtues the unusual disposition to care.

Another reason that the three were regarded in ascending order of esteem was that, apart from their relative priority in

27

moral splendor, they were identifiably unequal in their comparative frequency. Most men earned only some of what they could. Fewer managed to save. Rarest of all were those who, earning and saving in superlative fashion, possessed the seemingly contradictory capacity to turn it loose.

So the threefold precept worked its way into the life of our society. All three propositions were interrelated in that the second built upon the first and the third depended upon the other two. Giving was morally superior, less frequently practiced and thus more highly acclaimed than earning or saving. But they all went hand in hand.

Can we say as much now? I think not. In the American society of today something has happened to the practice and spirit of giving that bids fair to drive a wedge of separation between it and its two partners. To be more accurate, the change that has taken place is in the attitude of Americans toward giving, especially large-scale giving; that is, toward philanthropy. In this one regard at least, the value system that Americans believe in seems to have shifted, and we as a people may be in the process of doubting, perhaps even disavowing, a heretofore honored part of our ethical heritage.

It is important not to exaggerate the situation. Most individual Americans continue to make their modest contributions to worthy institutions and causes. Comparative statistics of annual benevolence are confusing—some agencies are up in their receipts and some are down. Particularities of time and circumstance affect such figures in ways that are beyond the interest of this essay. I do not mean that the mythical average American citizen is less generous than he used to be. I have no knowledge that this is so, and personally I don't believe it.

But what I do believe is that the attitude of the ordinary citizen toward those who, earning much and saving much, also give much has shifted from an earlier admiration to a present-day suspicion. This seems to me to be true whether the big donor is an individual, a family, a corporation or a foundation—or, for that matter, the Federal Government. Earning and saving continue to be widely praised if not as widely practiced. Small-scale giving is well regarded, especially if the recipient is tax-exempt. But large-scale giving is in disrepute.

Signs of the disrepute in which philanthropy is presently held are all around us. It would be easy at this point to back-track on our argument by referring to the various attacks on foundations, in Congress and out, to which we have already referred. But I invite the reader, instead, to cast an eye internally, to find within himself tokens of the attitude that seems to have invaded us all. My own exercise runs like this:

First, I feel that we Americans tend to greet the act of the large donor, whether personal or corporate, with the jaundiced question, What is he trying to buy? Something relatively harmless, perhaps, such as an honorary degree—and we are mildly amused. Or something insidious, such as a preferential stake in a business deal or a Government contract—and we are not amused. That he is buying something often goes without question. Why else would he spend the money?

Again, we hear of the large gift and immediately the question comes to mind, What is he trying to hide? There is more here than meets the eye, of course. What has somebody got on him? What guilt is he attempting to erase? Crossing the palm with silver is a time-honored way of reducing the heat. Big heat, big silver. We know we don't know all the pressures the donor feels, for surely his own explanation of the gift cannot be trusted. But we do know he feels them. Why else would he spend the money?

Or the reaction may be that he is putting on a show of generosity at our expense. Why does the Government let him get away with it? If he had not had some kind of favored position at the hands of Government—tax exemption, unlimited charitable deduction, opportunity to write off business losses—he wouldn't be able to play Galahad. The taxes we pay are higher than they ought to be. One reason is that we have to pay his share, because he is allowed to escape. He gets the glory but we foot the bill. How else would he have had that much money to spend?

The next reflex feeling has two versions, depending upon our

29

political stripe. Both are summarized in the position: He is trying to change the social order and we don't like it. He wants to
force his notions on all the rest of us. This is a democracy, isn't
it? By what right does he manipulate things to his liking,
masquerading as benevolent, when our view and our vote, supposedly equal to his, don't count? If he didn't mean his money
to be effective on behalf of his own wrong-headed desires, why
else would he spend it?

One version of this attitude points rightward, the other looks
off to the left. The first says, That big donor is a reactionary, turn-
ing the clock back to an outmoded time. He supports this radio
station, that college and the other community organization because he knows they will preach his gospel of laissez faire, funda-
mentalism or Communists-under-the-bed. The second says, That
big donor is a revolutionary, tearing down our system and soil-
ing our flag. He supports this TV program, that university and
the other social agency because he knows they will spout his
line of socialism, modernism or Birchites-under-the-bed. The
two reactions amount to pretty much the same thing: when the
gift doesn't go down our own ideological alley, we resist its
nefarious overtones and resent its being made.

It all adds up to the querulous attitude: By what right does
one wealthy person or one well-heeled trust have the chance to
be charitable? Because of his or its money, that's all. Does that
possession automatically bestow on him or it the liberty of being
benevolent? If the factual answer is Yes, the atmospheric answer
of much of the public is, We don't like it. We don't like a situation in which someone else, just because he has more money
than we do, gets to exercise his generosity.

Moreover, we don't like the rich man's expectation that we
will applaud him. Maybe he had earned and saved his money in
meticulous fulfillment of the old, selfish ethic, but that is no
assurance that he has gained and maintained a sufficient store
of wisdom to support his now trying to become unselfish.

Such a line of thought is fashionable these days. The disrepute
into which philanthropy, especially large philanthropy, has fallen
is a fact of our times.

30

G. The Changing Attitudes of Donors

This disrepute can be seen, by reflection, in the changing attitudes of donors themselves, whether they are individuals, foundations or other organizations. Not long ago giving on a large scale was likely to be, in general, almost as routine as small-scale, personal donations. In a particular case, of course, a large gift was a circumstance of special import for both donor and recipient. But the overall pattern of philanthropy, large as well as small, followed a relatively unvarying formula, consisting of a combination of predictable actions and attitudes:

—the decision of the donor, made on his best understanding of the merits of the case;

—the gift itself, with very few extraneous considerations and conditions;

—sincere appreciation on the part of the recipient;

—genuine satisfaction on the part of the donor;

—and unmixed approbation on the part of the public.

Times are no longer so simple. Attitudes of the general public and even of recipients have come to be adulterated with doubt and criticism, both of the terms of the gift and of the intentions of the donor. Thus the donor, unsure of the gift and its reception, begins to make his decisions on factors other than just the merits of the case and to surround the gift with various kinds of protective understandings. His whole attitude toward the transaction may change.

Take his feeling about publicity, for example. The norm has always been, and still is, that most gifts of unusual size are appropriately announced, at least by the recipient if not by the donor. But ever since philanthropy began to be a fairly common practice among people of wealth, some donors have tried to eschew the limelight. Why? Put yourself in their place, if you can, and you will begin to sense something of what they have come to feel.

Let us play the game. The imaginary time is the teens of this century, and you want to make a donation of a million dollars to establish some high schools for (as you probably call them)

31

"colored people." Schools for them are awfully poor, everybody knows, and they badly need education. But you don't want the gift publicized because you are a genuinely modest person. You don't want to be lionized, so you make it anonymously.

That's all right. We understand that. And if we happen to find out about your gift, we admire you all the more.

Now it's the forties. You plan to give two million dollars to a group of what are called "Negro" colleges. Everybody knows that separate isn't equal, and Negroes ought to have a chance at higher education, too. But those who can make that size of gift run the risk of being called "malefactors of great wealth," and you'd prefer not to be thought of in that category. You want secrecy not because you are doing anything wrong, but just because you don't want to be misunderstood and bothered.

That's all right, too. We accept your feeling. Anyway, it's your money and you ought to be able to do with it as you please, without interference.

But it's not the teens or the forties. It's the seventies. This time you want to give five million dollars to the "blacks." They need an opportunity to go to good schools and colleges, of course, but they need a lot more too. So you may spread it around a bit: some to fellowships earmarked for black students in professional schools, some to a black medical school, some for voter registration drives, some for financing black business enterprises, some for rehabilitation of the ghettos and fair housing programs.

But the last thing you want is publicity. Not because you are unduly modest, and certainly not because you hope not to be bothered—for if you've got that kind of money to give, you know you're going to be bothered anyway. Rather, because you simply don't relish the idea of being criticized for your efforts.

You are aware that the criticism will come from all points of the opinionated compass: segregationists will be livid, seeing all that money go to the blacks. Integrationists will also be irate, feeling that you are contributing to continued separatism. You can't win. So if you are still determined to put your money to good use on behalf of those who need it, you may tread softly, welcome silence and hope that some other philanthropic outfit draws the fire. You just don't want to put up with the inevitable flak.

This time it is not quite all right. Modesty and privacy are values to be prized, but a desire to escape criticism sounds craven. We who are your public, then, are likely to be doubly critical if we think you can't stand for us to be critical. All you want is praise? You'll get none of it from us.

The trouble with imaginary illustrations is just that: they are not real. All that they are meant to be, however, is suggestive. Anybody who ever wanted to give a million dollars was impelled by more than a sense of modesty; two million dollars, by more than a desire for privacy; five million dollars, by something quite different from a fear of criticism. These feelings are peripheral to the act of giving itself, and may even be antithetical to the impulse of generosity. That is, one makes the gift notwithstanding his modesty, at the risk of his loss of privacy, and in spite of his distaste for being criticized.

Somewhere along the line, however, these peripheral emotions may develop sufficient force to cut the donor's nerve of endeavor. When a potential benefactor comes to understand the negative reactions that his gift is likely to provoke—what's he trying to buy? to hide? to manipulate? and all the rest—his prudential stance of self-protection may well override his philanthropic impulse. If he doesn't lose the urge entirely, at least his joy in giving is considerably muted. Sooner or later he may begin to ask himself, Why bother?

Such a feeling on the part of today's philanthropists is not imaginary. As far as I am aware, no systematic research into a donor's shifting degrees of personal satisfaction has ever been undertaken. Graphs that tried to depict the changing patterns of a benefactor's attitudes would be silly. Such things are hardly susceptible to questionnaires, charts and the paraphernalia of analysis. But one cannot escape the impression gained from several decades of contact with donors and donations. As both recipient of and surrogate for philanthropy, I have watched at close range its moods and tempers as well as its acts and achievements.

And the summary impression I have gained is this: the benefactor today, large or small, is likely to be unhappy about his giving. In comparative terms, he is almost certain to be less starry-eyed, less sanguine about his gift's beneficent results, less glad, than was his predecessor of fifty or even fifteen years ago. Self-interest aside—and to the cynic it needs to be said that self-interest could indeed be often put aside—he feels less sure than he once did that his gift will accomplish anything worthwhile. Church treasurers, secretaries of college alumni funds, financial officers of hospitals, museums and symphony orchestras, can all testify to this fact, for their money-raising efforts and their daily mail give evidence of it.

Something of this sort is true, I believe, not only for individual donors but also for organized philanthropy; that is, for foundations, family and community funds and corporation charitable trusts. The money is there to be given, and so it is. But the dream of what it could help to do has lost some of its luster, and the pleasure in the doing is tempered. Rumors are not to be trusted, of course, but the fact of their currency tells something about the atmosphere of the times. In the last few years in the foundation field, rumors have been rife that the X Foundation intended to spend itself out of existence immediately, or that the Y Charitable Trust of the Z Corporation was going to give up its incorporated status and revert to being simply an annual benevolence program of its parent business. Rumor outruns fact, to be sure, but some such transformations have already taken place, more may be in the offing, and the moods of uncertainty and unhappiness becloud the scene.[33]

Short of dissolution, or giving up the war without a battle, foundations take a number of tacks in their response to criticism. Answers to specific charges will be discussed in the succeeding two chapters; now we mean simply to note some of the general reactions.

First is silence. But the immediate thing that must be said

33. The uncertain and unhappy mood is reflected in the tables of contents of recent issues of both *Foundation News* and *Non-Profit Report*; the latter has begun to run a fairly regular listing of "Terminated Foundations" (e.g., November, 1971, p. 8; December, 1971, p. 12; January, 1972, p. 15). It is reflected also in the agendas of nearly all the host of conferences on and for foundations that take place regularly.

about it is that it is seldom practiced. "The public be damned" was once thought to be the attitude of more than one tycoon, but swashbuckling has gone out of style, and though answers to the attack occupy a broad spectrum of reaction, almost nobody emulates the ostrich.

But a number of big donors, including foundations, are genuinely surprised. Who, me? The era of good feeling toward philanthropists and foundations lasted so long that many were ill prepared for the suspicion and even censure with which they have recently been visited. How could anyone possibly say that they were feathering their own nests? Isn't it obvious that their only desire was to do good?

Lest the surprise be thought to be ingenuous, even feigned, we need to be mindful of the self-image of a person or organization engaged in philanthropic pursuits, a self-image that is undoubtedly one of the occupational hazards. Like the minister, the teacher, the doctor or the lawyer, he accepts as a premise of his work the belief that it is disinterested, patently directed toward the welfare of others. When his vocation is attacked, therefore, and when his selfless practice of it is questioned, his surprise is genuine.

He is likely to protest his innocence. Surely a foundation's protestation is a justified as well as predictable reaction, when the charges are blanket and free-swinging in character and when the foundation knows that they don't legitimately apply to it.

Confession is also an occasional reaction. Those few who are indeed guilty of serious wrongdoing are not likely to admit it, of course, any more than any other kind of criminal. But the confession of having transgressed the less serious levels of proper behavior is sometimes expressed. The most popular form of confession among foundations is the recognition that they have failed to keep the public completely informed about their doings and that they have practiced poor public relations.

Two further types of reaction, seemingly contradictory in nature, often go hand in hand. First is resignation, the recognition that criticism is the price a foundation must pay for operating in the public sector. If one is to do anything worthwhile, it is bound to make some people unhappy. Foundations are in the business of making people unhappy, for those whose appeals are turned down far outnumber those whose projects get supported. Even if some of the critics are not among the company of those who have been rebuffed, their attacks are to be expected, and sooner or later they will be made.

But nobody has to like it. The partner to resignation is indignation, and foundations increasingly express themselves, often in private, sometimes in public, in feelings of outrage at the terms of the attack upon them. On rare occasion the anger may be only faintly concealed and may even descend to ad hominem types of argument. Consider the source! What is the critic really after? Economic, social or political gain of his own? Even if such questions are sometimes in order, the flint shows through, and the resentment and exasperation of foundations at what they take to be unprovoked and undeserved attacks are among the responses now being made.

Self-examination is a reaction of an entirely different kind of which we shall take note in succeeding chapters.

One way or another, all of these reactions add up to a defensive and dispirited posture.

It is rare indeed that second- or third-generation members of a family take as much delight in their fund's activity as did its founder. In many corporations chief executive officers turn over the chore of supervising the benevolence programs to junior personnel. Board memberships and positions on the staffs of large foundations are not the sinecures they were once thought to be. Annual reports of such organizations tell more than they once did, but much of what they tell is not merely reportorial but in a tone of self-justification. Let it be clearly stated: Those who are in any way intimately connected with philanthropy are now being disabused of the earlier notions of its splendor, its public approbation and its fun.

H. CONCLUSION

We find ourselves, then, in a strange time. As non-governmental endowed agencies devoted to the general welfare, foundations have grown remarkably in numbers, size of resources and diversity of structure and program. They have a right to be genuinely proud of their brief history. Motivations that explain their founding and have inspired their functioning are, like those of all other organizations, both selfish and selfless, and both kinds need to be credited and observed.

The work of foundations has inspired a variety of feelings and attitudes, many of them appreciative. But man-bites-dog is always the newsworthy item, and the charge that foundations are biting the public hand that feeds them is the attitude that has caught much of Congressional and general attention. It is of a piece with the general disrepute into which giving of all sorts and sizes seems to have fallen, and this widespread suspicion of decent reflexes, generous impulses and good works may represent a serious shift in American values. As agents for much of American philanthropy, foundations are victim to this suspicion. They have been caught in the act of helping, and their effectiveness in so doing will be seriously proscribed if they cannot make persuasive answer to the charges leveled against them. Among the attitudes to which they must respond are those that philanthropists have themselves begun to feel—a distaste for being criticized, a loss of satisfaction in the work of benevolence, a retreat into a defensive posture.

To whatever extent this brief outline of fact and feeling is true, it behooves us to ask why. The purpose of this book is to participate in that inquiry and, further, to postulate as to ways in which philanthropy may come again, deservedly, into the good graces of the public. My chief interest is in organized rather than personal philanthropy, not only because my experience in the latter is so modest, necessarily, as to be of no moment to anyone else, but also because my employment is with the former. As a foundation executive I am concerned about what has happened to foundations in recent years and, more, what their future may be. But beyond foundations I am interested in the survival of the American spirit of magnanimity and the strengthening of the American urge to face problems squarely and seek to solve them. Though foundations are only one type of institution that can manifest that spirit and that urge, an analysis of their current state of mind and manner may be suggestive for other institutions and for the citizenry in general. What are the specific charges against foundations? Are they valid? What are they doing about it? Is there a hopeful future? To the discussion of these questions the following chapters are directed.

II

Attack and Defense: Structure and Finance

A. INTRODUCTION: PROBLEMS IN MEETING THE ATTACK

CRITICISM of foundations is of two main types. The first is the constellation of charges having to do with structure and finance, with the establishment, management, administration and governance of foundations. These charges will be the subject matter for this chapter. The second type of criticism is directed to the programs of foundations and their operating policies, and to the effectiveness of their work; this will be the subject for the next chapter.

Before examining the major charges in detail it may be well to take note of some of the peculiar difficulties inherent in the give and take. Critics have their problems, and no less so do donors, trustees and staff members of foundations. If it were not for peculiar difficulties in getting a hold of the foundation field, the public might well have heard even more criticism than has been the case, or heard it earlier; and certainly foundation people would have been more outspoken and convincing in their responses.

The problem of the conscientious critic is a peculiar one. If he desires to be something other than a bushwhacker, lashing out indiscriminately, he soon realizes that the foundations needing criticism are the ones he can learn almost nothing about. Conversely, the ones whose affairs are public knowledge serve, in the main, as poor illustrations for the criticisms he feels duty-

39

bound to launch. It is not surprising that insinuation and innuendo are often the critic's stock in trade, for hard evidence is rare.

Once the charges are made, whether well or poorly based in facts, the respondents often find it difficult to reply. If the charge is true, it may not be the whole truth. If the charge is false, the lack of hard evidence which should have deterred the critic may also apply to the respondent, whose attempt at refutation may seem the more feeble by virtue of its being more honest.

Any foundation supporter is likely to wear two or more hats, for his relationship with a foundation is likely to be one among multiple relationships, with profit and non-profit institutions. On behalf of some, he would work for higher personal gain for himself and his associates; on behalf of others, he would work for larger contribution to other individuals and to society as a whole. His being a convincing protagonist for a business corporation may make him an unconvincing defender of a philanthropic foundation, or vice versa.

Foundation defenders, therefore, may seem to be mixed up in their motives and values. At one moment they play the part of seeking personal benefit; at another, when they wear their foundation hat, they must play the role of desiring the public benefit. When these roles are at great odds with each other, then the transfer from one to the other and back again constitutes a major problem for the foundation supporter.

Beyond these moral and psychological problems, the person who would like to respond constructively to criticisms leveled against foundations is often aware that he lacks basic information about the field that would be helpful to him. For example, patterns for the structure of foundations are hard to come by. Literally thousands of small foundations that are no more than incorporated family giving programs are presided over by some well-intentioned, generous individual who simply does not know how to organize his philanthropy or what to do. He hates to be called a tax dodger, and he genuinely wants his foundation's money to be put to good use for the benefit of others, but he has no capacity for developing a philanthropic program that would escape being subject to the charges he hears. He wants to be innocent of the charge that he himself is gaining some special privilege through his foundation, but he is uncertain how to set things up so as to establish and maintain his innocence. Even in some field in which his business experience may have made him expert, such as investments, he may still not know how to pursue a sound investment policy for a foundation as distinct from a business. When the donors or managers of small foundations and family funds find it difficult to respond to criticisms, they have some legitimate excuse, for philanthropy is only a part-time occupation for them.

But the chief interest of this essay is in the large foundations. When charges are leveled against them of errors of omission or commission in the field of organization and financial management, one would be justified in expecting that they could make convincing reply. Is this the case? In the following sections we shall note six main criticisms brought against foundations in the area of structure and finance, and in respect to each criticism answer will be made in terms of what seems to be the prevailing situation among the large foundations at the present time.

B. Criticism and Response:

1. *Tax Dodge?*

The most widespread and inclusive charge against foundations of all sorts and sizes is that the foundation as a type of institution is a tax dodge. The larger the foundation, the greater the intended escape from the payment of just taxes. No matter the good causes or the worthy organizations that may be helped, the money is in some sense tainted, for it has been siphoned out of the general purse by peculiar advantages that the wealthy benefactor has received.

This criticism is not as simple as it sounds. More than one target is in the critic's sights. First, the tax laws themselves are often thought to be designed in favor of the well-to-do. Second, even if the tax laws are relatively sound and non-prejudicial, they almost inevitably have loopholes, and to some critics the existence of any foundation is ipso facto evidence that the original donor found them. Legality is not exactly the issue, they say, for the more sophisticated philanthropists manage to refrain from doing anything illegal and thereby earn the greater censure. Thus legislators who write leaky tax laws share the blame with donors and their lawyers who take advantage of them.

The complaint, further, is really against the electorate at large, though it is seldom phrased in these terms. The American public, short-sighted as to its own self-interest, is willing to put up with representatives in Congress who turn on their true constituencies and pander to the wishes of the elite. A new strain of populist sentiment is evident here, but neo-populism is not the whole story, whether in its Patman, Wallace or some other version.

The heart of the matter is that the citizenry of this nation, deeply resistant to unfair taxation, is prepared to vent its spleen on anybody and any outfit that seems to get by or to let others get by. The net of resentment is cast widely, but when it is pulled in, foundations are sometimes thought to be in the center of the haul. If a foundation were to protest, "I'm not the fish you were really after," the reply might well be, "Anyway, I caught you." The fact is, foundations look to many people like tax dodges, or like part of the total paraphernalia of tax-dodging which the wealthy are supposed to employ.[1]

A few quotations from representative critics will suffice to document the full seriousness of this charge:

—Representative Wright Patman in testimony before the House Ways and Means Committee in 1969: "Philanthropy—one of mankind's more noble instincts—has been perverted into a vehicle for institutionalized, deliberate evasion of fiscal and moral responsibility to the Nation."[2]

1. See, for example, Lundberg, *op. cit.*, chap. 10; Goulden, *op. cit.*, chap. 7; Branch, *op. cit.;* George Meany, "Remarks before the House Committee on Ways and Means," in Reeves, *op. cit.*, pp. 209–218; and various Patman Reports, *op. cit.*
2. House Committee on Ways and Means, *Tax Reform, 1969,* Hearings, Part I, Washington, D.C., Government Printing Office, 1969, p. 12. (Hereafter referred to as Ways and Means Committee Hearings.)

—Joseph C. Goulden, author of the 1971 diatribe, *The Money Givers:* "Foundations are tax dodges, created by the greedy rich to cheat the Internal Revenue Service. ... the world of foundation philanthropy reeks with business and tax abuses—many of them on the verge of criminality. ..."[3]

—Ferdinand Lundberg, who created a sensation in 1968 with his best-selling exposé of *The Rich and the Super Rich:* "Nearly all of the American foundations have come into view since the enactment of the income tax and estate tax laws. ... One does not know in each case that the founder sought to escape taxes, but common reason would indicate it."[4]

—A 1970 cartoon by "Mal," circulated by the *Washington Star* syndicate: To a nondescript creature standing at respectful attention, the seated, cigar-chomping power figure says, "Sure, I look on charity as a moral obligation. I also look on charity as a convenient tax dodge."[5]

It would be idle to pretend that there is nothing at all to this charge, and it would be equally absurd to argue that tax-dodging is so endemic that all foundations are permanently flawed. Eschewing either extreme, let us pick our way through this tricky terrain to see what it is that so many complain about and whether it does in fact justify their complaints.

"Dodge" is, of course, a loaded word. The dodger, whether artful or no, is thought to be engaged in something immoral, and probably illegal as well. "Abuse," "avoidance" and "escape," equally popular as perjoratives, are equally effective in suggesting that serious shenanigans are involved.

Yet the fault is not that foundations have themselves dodged the paying of taxes. They are, after all, "tax-exempt." Even though the Tax Reform Act of 1969 puts them into a misty mid-region between exemption and non-exemption, they have not yet been accused of failing to abide by the law's requirements that they pay a kind of "excise tax" or audit fee. At the moment

3. Goulden, *op. cit.*, pp. 6, 16.
4. Lundberg, *op. cit.*, p. 468.
5. *Washington Star*, May 30, 1970.

of writing they have not yet had time or chance to be derelict in this fiscal duty, and all of them are now lining up at the pay-window.[6]

What does it mean, then, for a foundation to be accused of being a tax dodge? It does not mean that the foundation itself is doing something immoral or illegal. Rather, it has reference to the attitude, or motive, or action of the donor or donors in the establishment of the philanthropic fund. The criticisms to follow in this and the next chapter can be said to apply to the current life and work of foundations themselves, and to their managers, whether on trustee or staff level; whereas this charge of tax-dodging is a sort of pre-existence criticism.

How, then, can a foundation reply? Imagine the problem as it might apply to some of the nation's leading colleges and universities which bear proudly the names of nineteenth-century entrepreneurs who, during their lifetime and after, were sometimes looked upon as engaged in activities that, if not illegal, were at least detrimental to the general welfare. The honor roll is long: Carnegie, Drew, Duke, Rockefeller, Roosevelt, Stanford, Vanderbilt and many another. These institutions would have to plead innocent to any charge that predated their founding.

By the same token, and as President of the Danforth Foundation, I rise to a point of righteous order and proclaim, "The Danforth Foundation is not a tax dodge. As an honorable tax-exempt agency we intend to pay every tax that is legitimately imposed upon us, however inadvisedly."

The critics would not let us off the hook so easily, of course. They would want to ask whether the original Mr. Danforth received any encouragement or benefit from the tax laws when he established, or when later he made further contributions to, "his" foundation. The answer, of course, is Yes—even as it would be the same answer for you or me when we make a contribution to, say, our local church and itemize deductions on our annual income tax return.

The tax laws of this nation, though changing from time to

6. See "Foundation Excise Payments," *Non-Profit Report,* July, 1971, pp. 1–2; further notices in *Ibid.,* September, 1971, p. 16; December, 1971, p. 8; March, 1972, p. 20, etc.

time, have consistently given recognition to the contributions that citizens make for educational, scientific, religious and charitable purposes. When John Q. Citizen pledges to his local church, or when John D. Richman sets up a multimillion dollar foundation, each is able to do so because the law allows it. When he reports his act to Government, he receives whatever "concession," though that too is a loaded word, that is approved in the eyes of the current law. Once he has made his gift, small or large, he pays his tax as the law prescribes; and as long as he does so, whether poor or wealthy, he is not properly subject to a charge of dodging or avoiding his taxes.

But we cannot leave the matter here. Two important things remain to be said. First, the system of taxation may be unfair. That is, the tax laws may be poorly drawn, or prejudicial to the interest of some one group of people in comparison with other groups, or otherwise inimical to the best interests of the public as a whole. Between the time of the Second World War and the passage of the Tax Reform Act in 1969, foundations were established at an extremely rapid rate, and the justifiable conclusion is that the tax laws made such establishment highly attractive to citizens of large and even quite small means. Those who criticize this development have a legitimate complaint against the tax laws themselves. The kind of recognition that a Government, obliged to support itself with taxes, should give to educational, religious and charitable organizations is always a matter of proper debate in a democracy. But when and as individuals or institutions, including foundations, abide by the tax laws of the land, then there is no justification for pointing the finger of misbehavior at them.

The second thing to recognize is that both individuals and institutions are capable of misbehavior, that is, are capable of taking advantage of the law. It is on this point that Mr. Patman's investigations have been of benefit, for he succeeded in documenting a number of individual instances of abuse.[7] The Treasury Department Report on Foundations of 1965 gives other instances,[8] and many of the critical writings of recent

7. See Patman Reports, *op. cit.*
8. See Treasury Department Report, *op. cit.*

45

years have referred in general to such tax abuses, though illustrations by name have been hard to find.[9]

The specific tax abuses, as distinct from self-dealing and other kinds of faults that will be dealt with below, consist in false claims as to the value of contributions that a donor makes to his foundation. Claims for gifts that were never made, or that were never worth what was claimed, are ways of cheating that can and have applied to foundation donors as well as to other supposed benefactors. A false claim of any sort raises question as to the genuineness of the donor's altruistic purpose, and thus gives ground for suspecting that the central purpose is self-protective, not benevolent, that enhancement of one's estate is the chief aim, and that avoidance of taxes is indeed the special effort of the alleged philanthropist.

Until the passage of the Tax Reform Act of 1969, tax laws applying to foundations were so lax that various kinds of tax avoidance schemes were possible. One such plan came to be known as "boot-strapping," whereby income from a business was accorded favored tax treatment when only some small part of it accrued to the advantage of a tax-exempt institution.[10] Again, Mr. Patman exposed the efforts of an outfit called Americans Building Constitutionally, or ABC, to charge size-able fees for giving advice as to how people of means could set up foundations for their own special advantage.[11] Mr. Patman himself has been criticized because he did not, in his home state of Texas, expose some of the activities of foundations that found ways of gaining tax advantages without contributing significantly to charity.[12] In all the abuses that have been discovered, it has been made abundantly clear that the situation could be greatly improved if there were regular audits of all foundations by the Internal Revenue Service. Since the Tax

9. See, for example, Lundberg, *op. cit.*, chap. 10; Goulden, *op. cit.*, chap. 7; Meany, *op. cit.*

10. See Goulden, *op. cit.*, pp. 213 ff.; Luis Kutner, *Legal Aspects of Charitable Trusts and Foundations,* Chicago, Commerce Clearing House, 1970, pp. 252 ff., 427.

11. See Report of Peterson Commission, *op. cit.*, p. 54; Goulden, *op. cit.*, p. 187.

12. See Lundberg, *op. cit.*, p. 504; Goulden, *op. cit.*, p. 233.

Reform Act of 1969 provides for this possibility, tax avoidance in the future will be harder to practice and easier to identify.

Perhaps a word should be said about the role of tax lawyers. It is sometimes charged: "The tax lawyer can make a philanthropist of the meanest of men. He is disturbingly pragmatic, more interested in tax savings for his client than in benefits for charity, and his professional literature and trade meeting oratory reflect the preference."[13] It is hardly fair, of course, and certainly unrealistic, to expect tax lawyers to have a higher code of ethics than the men of wealth who employ them to protect their fiscal interests. Reputable tax lawyers resent the suggestion that they are solely responsible for tax abuses.[14] But magazine articles in tax journals and their own participation by way of giving lectures and leading discussion groups in foundation meetings testify to the fact that they keep fully alert to all possibilities whereby a foundation donor can benefit himself as well as the general public.[15]

It has already been noted that when an effort is made to give individual illustrations of tax abuse, the specific examples turn out to be quite few in number. Mr. Patman made wild charges but cited only a few, and the work of other critics has produced only a small additional number.[16] In the 1967 volume, *U.S. Philanthropic Foundations: Their History, Structure, Management and Record,* Warren Weaver refers "to the bad apple that taints the barrel of good apples. For it is reprehensibly true that a very few foundations have abused tax-free privilege." His own long experience in the field, however, persuaded him that "for every foundation which has cheated on tax exemption there are hundreds of foundations which have conformed meticulously to the letter and spirit of the law."[17]

13. *Ibid.,* p. 184.

14. See statements of Norman Sugarman and F. Emerson Andrews in Henry Sellin, ed., *Proceedings of the Eighth Biennial Conference on Charitable Foundations,* New York, New York University, 1967. (Hereafter referred to as NYU Proceedings, with appropriate biennial number.)

15. See Goulden, *op. cit.,* chap. 7 and footnotes.

16. See *Ibid.;* Lundberg, *op. cit.,* chap. 10; and Patman Reports, *op. cit.*

17. Weaver, *op. cit.,* pp. 189–190.

In the same vein the Peterson Commission concluded their discussion of the "financial abuses of foundations" by saying:

Every abuse, by definition, is bad. Yet it needs to be repeated that the air of the illicit that has settled on foundations generally is at least partly due to the fact that so little has been known about the actual frequency of abuses charged against them. In place of the careful inquiries we need, we have had guesses made airborne by the winds of suspicion. In place of the stable body of hard facts we need, we have had a mental process whereby a person looking at the foundation picture finds only what he is looking for. Worst of all, instead of isolating the spectacular case of an abuse so that it can be carefully examined to determine whether it is unique or part of a pervasive pattern, we have set it loose to undercut public confidence in all foundations and even charity as a whole—and this at a time when charitable organizations desperately need added support.[18]

What, then, is the answer to the question as to whether a foundation is a tax dodge? The answer is clear. It is no more so than is a church, a school, a hospital, or a symphony orchestra. Donors to any one of those organizations receive recognition from government for their benevolence; that is, their payment of taxes is affected in various ways by their philanthropic contributions. Donors can indeed misuse the tax privileges they receive from Government, and abuses in the foundation field have occurred. How many and to what extent are not known. But the charge that foundations in general are tax dodges simply does not stand up.

2. *Business and Family Advantage?*

Much more serious is the charge that a foundation constitutes an unfair advantage in personal or business affairs. As we have already noted, it is exceedingly difficult for a foundation, once established, to be a tax dodge, and without doubt it is exceedingly rare. In respect to business or family advantage, however, both the possibility and the actuality are entirely different. If the donor or any member of his family continues to have any relationship at all to the foundation he established,

18. Report of Peterson Commission, *op. cit.,* p. 62.

48

then the possibility that he or his family will benefit from the activity of his foundation is ever present and inescapable. If the donor or any member of his family continues to pursue business interests in one or a multitude of companies, the possibility cannot fail to exist that some relationship between those interests and the foundation takes place. Before we inquire as to the actuality, however, let us examine the charge more fully.

The line of argument goes something like this: It takes a person of considerable wealth to establish a foundation. Likely, he worked hard to make his money, and thus he developed the habit of working at whatever he did. At the very least he would not allow his non-business efforts to harm his business. His foundation may or may not be structurally tied in with his company, but you can be sure that his right hand knows what his left hand is doing and vice versa.

The foundation, then, is something of a masquerade. It is a disguised advertisement for him and his business. If some philanthropist is not so gross as to advertise his product directly by his foundation, this does not make him morally superior. It only means that he is smarter at public relations. As long as his foundation stays out of trouble, he, his family and his company all benefit. He knows this. He didn't get where he is by not knowing where his own interests lie.

If the donor or his family are no longer in business, or if they have other important interests besides the family business, the critic would feel that the same argument would still apply. Personal advertisement and social benefit could continue to be gained, and increased public esteem could be the outcome. Obviously the foundation would have to keep away from controversy. It would need to build up a reputation of being a safe, helpful agency devoted to good works. But if the foundation stayed out of trouble, then the non-business as well as business interests and activities of the donor and his family would be bound to benefit.

This accusation begins to have sharper bite when the specifications of self-serving get more precise. Critics point out that the unfairness in the advantage that the donor-businessman attains consists in something much more tangible than the

49

rubbing off of the foundation's good name on his business activity. It can consist in the interlocking arrangements between company and foundation that the donor creates and continues to practice. He can fix the foundation so as to enable him or his family to maintain control of the company. He can play each off against the other, vote the foundation's stock holding as if it were his own, manipulate the assets of both back and forth and protect his interests by filling both boards with relatives and cronies. Consequently, his foundation is something worse than a masquerade; it is a fraud. Its existence is understood as a desire not to turn loose but to hang on. It is an embodiment not of the donor's generosity but of his greed.

An easy answer to at least part of this charge would be to take note that it is now largely out of date. The Tax Reform Act of 1969 prohibited many types of conflict-of-interest and self-dealing, and the influence of the Act will clearly be in the direction of discouraging others not specifically outlawed. We shall look at this more carefully in Chapter V.

But such an answer will not do here, because we still need to know how widespread were the faults that the Tax Reform Act was designed to rectify, and whether or not there continue to be forms of this misbehavior that the Act does not touch. Much of the spleen visited upon foundations by their unforgiving enemies centers in this charge. The evidence that some critics see for the tax-dodge criticism noted above belongs here rather than there, for many a time when a foundation is not dodging the paying of appropriate taxes in any fashion, it may still be bestowing special privilege on some family or business.

The ways of receiving special advantage are many and complicated. Some are gross, some are subtle. If foundations are ever to possess again the good opinion of a large section of the public, they must make convincing answer to this charge, or else change their ways of behavior, or both. In any event, this is a criticism to which we simply cannot give short shrift.

The most heinous examples of self-dealing were indeed so bad that the law finally took notice of them, and presumably they are in process of being cleaned up. Mr. Patman put a few of them on public record. The dust he began to raise in 1961

50

persuaded the Internal Revenue Service to look more carefully into possibilities of self-serving.

The Commissioner of Internal Revenue, Mortimer Caplin, wrote in 1963: "What have we found, enquiring into foundation practices? There have been abuses. We have found self-dealing between the foundation and insider groups; some losses of exemption have resulted. We have found unreasonable accumulations. . . . speculative investments. . . . We have found foundations actually going out and competing for interest income, and for rental income. We have even found manipulation of leases. . . . In short, we have found a wide variety of transactions close to, as well as on the other side of, legality—violations of the spirit, if not always of the letter, of the law. Congressman Patman's investigations have been of considerable assistance—and impetus—to us, in these matters." [19]

The Treasury Department's Report on Private Foundations, published in 1965, discussed "six categories of major problems" in the foundation field. Of these six, four are illustrative of the charge that foundations are used as a business and family advantage:

A. Self-Dealing.
Some donors who create or make substantial contributions to a private foundation have engaged in other transactions with the foundation. Property may be rented to or from it; assets may be sold to it or purchased from it; money may be borrowed from it or loaned to it. These transactions are rarely necessary to the discharge of the foundation's charitable objectives; and they give rise to very real danger of diversion of foundation assets to private advantage. . . .

C. Foundation Involvement in Business.
Many private foundations have become deeply involved in the active conduct of business enterprises. . . . Serious difficulties result from foundation commitment to business endeavors. Regular business enterprises may suffer serious competitive disadvantage. Moreover, opportunities and temptations for subtle and varied forms of self-dealing—difficult to detect and impossible com-

19. Mortimer Caplin, "Foundations and the Government: Some Observations on the Future," *Foundation News*, May, 1963, quoted in Reeves, *op. cit.,* pp. 174–175.

51

pletely to proscribe—proliferate. Foundation management may be drawn from concern with charitable activities to time-consuming concentration on the affairs and problems of the commercial enterprise. . . .

D. Family Use of Foundations to Control Corporate and Other Property.

Donors have frequently transferred to private foundations stock of corporations over which the donor maintains control. The resulting relationships among the foundation, corporation, and donor have serious undersirable consequences. . . .

E. Financial Transactions Unrelated to Charitable Functions.

Private foundations necessarily engage in many financial transactions connected with the investment of their funds. Experience has, however, indicated that unrestricted foundation participation in three classes of financial activities which are not essential to charitable operations or investment programs can produce seriously unfortunate results. Some foundations have borrowed heavily. . . . Certain foundations have made loans whose fundamental motivation was the creation of unwarranted private advantage. . . . Some foundations have participated in active trading of securities or speculative practices. . . .[20]

Commentators friendly to foundations recognize the fairness of the Treasury Department's Report. Here and there across the country the Internal Revenue Service took action against flagrant abuses. Muckrakers described hypothetical situations, and when they were protected against libel, sometimes named names, dates and places.[21] It was still hard to pin down specific instances of gross misbehavior or to know how widespread they were.

When the Peterson Commission came to review the "financial abuses of foundations," they described at some length various ways in which donors could manipulate their foundations to their own personal or business advantage. But the report continues: "The Commission recognized the self-evident potential for abuses in the foregoing kinds of transactions. But how *often* and how *serious* have these abuses actually been? The question, which goes to the heart of any reformist proposal, was difficult

20. Treasury Department Report, *op. cit.*
21. See Staff of the Russell Sage Foundation, *op. cit.*; Goulden, *op. cit., passim*; Weaver, *op. cit.*, pp. 185–186.

for the Commission to answer because it had no subpoena or auditing power to get at the hard facts. Thus, the Commission had to use various indirect approaches."[22]

One of the things they did was to examine approximately five hundred returns of the sort that foundations made annually to the Internal Revenue Service on Form 990-A. Until the Tax Reform Act of 1969, some self-dealing transactions between donor and foundation were approved if they were "at arm's length" or met a standard of reasonableness, but these transactions had to be reported. The Commission notes that the "percentage of foundations reporting" on various transactions was quite small in every case. For example, only 1.5 percent reported "borrowing income or corpus"; only 2.5 percent, "receiving compensation for services"; only 3.5 percent, "purchasing securities or other property"; and only 5.5 percent, "selling services or property." The Peterson Commission concludes that though "some foundations may not have reported transactions at all, . . . the vast majority did not report any self-dealing transactions."[23] A confirmed critic of foundations, however, might emphasize the other side of the coin, that as large a number as 5.5 percent of the foundations admitted some form of self-dealing.

All of this, however, is now supposed to be at an end. The Tax Reform Act of 1969 will see to that, provided that conscientious audits will be made by the Internal Revenue Service at fairly frequent intervals, and provided further that enforcement of the laws against self-dealing will be firm, impartial and swift.

But these were always the easier types of advantage to identify and to condemn, and the more subtle forms of special advantage remain. To make clear what these peculiar privileges consist in, perhaps we should review our understanding as to the nature of a foundation and thus as to something of the proper relationship between foundation and donor.

Undue family or business advantage gained from the creation and activity of a foundation is not merely the result of some

22. Report of Peterson Commission, *op. cit.*, pp. 57–58. (Italics are the Commission's.)

23. *Ibid.*, p. 58.

monstrous and now illegal act of self-dealing, some clever financial manipulation. Such advantage may accrue in terms of social prestige, or political preferment, or even something as relatively innocuous as perquisites and personal immunities.

Objection to special advantage can itself get picayunish. One does not go so far as to say that any benefit at all that a donor receives is by that very fact improper. If a foundation is in fact established for the motives that justify its being given tax exemption, then it stands in the same position vis-à-vis the donor that any other educational, scientific, religious or charitable organization, justifiably receiving tax exemption, stands. A foundation is in fact a kind of midwife between the donor and the ultimate recipient, and it owes its existence and its legitimacy to the proposition that, like the distributor between the wholesaler and the retailer, the foundation can do a more thoughtful, more careful, more balanced job of philanthropy than would be the case if the donor tried to deal directly with all the various individual recipients.

If the foundation were in fact the donor's back pocket, then it would partake of the donor's character, and he could properly manage it to whatever extent and in whatever way he chose. In point of fact, however, the donor receives his tax deduction not when his foundation makes the grant to some recipient agency but earlier, when he establishes the foundation. Thus the foundation partakes more of the character of the charitable recipient, it is recognized as a charity, and the donor's relationship to it should properly be of the same order as his relationship with any other educational, scientific, religious, cultural or charitable agency to which he might make a gift.

This is not to say that the donor should have no relationship at all. On the contrary, when I make an annual gift to my church or my college, I continue to be a member of that church and an alumnus of that college. I expect that relationship to be a meaningful one for me, one which will allow me room to express my views from time to time about what the church or the college is doing or proposes to do. I expect to have no peculiarly advantageous relationship, but I do stay related to the recipients of my gifts.

54

Correspondingly, the donor stays related to his foundation. By the act of its receiving tax exemption, it is no longer "his" foundation in the sense that it can be used for special privilege for him. But it is still his foundation, in the sense that he can use it as a channel through which he can express his desire to be of service to those around him. The test, then, is a difficult one of whether he remains related to and uses the foundation to make it serve him or to enable it to serve others.

Even this is too neat, of course. He may believe he is serving others when in reality he is exploiting them. He may see no conflict at all in his making foundation grants to those who can be potential customers of his business products. He may see no harm in his paying himself a salary from his foundation receipts, or in his putting some of his close friends or family on the pay-roll. He may simply not realize he is getting old.

The point is, there are a hundred ways in which a foundation can be used by a donor for some special sort of advantage for him, his family, his business, or his own narrow interests. The foundation might be as innocent as the donor's plaything, and as sinister as the donor's tool for overturning society. Either way, it could be employed to bestow some special preference on the donor that the nature of its incorporation as a tax-exempt agency devoted to the public welfare does not justify.

Not long ago I had occasion to inquire of a distinguished scientist, who has also been a foundation executive, about the relationship he had had with one of the foundations with which he had been connected for a number of years. In his recent auto-biography he had written about that foundation's programs: "The actions themselves—at least speaking of areas within which I had had training and experience—seemed to me first-rate and unquestionably in the public interest. But the extent to which all this depended upon the special genius of a man approaching ninety seemed to me worrisome."[24] There was no doubt in the scientist's mind that the donor of the foundation was a remarkably intelligent, generous, toughminded man who was quite prepared to bend his sizeable philanthropy to serve

24. Warren Weaver, *Scene of Change: A Lifetime in American Science,* New York, Charles Scribner's Sons, 1970, p. 125.

55

his own special tastes and interests. In light of that fact, I referred to the quotation, said I was surprised at the use of the word "worrisome" and asked him whether he had considered using any other word. "Yes," he said, "I thought of saying 'illegal'. "

"Worrisome" was protective and tactful, but "illegal" would be harsh and inaccurate. As the law now stands, it was unlikely that anything that Mr. Sloan was doing to mold his foundation to his own desires was against the law. "Reprehensible" might have been the right word.

Donors are occasionally so ill-advised as to try to gain political advantage through their foundations. The cause célèbre of this kind of self-dealing was the activity of the Frederick W. Richmond Foundation in Brooklyn during 1967 and 1968, which happened to coincide in time and geographical location with a campaign for a Congressional seat by Frederick W. Richmond himself. The incumbent against whom Richmond was running was Representative John Rooney, and once he had disposed of Richmond in the Democratic primary and had been re-elected to Congress in the fall of 1968, he let his colleagues in Washington know about the threat that awaited them from foundations subject to the bidding of potential political opponents. He was one of the first to testify in February, 1969, at the hearings of the House Ways and Means Committee on foundations. As Rooney phrased it, "I am the first known Member of Congress to be forced to campaign for re-election against the awesome financial resources of a tax-exempt foundation."[25]

The Richmond Foundation case was so blatant and mismanaged as to be of no effect, except in reverse: Rooney not only got re-elected but foundations far and wide were hurt by his charge that donors could receive political advantages. But what about more subtle relationships and more low-key campaigns? Now and again one hears, though seldom sees in print, the snide question as to whether any of the several Rockefeller foundations have been of help to any of the Rockefeller politicians, in New York, Arkansas, West Virginia or wherever. It is a tribute, both to the integrity and maturity of the various

25. Ways and Means Committee Hearings, *op. cit.,* Part I, p. 213.

Rockefeller foundations and the generally high regard in which Rockefeller politicians are held by friend and foe alike, that there has been so little mention of such possible relationships.

Whenever a member of a foundation family enters public life, however, some question may arise in respect to the role that the foundation may be playing in his career. In the fall of 1970 it was necessary for some of us on the staff of the Danforth Foundation to wage a two-way struggle to preserve the Foundation's independence against political incursions from opposite directions. John Danforth, a grandson of our founder and formerly a Trustee, until he resigned upon his election as Attorney General of Missouri, ran for the U.S. Senate against the incumbent, Stuart Symington. Danforth's supporters hoped that locally well-regarded grants would rub off to his credit; Symington's, that some of the Foundation's allegedly controversial activities in the inner city would hurt his opponent in the suburbs. In each case such use of the Foundation would have been based on the false premise that John Danforth had had something to do with those Foundation programs that post-dated his service on the Board. In my opinion the political partisanship of both sides failed, but the danger was always present that the Foundation might be made to appear either a peculiar advantage or an unwarranted disadvantage to a member of the donor's family.

Is it possible that a donor could actually fail to receive some advantage from his foundation? Or is the situation so automatic that no matter how carefully the donor may protect himself and his foundation against unfair benefit, he or his family will still be a beneficiary? This is not an idle question, for unless the foundation develops a bad reputation, it is almost impossible for some of the credit that the foundation has earned not to apply to the people responsible for it.

How much credit is a proper amount? How much connection between a foundation and its donor is justifiable? How far can the donor go in fostering the relationship with his foundation, without stepping over the line of unfair advantage?

Surely he can call the foundation by his own or the family name. Surely he can retain a place on the foundation's board of trustees, and provide places for some of his family and close friends. Surely he can continue to take an interest in the foundation's activities throughout his own lifetime. And when a grateful recipient wants to say thank you, surely he can accept the appreciation if it is expressed in proper bounds of taste and attribution.

But even for these things, some limitations must be observed. If his foundation is larger than simply a modest family giving program, he must be careful to refrain from establishing its structure so as to be nothing more than his own alter ego, and from establishing its practice so as to be completely subservient to his own command. He must seek expert counsel on board and staff. He must try to make sure that neither he nor any members of his immediate family, nor his business interests and business associates, occupy preferential positions in the scope of the foundation's activities and receive peculiar advantages or benefits at the foundation's hands. It is not enough that the advantages to be eschewed be fiscal or financial in nature. He must also see to it that no special political or social advantages are bestowed. But all of this is very hard and takes time. And one of the most difficult things for anyone, even, or perhaps especially a close associate to try to say to a foundation donor is, "You are receiving and accepting unfair advantage from your foundation."

The possibility that a foundation be an unfair business or personal advantage can apply to staff members of a foundation as well as to the donor or members of his family. All of the paraphernalia of special advantage—business tie-ups, self-dealing, high salaries, social or political advantage, personal amenities, etc.—can be made to accrue to non-family trustees or officers of the foundation. Complaints are heard less often, because donors are more likely to be beneficiaries; but the possibility still remains.

Insensitivity to the danger of special advantage can be of two sorts: (1) the person benefited may simply not recognize, or be able to recognize, that he is receiving some improper advantage; and (2) when and if he recognizes it, he may not be prepared to admit its impropriety. There is an easy acceptance of the role that having or working for a foundation enables a person to play, and there is a strange reluctance to admit it, much less to disavow it. Advantages can exist in foundations of any size, but some types of advantage are easier to accept, and hide, in small foundations than in large ones. The older the foundation, the more likely it will possess the kind of maturity that can see, and seeing, reject, the acceptance of special advantages.

And yet when all the possibilities of misbehavior are taken into account and all the instances of actual self-dealing and other kinds of advantage-taking have been added up, the surprise is how little there is to complain about. The Treasury Department's Report that pointed out ways in which advantage could be taken concluded that "most private foundations act responsibly and contribute significantly to the improvement of our society."[26]

3. *Investment policy?*

The cut of this criticism runs as follows: One of the chief ways in which a donor manages to receive advantages from his foundation, or more correctly, manages to continue to enjoy advantages he possessed prior to his establishing the foundation, is by practicing an investment policy that is aimed not at making the largest possible amounts of money available for charity but at protecting the value of the donor's own holdings. Most foundations are established with a gift of stock or other property. Most gifts of stock are concentrated in the holdings of the donor's own business or corporation, for very few foundations start out life with a diversified portfolio. The natural thing is for the foundation to keep the stock with which it started. But, says the critic, that is often the wrong thing, from the point of view of the best interests of the general welfare which the foundation is supposed to serve.

The point at issue is whether the foundation is spending its money in desirable measure, or whether, on the contrary, it is hoarding it or not even earning it. Charges are made that

26. Treasury Department Report, *op. cit.*

foundations do not manage their assets well, that the rate of return on their assets is absurdly low, and thus that their pay-outs to charity are pitifully small in comparison with the size of their resources.

The answer that must be made to this general criticism is that foundations are guilty—some more than others, of course; some over a longer period of time than others; some consciously and intentionally, others inadvertently. But on balance and across the board, the situation seems clear that foundations have pursued policies of investment and expenditure that deserve much of the criticism they have received. Many of these abuses will soon be a thing of the past, for the Tax Reform Act of 1969 has much to say, directly or indirectly, about concentrations of stock, amount of return and especially amount of annual pay-out. The significance of the act in this regard will be discussed in Chapter V.

The first effort to establish some standard of good performance in this area was the Revenue Law of 1950 which prohibited a foundation from piling up an "unreasonable" accumulation of its resources.[27] The aim, of course, was to make foundations pay out their income on a current basis, but "unreasonable" was never very clearly defined. Moreover, enforcement was sporadic at best.

The Danforth Foundation came in for attention, for just at the time the new law was introduced, the Foundation was engaged in expanding its staff and its activities. Setting aside money for the support of programs being designed, the Foundation fell afoul of the Internal Revenue's understanding of "unreasonable accumulation," and the outcome of a long and complicated challenge was that the Foundation was judged to have spent less than it should have spent in the years 1951 and 1952. This matter is now quite academic for us, for the Danforth Foundation has overspent its income every year since 1953, often by margins of 200 percent or more.

27. See Marion R. Fremont-Smith, *Foundations and Government: State and Federal Law and Supervision*, New York, Russell Sage Foundation, 1965, pp. 159–193; F. Emerson Andrews, *Philanthropic Giving*, New York, Russell Sage Foundation, 1950, *passim* and pp. 294–301 (the Act itself).

60

The Peterson Commission gave considerable attention to investment and pay-out performance, and many of their findings are pertinent to the charges we are now examining. For example, "The most important type of appreciated intangible property has been stock in a company in which the donor and his family owned a substantial interest (20 percent or more). Such stock has accounted for 44 percent of all contributions to foundations and 70 percent of the contributions to foundations with over $100 million in assets."[28]

Whether the foundation itself owned controlling interest in a corporation, however, is a different matter, and foundations have often been insensitive to this point, even before the Tax Reform Act of 1969 set standards in such matters. The Peterson Commission discovered: "While ownership of a 'controlling' interest in a corporation (20 percent or more) by a foundation has been, and continues to be, relatively infrequent, it is found primarily among large foundations. . . . At the time of our survey, our data suggest that only 4 percent of foundations still owned a 'control' block. But 27 percent of those with over 10 million in endowment held control stock, and, in all, foundations with a controlling interest in a company held nearly three-tenths of all foundation assets."[29]

Whether foundations have had a controlling percentage or a much smaller, though still substantial, proportion of the ownership of the donor's company, they have been slow to change their holdings or to diversify their total portfolio.[30] For example, though the Danforth Foundation never held control of the Ralston Purina Company, at one time it did own around 19 percent of the outstanding stock. In the fall of 1970, however, it reduced this holding by approximately one-half. Such an action does not represent any change in the actual relationship between the two organizations, the Foundation and the Company. From the beginning of the Foundation they have been

28. Report of Peterson Commission, *op. cit.,* p. 72.
29. *Ibid.*
30. Ralph L. Nelson, *The Investment Policies of Foundations,* New York, Russell Sage Foundation, 1967, Appendix V, Table E, pp. 186–188.

organically separate, though members of the family have been members of both Boards. The Danforth Foundation's selling of approximately one-half of its Ralston stock did not represent any loss of confidence by the Foundation in the Company. It grew simply out of the fact that in light of the need to keep income and expenditures in rough balance, as well as the desirability of not holding too large a share of any one company's stock, it seemed wise to reduce the amount of Ralston stock in the Foundation's portfolio.[31]

Unlike Danforth, some of the larger foundations do own control of business corporations, and as a result of the Tax Reform Act they are going to have to divest themselves of a considerable amount of holdings in their related companies. Among the foundations that will be affected are: Duke, Hartford, Kellogg, Kresge, Lilly, Moody, and Pew.[32] The point of all this voluntary or mandatory diversification of foundations' portfolios is to make sure that charitable institutions are not engaged in some conflict of interest with profit-making organizations, to the benefit of either or both, and to the possible detriment, therefore, of competitors of the business.

How have foundations managed their assets? One of the six major problems that the Treasury Report of 1965 identified was "delay in benefit to charity." The Treasury Department's position was succinctly stated: "The tax laws grant current deductions for charitable contributions upon the assumption that the funds will benefit the public welfare. This aim can be thwarted when the benefits are too long delayed ... the purposes of charity are not well served when a foundation's charitable disbursements are restricted by the investment of its fund in assets which produce little or no current income."[33]

The Peterson Commission examined this question carefully and concluded "that the investment performance of foundations

31. See *The Danforth Foundation Annual Report,* 1970–1971, p. 23; "Danforth: Momentum Past Moratorium," *Non-Profit Report,* November, 1971, p. 6.
32. Nelson, *op. cit.,* Appendix V, Table E, pp. 186–188. Kresge is currently engaged in selling and exchanging large amounts of S. S. Kresge Co. stock; see *Wall Street Journal,* April 26, 1972.
33. Treasury Department Report, *op. cit.*

is below par, and perhaps significantly so." The limited available information bore out this conclusion. The Commission presented a table giving the "median total return on assets" in percentages of the total assets themselves; their figures for 1968, the year for which they had collected fairly reliable data, showed that the median total return for foundations over one hundred million in size was 8.5 percent of their assets, but the "weighted figure for all foundations" of whatever size was only 5.6 percent The rate of return on assets included interest, dividends and realized and unrealized capital gains. The percentages for other endowment funds were considerably higher for 1968 than the percentages of return for foundations—14.9 percent for balanced funds, 15.3 percent for common stock mutual funds. The conclusion was reached "that, in every category, foundation investment performance is substantially lower than the balanced funds performance of nearly 15 percent in 1968."[34]

For other kinds of tax-exempt institutions to receive as poor a rate of return as has been the case for foundations would probably be considered a serious mismanagement of their resources. Universities or hospitals have got to be able to get a better return on their endowment in order to operate. At one time it would have been thought that this was hardly a matter of major moment to people outside the foundation. If the foundation's investment policy didn't produce any larger return, it was too bad that it didn't have more to spend, but after all it was the foundation's own business.

But a change in the attitude of the public is taking place. As the Peterson Commission states the matter: "The public, whether it is aware of the fact or not, has a stake of its own in the matter, and for the following reasons: Since each percentage point of added total return on foundation investments would yield between two and three hundred million dollars of additional funds for charity, the costs to society of a lackluster management of these investments could be on the order of hundreds of millions of dollars annually."[35]

The investment performance is important because it is re-

34. Report of Peterson Commission, *op. cit.*, p. 74.
35. *Ibid.*, p. 75.

lated to expenditure performance, or pay-out. Whether or not the actual investment policies of foundations will be improved in the years immediately ahead, the Tax Reform Act of 1969 has seen to it that pay-out will have to be. This means that, if investment performance doesn't begin to match the required pay-out provisions of the act, foundations may find themselves slowly going out of business.

The requirement of the act is that by 1972 foundations must achieve a pay-out at the rate of 4½ percent of the market value of its assets at the beginning of the year; and must increase this pay-out rate by ½ of 1 percent per year until the foundation achieves a 6 percent pay-out by 1975. On the basis of what other endowments expect to produce, and do produce, for the use of their tax-exempt institutions, these percentages hardly seem excessive. Yet their imposition will force a major change in the behavior of many of the larger foundations, as well as smaller ones, all across the country.[36]

The reason so many foundations have been low in annual pay-out is that their actual expenditures have been tied to their cash income, without reference to capital gains. When and if a foundation held stock that produced very little in the way of dividends, though its capital gains may have been enormous, it tended to spend each year a sum closely approximating its cash income, even though this may have represented a very small percentage of the market value of its assets.

A comparison of the figures for the large foundations on market value, income and expenditures shows the great variance among foundations in respect to both investment policy and

36. See *Tax Reform Act of 1969*, P.L. 91–172, Chicago, Commerce Clearing House, 1970, Code Sec. 4942 and Act. Sec. 101(1)(3). (Hereafter referred to as TRA, with appropriate Section no.) Among scores of comments see Laurens Williams in *Foundations and the Tax Reform Act of 1969*, New York, The Foundation Center, 1970, pp. 8–12. The pay-out percentages given apply to foundations in existence before May 27, 1969. Efforts have been made to amend the law; see "HR 11197: New Foundation Bill," *Non-Profit Report*, November, 1971, pp. 1–2, and "Memorandum to Members," 72–2, Council on Foundations. The Secretary of the Treasury is given authority by Sec. 4942(e)(3) to change the percentages from time to time as changes in money rates and investment yields dictate; he did so on April 17, 1972 (TIR 1164); see "Memorandum to Members," 72–3, Council on Foundations.

expenditure policy, and, for those whose performance is weak, gives ground for the criticism increasingly being leveled on this score. The huge degrees of variance, however, suggest how desirable it is that critics inform themselves about the actual practices of various foundations, for if there are indeed some foundations whose performance deserves complaint and condemnation, there are many others whose performance is worthy of approval.

Take, for example, the matter of income. Among the approximately thirty foundations that were reported in 1969 as having assets of over $100 million in market value, nine had cash income of less than 2 percent of their assets. Several of these had large capital gains, of course, but when their expenditures were tied to their cash income, rather than to their total return including capital gains, this meant that the percent of their expenditures in comparison with their assets was tragically low, well below what the new tax regulations will require. The other side of the picture is that twelve of the number had cash income of over 4½ percent of their assets; and since many of these also spent some of their capital gains, their expenditures achieved levels fully within the requirements of the Tax Reform Act.

It may be useful to learn a new way of ranking foundations in respect to size. The traditional method is to list them by reference to the market value of their assets. On this basis the thirty-two over $100 million, according to the latest edition of the *Foundation Directory,* line up in the following order.*

Name and Location of Foundation	Market Value of Assets (in millions)	For FY ending in:
1. Ford Foundation, New York City	$2,901.5	9/30/70
2. Lilly Endowment, Indianapolis	777.6	12/31/69
3. Rockefeller Foundation, New York City	757.1	12/31/69
4. Duke Endowment, New York City	509.8	12/31/69
5. Kresge Foundation, Detroit	432.6	12/31/69
6. Kellogg Foundation, Battle Creek	392.6	8/31/70
7. Mott Foundation, Flint	371.5	12/31/69

* Explanatory footnote begins on p. 68.

65

Name and Location of Foundation	Market Value of Assets (in millions)	For FY ending in:
8. Pew Memorial Trust, Philadelphia	367.0	12/31/69
9. Sloan Foundation, New York City	302.9	12/31/69
10. Carnegie Corporation, New York City	283.4	9/30/70
11. Hartford Foundation, New York City	277.4	12/31/69
12. Mellon (A. W.) Foundation, New York City	233.8	12/31/69
13. Longwood Foundation, Wilmington	226.1	9/30/68
14. Houston Endowment, Houston	209.2	12/31/69
15. Rockefeller Brothers Fund, New York City	198.2	12/31/69
16. Woodruff Foundation, Atlanta	187.2	12/31/69
17. Bush Foundation, St. Paul	163.3	11/30/69
18. Danforth Foundation, St. Louis	161.9	5/31/70
19. Mellon (R. K.) Foundation, Pittsburgh	139.7	12/31/69
20. Kaiser Family Fund, Oakland	136.4	12/31/69
21. Moody Foundation, Galveston	129.0	12/31/69
22. Alcoa Foundation, Pittsburgh	124.7	12/31/69
23. Irvine Foundation, San Francisco	124.0	3/31/70
24. Clark (The Edna McConnell) Foundation, Wilmington	113.6	9/30/70
25. Commonwealth Fund, New York City	113.5	6/30/70
26. Clark (Edna McConnell) Foundation, New York City	113.2	12/31/70
27. Cleveland Foundation, Cleveland	112.0	12/31/69
28. Scaife Foundation, Pittsburgh	109.6	12/31/69
29. Brown Foundation, Houston	108.6	6/30/69
30. Richardson (Sid W.) Foundation, Fort Worth	106.3	12/31/68
31. Surdna Foundation, Yonkers	103.2	6/30/69
32. Johnson (R. W.) Foundation, New Brunswick	102.4	12/31/69

Look what happens, however, when the listing is by order of their actual philanthropic activity rather than by the market value of their portfolio. Their ranking by expenditures goes like this.*

*Explanatory footnote begins on p. 68.

Name of Foundation (with rank in assets in parentheses)	Expenditures	
	Amount	% of Market Value
1. Ford Foundation (1)	$282,675,684	9.7%
2. Rockefeller Foundation (3)	38,932,927	5.1%
3. Duke Endowment (4)	22,520,920	4.4%
4. Sloan Foundation (9)	16,975,832	5.6%
5. Kellogg Foundation (6)	16,835,799	4.3%
6. Hartford Foundation (11)	16,123,229	5.8%
7. Mott Foundation (7)	14,757,205	4.0%
8. Houston Endowment (14)	14,600,712	7.0%
9. Carnegie Corporation (10)	13,985,949	4.9%
10. Mellon (A. W.) Foundation (12)	12,157,072	5.2%
11. Danforth Foundation (18)	10,497,076	6.5%
12. Kresge Foundation (5)	8,999,068	2.1%
13. Rockefeller Brothers Fund (15)	8,981,471	4.5%
14. Lilly Endowment (2)	7,997,193	1.0%
15. Longwood Foundation (13)	7,375,004	3.3%
16. Pew Memorial Trust (8)	6,854,000	1.8%
17. Commonwealth Fund (25)	6,498,359	5.7%
18. Cleveland Foundation (27)	6,270,431	5.6%
19. Woodruff Foundation (16)	6,220,500	3.3%
20. Mellon (R. K.) Foundation (19)	6,036,469	4.3%
21. Surdna Foundation (31)	5,040,225	4.9%
22. Scaife Foundation (28)	4,913,650	4.5%
23. Bush Foundation (17)	4,252,999	2.6%
24. Irvine Foundation (23)	3,816,838	3.1%
25. Brown Foundation (29)	2,930,231	2.7%
26. Alcoa Foundation (22)	2,909,557	2.3%
27. Moody Foundation (21)	2,554,363	2.0%
28. Clark (Edna McConnell) Foundation (26)	2,229,687	2.0%
29. Richardson (Sid W.) Foundation (30)	2,150,642	2.0%
30. Clark (The Edna McConnell) Foundation (24)	1,220,487	1.1%
31. Johnson (R. W.) Foundation (32)	611,126	0.6%
32. Kaiser Family Fund (20)	251,300	0.2%

Comparisons are invidious. When the criterion is the extent to which a foundation's resources are being put to use, some sharp changes in the relative order of rank take place. For

---

* Figures in the two tables in the text are compiled from the *Foundation Directory*, IV, *op. cit.*, and overall are more accurate than any other published material. Rankings and comparisons, however, can never be precise, because of different accounting and reporting procedures. Sometimes different figures, available from individual foundation reports, serve as better bases for comparisons; and in a few cases differences are so large as to make the tables based on the *Directory*'s figures misleading.

For example: sounder comparisons might be made if closer fiscal-year endings were observed. The fiscal year for the majority in the tables ended on 12/31/69. The more comparable Ford figure, therefore, would have been for the FY ending 9/30/69, which was $2,779.3 million in assets, though almost the same amount in expenditures—$284,279,000. It makes little difference for Ford, but for Commonwealth it makes a lot: figures for FY ending 6/30/69 read $142.4 million in assets (twentieth in rank that year) and $11,036,000 in expenditures (eleventh in rank). Other dissimilarities based on different fiscal years seem minor.

The problem with Longwood and Sid W. Richardson is not so much a different fiscal year as it is their inadequate reporting. As the table shows, the latest or most reliable figures available to the *Directory* were for 1968 FYs. The asset figure for Longwood in 1969 was $193.6 million, and the expenditure figure was $6,826,000. Sid Richardson's 1969 figures were also delayed in being sent the *Directory*: assets fell to $86.1 million, making it slightly smaller than the Smith Richardson Foundation of Greensboro, North Carolina, with $87.3 million, and expenditures rose to $6,567,000 in 1969. Thus Sid Richardson may no longer belong in the list of foundations with over one hundred million in assets, taking its place with several other recent ex-100-millionaires: the Bishop Estate of Honolulu, the William R. Kenan, Jr., Charitable Trust of New York City, Edwin H. Land–Helen W. Land, Inc., of Cambridge, Massachusetts, and the Phoebe Waterman Foundation, now called the Haas Community Fund, of Philadelphia. Bishop, with $131.9 million in assets reported in the third edition of the *Foundation Directory*, decided to give up its status as a "private foundation." Kenan had $110.7 million in 1969, but fell to $83.1 million in 1970, in time to be included in the fourth edition of the *Directory* at the latter figure. Land's decline was even sharper: from $139.4 million in 1969 to the *Directory* figure of $75.4 million in 1970. Waterman-Haas's decline paralleled Richardson's in date and amount: it went from $114.8 million in 1968 to $87.6 million in 1969; but unlike the case for Sid Richardson, the *Directory* was given the Haas figure for 1969 rather than for 1968. Of all these, only Haas issues annual reports.

Losses from the 100-million-asset list are likely to be more than met by additions from time to time. For example, the Max C. Fleischmann Foundation of Reno has flirted with the one hundred million line for

example, Sloan moves from ninth in the first list to fourth in the more meaningful second ranking; Hartford from 11th to 6th, Danforth from 18th to 11th, Commonwealth from 25th to 17th,

several years: $95.1 million in *Directory* III (1966 figure), $98.6 million in 1969, though down to $82.9 million in *Directory* IV (1970 figure) and headed for liquidation by 1980. The Charles F. Kettering Foundation of Dayton was $120.9 million in *Directory* III (1965 figure), $98.0 million in 1969, and $93.3 million in *Directory* IV (1970 figure). Both Fleischmann and Kettering issue annual reports, and either is likely to nudge above the line at any time the market turns up. If either was in the above table on expenditures, it would rank higher than any of the last ten on the list: Fleischmann's expenditures in 1970, according to *Directory* IV, were $4,420,588; Kettering's, $4,842,554.

Let the reader be advised against reading too much into the tables. For example, it should not be concluded that the Robert Wood Johnson Foundation was thirty-first among all foundations in its expenditures for 1969. It *was* thirty-second in assets in *Directory* IV, but it was thirty-first in expenditures only among those thirty-two. Not just Fleischmann and Kettering but a considerable number of other foundations, smaller in assets, would muscle their way higher into any true ordering based on annual expenditures.

Mention of the R. W. Johnson Foundation calls for another caveat. As of January, 1972, the market value of the assets of this foundation was rated at approximately $1.1 billion, making it number two on the list, next to Ford. Sharp ups and downs are possible at any time. Listing A. W. Mellon as having $233.8 million in assets as of 12/31/69 (in the table, above) the *Directory* goes on to note: "During 1970 the Foundation received distributions from trusts established by the late Ailsa Mellon Bruce, bringing total assets at 31 December 1970 to approximately $698,000,000." (*Foundation Directory,* IV, *op. cit.,* p. 314). Since its expenditures, however, could not have been fairly related to the recently acquired assets, the figures in the tables above are consistent with each other, properly comparable with those for other foundations at that time, and for the present moment, therefore, badly out of line.

The figures pose other puzzles. Since the tables are based on *Directory* IV entries, the Houston Endowment has to be carried as eighth on the list of expenditures; but the *Directory* notes that of the $14,600,-712 expended, only $4,668,008 went for grants, which compares with its 1968 figure of $3,973,000 for grants. If the full story were known, and if comparable figures were being used throughout the list, Houston ought perhaps to be ranked about twenty-second or twenty-third in expenditures.

It is certainly the case, however, that sharp swings are possible from year to year, or even within a single year, especially for foundations that do not have clearly defined programs and procedures or sizeable professional staffs. The first figure for Pew's assets in 1969 was $541.3 million; for Kresge's expenditures, $7,139,000; for Woodruff's expenditures, $4,080,000. If these three figures had appeared in the *Directory,*

Cleveland from 27th to 18th, etc. A careful observer will note that, for other foundations, the situation is reversed.

Even more revealing are the percentages of market value of assets that foundations are expending. For some foundations low in the list there are probably extenuating circumstances—new establishments, with programs not fully developed; misunderstood legal requirements; errors.* But these excuses hardly apply to mature, long-established funds whose programs are geared to what they want to spend. For supposedly reputable foundations to be spending less than 3 percent of their market value, some of them even less than 2 percent, is exactly the sort of behavior that brings serious criticism on the whole field of philanthropy. Who is to say it is unjustified?

Comparisons can be downright odious. Though the figures in the tables above, verifiable from the *Foundation Directory,* reveal large differences in the behavior of the foundations mentioned, even greater contrasts are disclosed by reference to 1969 figures for all, not just for some on the list. In the 1969 ranking by assets Lilly was number two, Pew with $541.3 million on first report was number four, and Kresge was number six, whereas Kellogg, Mott, Sloan, Carnegie, Hartford and A. W. Mellon, each of which is smaller than any one of those three, spent considerably more that year.

---

the percent of their assets which were expended would have been even lower than the table above shows.

What is one to make of the expenditure percentages for, say, Brown, Bush, Irvine or Kaiser? How will the confusion between the Edna McConnell Clark Foundation, Inc., of New York City and The (sic) Edna McConnell Clark Foundation (no-Inc.) of Wilmington (with a New York mailing address) be resolved? Moody is a more understandable situation: it has been, and continues to be, disrupted by litigation, and its peculiar assets are subject to huge pendulum swings of value. *Directory* III gave its 1965 asset figures as $243.7 million, and as late as 1971 Mr. Patman thought it was one of the fifteen largest. Its own annual report for FY ending 12/31/70 gives its assets as $128.6 million and its grants for the year as $6,694,578.

Because these tables are full of imprecise figures they give a *dependable* picture of the uncertainty in the field, the wide variations in performance from well-run to reprehensible outfits and the sum total of improvement in financial management that foundations must achieve.

* Explanatory footnote begins on p. 68.

Or look at two others, Commonwealth and Danforth, that are not even as large as the ones just mentioned. In their fiscal years ending in 1969 their assets were $142.4 million and $172.5 million respectively, totalling $314.9 million; whereas the combined resources of Kresge, Lilly and Pew totalled $1,751.6 million, or over five times as large. But when reference is made to what these foundations were doing, the expenditures of Commonwealth and Danforth, each over 11 million in 1969, totalled $22,939,000, whereas the expenditures of the three giants (counting Kresge's first figure of $7,139,000 rather than the later one of $8,999,000 above) totalled only $21,990,000. In that year Commonwealth and Danforth were two of only three foundations, the third being Ford, that exceeded a 6 percent pay-out figure.

In 1971 Mr. Patman turned his attention to the investment and expenditure policies of what he thought were "The Fifteen Largest United States Foundations." The report of that title, ostensibly prepared for the House Committee on Banking and Currency but actually given wide public circulation without benefit of hearings or correction, took to task those fifteen, and by implication the whole foundation field, for inadequate income and pay-out, along with other faults. Trouble was, his figures were questionable, his interpretations often mistaken and even his list wrong. But the worst error was the lack of discrimination between foundations that are seeking to make large use of their resources for the general welfare and those that are not.[37] Critics badly need to begin to differentiate.

In any event, the pay-out requirements in the new Tax Reform Act will produce a considerable change for most foundations in the management of their finances. Though some kinds of criticism have been unfair or unbalanced, this is an area in which foundation practice as a whole could stand a great deal of improvement.

37. *The Fifteen Largest United States Foundations,* Committee on Banking and Currency, Washington, D.C., Government Printing Office, July 15, 1971.

71

4. *Center of Power?*

Another major criticism of foundations is that they are centers of immense and perhaps inimical power. A foundation, the charge runs, seldom goes off to a quiet corner to do its good works. (But in another connection, as we shall note in item number six below, the foundation is charged with secrecy.) On the contrary, it wields large influence on public affairs. It exercises control over many institutions of society, and thus over many individuals. It shapes, and moves and works its own will.

Small foundation, small power—and the critics don't worry much, unless the foundation does something spectacularly outrageous. But large foundation, huge power—and then the outcry begins to be considerable.[38]

The point at the moment is not to take note of criticisms of a foundation's use of its power, that is, of what it does. Various objections to the programs of foundations will be covered in the next chapter. Now, attention is focused simply on its possession of power by virtue of its existence as a financial resource. Criticism stems from the premise that all power is bad; or if not all power, private power, unchecked by the public or Government; or if not private power in general, somebody's other than the critic's. In the company of those who deplore the alleged massive influence of foundations are both lovers and haters of big Government. The lovers resent competition from the private sector; the haters dislike the mirroring of what they hate. Power, it is assumed, leads to corruption, to the problems noted in items one, two, and three above, and to many others besides.

Just about the only way to reply to this kind of criticism is with the banality "You have a point there." Maybe even two

38. See, for example, Lundberg, *op. cit.,* chap. 10; Weaver, *U.S. Philanthropic Foundations, op. cit.,* pp. 217–218; Goulden, *op. cit., passim;* Adolph A. Berle, *Power,* New York, Harcourt, Brace & World, 1967, pp. 220–221; Joseph Bensman & Arthur J. Vidich, *The New American Society,* Chicago, Quadrangle Books, 1971, chap. 10; William Hoffman, *David: Report on a Rockefeller,* New York, Lyle Stuart, Inc., 1971, *passim;* Dwight Macdonald, *The Ford Foundation: The Men and the Millions,* New York, Reynal & Co., 1956, *passim.*

points. First, among the various kinds of non-profit institutions that possess various degrees of influence in our national society foundations rank well up the list. It would be a wild-eyed opponent or equally blind partisan, however, who would credit foundations with more power than, say, universities or churches. Of course, churches seldom, if ever, wield power as a total group, and ditto for universities; and the very same thing is true for foundations—they have never learned to speak with one voice on anything.

The second point is that, possessing some indeterminate amount of power, foundations are capable of misusing it. Again, the same thing can be said for any other kind of institution that the fertile mind of man has ever established, and for individual people or groups of people as well as for their agencies. The objection that foundations have some undisclosed amount of power and that it might be misused is a mindless kind of complaint, and to deny it would be equally ridiculous.

But some of the refinements of the charge deserve further attention. Among those who are alarmed by the alleged power that foundations possess, size is thought to be a major factor. The trouble with the Ford Foundation, so the critics hold, lies in its being such a huge concentration of wealth and thus of power. In comparison with the rest of the foundation field, it is indeed large: Ford's assets are upwards of four times as great as those of the next largest, whether that next largest is Rockefeller as it has been for many years, or Lilly, whose market value assets have been increasing quite rapidly, or Robert Wood Johnson, only recently enrolled in the select company of the giants. Of the approximately twenty-six-thousand foundations in the United States, Ford alone holds well over 10 percent of the total assets.

But for those who are worried about the problem of size, the trouble is not just Ford, it is foundations in toto. The charge that bigness represents power for evil may be levelled in Flint against the Mott Foundation, in Indianapolis against the Lilly Endowment, in Pittsburgh against various Mellon funds or, perish the thought, in St. Louis against the Danforth Foundation. A quite small foundation may well be accused of wielding too much power in a quite small community; size, therefore, is a relative thing that can be made to serve the critic's purpose, depending on time and place and the particular foundation activity in question.

It is by virtue of the foundation's wealth, however, that it is presumed to possess too much power, whether on a local issue in comparison with local resources or on a national issue in comparison with the nation's total wealth. On occasion, but very rarely, the power of a foundation is thought to rest also in either the expertise or the bumptiousness of its staff. Again, Ford is more visible in personnel as well as in dollars, and thus is more likely to draw the fire of any who dislike the brand of leadership that foundation personnel may be giving in some areas of its interest. When and if the objection is to the actions of people, however, it is usually because they are supposed to have money back of them.

So foundations, it is alleged, own too large a share of the nation's total wealth. This has been the theme of Mr. Patman and of others who have picked up the cue from him. If comparisons are carefully chosen, foundations can be made to look as if their resources were adequate for the solution of all the nation's problems, providing only that government could get its hand on the money. "The aggregate receipts of the 575 foundations under study . . .," Mr. Patman wrote in 1967 in the *Progressive,* have increased sharply since the 1950s. During the four years 1961 through 1964, they took in $4.6 billion . . . nearly thirty percent higher than the combined net operating earnings—$3.6 billion after taxes—of the fifty largest banks in the United States . . . they had capital gains of $1.3 billion. . . . Here is a huge amount of income. . . . The pressure of the country's antipoverty needs, the nation's health needs, the nation's education, research, and scientific needs, and all other worthwhile causes demand that Congress force the distribution of these funds by law."[39]

That foundations don't really possess such an immense amount of the nation's wealth often goes unheeded by those who press the charge and even by the general public. In point

39. Patman, *op. cit.*

of fact, the total philanthropy in this country amounts to less than 2 percent of the gross national product, and foundation giving accounts for less than 10 percent of that total, less than two-tenths of 1 percent of the GNP. Moreover, it is growing less rapidly than the GNP.[40]

As a result of questions raised in the Senate Finance Committee hearings in connection with the Tax Reform Bill, the Foundation Center presented testimony on October 6, 1969, showing that "total foundation assets" were "only about eight-tenths of one percent of net debt instruments and corporate stocks in the U.S. economy . . . about seven-tenths of one percent of the value of all tangible U.S. wealth. . . . Annual foundation expenditures for charitable purposes are about half as much as Americans spend on the care and feeding of their pets, about one quarter as much as national spending on toiletries and cosmetics, about one sixth as much as national spending on tobacco products, and about one tenth as much as national spending on alcoholic beverages."[41]

But those who are frightened by concentrations of power in hands other than their own, and who equate power with size, are not persuaded by the actual figures. Foundations, in their view, are just too big.

Perpetuity is felt to be another factor making for unjustified power. The tremendous influence that foundations can exert is surely due in part to their being able to continue their work over a long period of years, even forever if they keep their books in balance. Power builds on power. Then, says the critic, they ought to be forced to go out of business after twenty, thirty, forty years of existence. Such a suggestion may come not only from opponents of foundations but also from "friends" who, appreciating their good works, complain at the progressive increase in their power. Even Democrats and Republicans are thrown out of office every so often. Why not foundations? Let them do good now and get it over with. Don't let them build

40. *Giving USA, op. cit.;* and Mary Hamilton, "Philanthropy and the Economy," in Report of Peterson Commission, *op. cit.,* pp. 256–261.
41. Manning M. Pattillo, testimony in Senate Finance Committee, *Tax Reform Act of 1969,* Hearings, September–November, 1969, Part 6, p. 5351. See also Goulden, *op. cit.,* pp. 10–11.

themselves up into centers of continuing influence and control.

This particular charge against foundations, accompanied by an effort to set some limit on their life span was, like many other criticisms, given wide currency by Mr. Patman. He proposed that foundations ought to go out of business after twenty-five years.[42] In the work of the Senate Finance Committee leading up to the passage of the Tax Reform Act of 1969, Senator Gore succeeded in introducing into the Senate's version of the bill an amendment to set the limitation at forty years, the result of a wearing-down process whereby earlier he had failed successively at getting the Committee to approve limits of twenty, twenty-five and thirty years. Many foundations were alarmed by this proposal and, when the Bill was reported to the Senate, they sought to persuade senators of its unsoundness. Whether through lobbying by foundations and their friends or because such efforts were not really needed, the Senate defeated by an overwhelming vote what Senator Mondale called the "death sentence amendment."[43]

The question as to how long a foundation ought to stay in business is of course a legitimate one. A few foundations, by their charters, have been required to spend themselves out of existence within a prescribed period of time. Some well-known and substantial liquidations, whether or not by specific charter requirement, are the Blakely-Braniff Foundation, the Children's Fund of Michigan, the Maurice and Laura Falk Foundation, the General Education Board, the James Foundation, and the Julius Rosenwald Fund.[44] In the other direction, some foundations are required by their charters to preserve their capital in perpetuity. Still others are given the option of continuing in existence or closing up shop, as the trustees themselves decide which would make the larger contribution to the foundation's purposes.[45]

But to say that a foundation may spend its capital is entirely

42. Patman Reports, *op. cit.*, I., 1962, p. 133; see also Reeves, *op. cit.*, pp. 27–28; Kutner, *op. cit.*, p. 382.

43. See *Congressional Record*, December 5, 1969, pp. S15755–15760.

44. See Andrews, *Philanthropic Foundations, op. cit.*, pp. 103–104; *American Foundations and Their Fields, op. cit.*, VII, p. xxiii.

45. See Weaver, *op. cit.*, pp. 93–97; Andrews, *op. cit.*, pp. 102–105; F. Emerson Andrews, *Legal Instruments of Foundations,* New York, Russell Sage Foundation, 1958, *passim;* Fremont-Smith, *op. cit.*, pp. 72–81 and *passim.*

different from saying it has got to do so in order to be considered as working in the public interest. The attack on perpetuity as an inimical feature of a tax-exempt institution is a new and dangerous development of a populist kind. Whether the critic attacks perpetuity in general or only as it applies to foundations, the response must be realistic enough to concede that perpetuity, or even longevity, does indeed enhance any institution's possibility of exercising leadership and influence. Longevity brings experience, which more often than not makes for wise use of resources. A time limit would mean the waste of experience and less effective philanthropy.

Foundations cannot deny their possession of some measure of power, as a result of their size or perpetuity or some other feature of their existence. In response to this charge, therefore, foundations have to say, Yes, but is that bad? The burden of proof is at least partly on the critics. They have an obligation to show in one or another instance that the power some foundation possessed was indeed misused.

But the burden of proof works both ways, not just one. Foundations themselves have an obligation to use their power responsibly; to make sure, in other words, that it is used on behalf of the general welfare rather than for some special advantage, and further, that the public has a chance to know the full story. In any event, the complaint that foundations are too powerful is one that must be answered pragmatically, on other grounds than the philosophical pros and cons of power itself.

5. Elitism?

The next charge is that, in its internal management, a foundation is a closed corporation. It is tight-knit, excluding the general public. It possesses its own sovereignty and is capable of being completely impervious to the wishes of the citizens at large.

The line of reasoning in this criticism seems to be that once a sum of money has been set aside for the general welfare, a representative section of the public to be served should determine how that service is to be rendered. Governors and managers of foundations are not sufficiently representative. The

77

smaller the foundation, the more likely it will be run out of someone's back pocket. But large foundations do not escape the danger, for one person, one family or one narrow point of view may still control the operation. Trustees can easily be cronies, and administrative staff no more than protégés. Thus even when the foundation does good, it doesn't do it right. It is an anachronistic throwback to the lord of the manor, bestowing his largesse on the peasants and knowing what is good for them.

Those who take this tack ask some embarrassing questions. How many blacks are on your board? How many representatives of other minority groups? How many women? Any non-management people? Any just plain consumers? Any poor? Are the staff your alter egos? Do they possess the same limitations as the board's? Or perhaps some of their own? All Ph.D.'s or "professionals"? Who can speak for the average citizen? Who can save the foundation from being a tight-knit, closed corporation?[46]

The first step in response is to disabuse the critic of the naive position that a foundation's being a closed corporation turns on visibilities of race, creed or color, memberships, degrees and size of personal bank accounts. The presence of a black on a foundation's board is no guarantee that that foundation will take seriously the problems of blacks in America today. One woman doesn't guarantee an end to masculine pretentiousness. One graduate of Podunk doesn't mean the relinquishment of Ivy dominance. Genuine representativeness on a foundation's board is not to be achieved by precise arithmetical proportioning, and whether or not a foundation is a closed corporation will turn on something other than simply the composition of the board or the staff.

Since the same thing is also true for other types of tax-exempt institutions, a second response to this criticism must consist in pointing out that, to whatever extent it is true, foundations are no more guilty than museums or colleges or even social welfare agencies working with the poor. Though such a rejoinder has a great deal of truth in it, it is a tu quoque kind of argument. Why

46. See, for example, Goulden, *op. cit., passim;* Lundberg, *op. cit.,* chap. 10; Patman, *op. cit.,* Reeves, *op. cit.,* pp. 7–17; Norman Birnbaum, "Reviews," *Change Magazine,* Summer, 1971, p. 69.

pick on me? You are guilty too; or if not you, at least that other fellow, that other institution.

Each of these responses, however, is no adequate answer to the charge; and it still remains for us to ask whether, not just superficially but in more significant ways, a foundation is a closed corporation.

The closest circle in which a foundation can operate is that of an individual's private philanthropic fund which, when it is incorporated, becomes a family fund. Since the overwhelming majority of foundations are quite small—too small to require the professional services of staff members or to challenge the interest of board members—the work of such foundations is inevitably going to be done by only one or two people, the donor or his successor. A recent study has disclosed that only 20 percent of all foundations have any paid staff at all, including secretaries, and only 5 percent have any full-time paid staff.[47] It would be rare indeed that a small foundation could escape the charge of being a tight-knit, closed corporation, for its very size would necessitate its operating in that way.

But our interest here is in the large foundations that, numerically a tiny minority of the field, are actually responsible for most philanthropic work of foundations. It is against the large foundations that this criticism has its chief pertinence, but reliable facts are not easy to gather. The Peterson Commission directed a good part of its investigation toward questions related to this criticism, and found that "an overwhelming majority of the trustees of the large foundations are white, Anglo-Saxon, and Protestant."[48]

In respect to board service, there are no reliable patterns of practice. On some foundation boards, trustees play a major role in grant-making; and in others they play almost no role at all. For some foundations, board members customarily suggest and discuss new program areas; in other boards such discussions seldom or never take place. A number of the largest foundations have regular, lengthy meetings, three, six, even twelve times a year; whereas the Peterson Commission discovered that

47. Report of Peterson Commission, *op. cit.*, p. 87.
48. *Ibid.*, pp. 89–90.

79

33 percent of foundation boards meet only once a year or less, 15 percent meet for only an hour a year or less, and 9 percent never meet at all.[49]

In 1936, Eduard C. Lindeman described the "typical trustee" as "a man well past middle age . . . of considerable affluence . . .; 'respectable' and 'conventional' . . . belongs to the 'best' clubs and churches . . . resides in the Northeastern section of the United States and has attended one of the private colleges in that region. . . . In short, he is a member of that successful and conservative class which came into prominence during the latter part of the nineteenth and early twentieth century, the class whose status is based primarily upon pecuniary success." More recent studies of trustees come up with similar composite portraits.[50]

The Treasury Department's Report of 1965 listed the "broadening of foundation management" as one of the six major concerns to which foundations or government should give attention. The report saw "close donor involvement" as the chief problem, and recommended that the donor or his immediate family not be permitted to constitute more than 25 percent of the foundation's governing body after the expiration of the first twenty-five years of the foundation's life, with a five- to ten-year adjustment period provided for those foundations that have already been in existence for twenty-five years.[51] The recommendation was not acted upon, and in light of the composition of trustee boards of many large foundations it is likely that such a rule would make little difference in the characteristics or points of view of board members.

Another cause of annoyance for those who feel that a foundation is a closed corporation is the practice of paying some trustees for their service on the board. Abuses in this regard are possible; and though it is difficult to substantiate actual instances, a few have supposedly been discovered and publicized, and then, like as not, defended by the foundation as altogether legitimate. Ford defends its policy of giving each trustee an an-

49. *Ibid.*, pp. 88–89.
50. Lindeman, *op. cit.*, p. 46. See also Andrews, *Philanthropic Foundations, op. cit.*, chap. 3; Reeves, *op. cit.*, p. 13; Goulden, *op. cit.*, pp. 51–58.
51. See Treasury Department Report, *op. cit.*

nual $5,000 honorarium, for they clearly earn it by the amount of time spent in the board's work. The Duke Endowment defends its giving much larger annual honoraria to its trustees by pointing out that the original indenture establishing the Endowment required such payments.[52]

Some slight attention, perhaps, should be directed to foundation staff members. On the one hand, foundations are sometimes criticized because staff members are obviously lackeys, "philanthropoids" (as distinct from philanthropists) who have no status except as they blindly do the bidding of the wealthy donor and his cronies. On the other hand, foundation staff members are at other times criticized because they, too, are Wasp, Establishment types, flitting back and forth from foundation offices to positions of distinction in Government or university life.[53] Whether they are thought to be pawns or chief actors on the foundation stage, their characteristics are taken to be one more evidence that the foundation is a closed corporation. Since there are relatively few professional foundation staff people, perhaps only about a thousand or so, employed almost exclusively by the large foundations, their positions are looked upon as signs of the elitism of the organizations they serve.

Is, then, the charge of elitism justified? Are foundations indeed closed corporations? If one observes the scene broadly and reports honestly on what he sees, there is no escape from a yes-and-no kind of answer. In the nature of the case, foundations are not egalitarian instruments. First, they are by definition the creation of those who had the financial means to engage in philanthropy. The donor may or may not have assumed—he had liberty to do either—that he himself had enough sense to know how his foundation ought to be run. But even if he chose the less elitist path of asking others to share with him the responsibility for managing the foundation, he could not escape two

52. For discussions of honoraria to trustees, see Weaver, *op. cit.*, pp. 105–107; Goulden, *op. cit.*, pp. 58–65; Andrews, *op. cit.*, pp. 84–87.
53. For discussions of staff characteristics, see Weaver, *op. cit.*, pp. 107–114; Goulden, *op. cit.*, chap. 4; Andrews, *op. cit.*, chap. 5; Arnold Zurcher & Jane Dustan, *The Foundation Administrator: A Study of Those Who Manage American Foundations,* New York, Russell Sage Foundation, 1972.

limitations, that in the first instance he himself was doing the asking, and, second, that he could ask only a small number who were bound to be, at best, only partially representative of the public. So a foundation, like many another valued institution in our democracy, is non-democratic in its structuring and management, and inescapably so.

But a foundation can reduce its unrepresentative mien by judicious effort to eliminate as far as possible its closed character. If a foundation is non-democratic, it need not be anti-democratic. On its board and staff it can make sure that there are people of broad-gauge understandings and sympathies, even if they are Wasps from New England. No foundation board is large enough to have every segment of the population represented on it, even every major segment. Moreover, there are few black Jewish nuns, too few to go around; and tokenism doesn't work, anyway. So a foundation, eschewing the will-o'-the-wisp of precise representation, must adopt the more difficult course of trying to make sure that there exists, on staff and board, a genuine balance in points of view, a variety of expertise and a sense of common cause. Whether or not charges of elitism stand up will turn ultimately on how the foundation behaves and what it does, and whether it tells its story fully and honestly to the public.

6. *Public Accountability?*

The last sentence leads directly to the final major criticism to be noted in this chapter. The charge is made that foundations are answerable to no one but themselves. Forgetful of why the government gives them tax-favored status, they have little sense of responsibility toward the public, it is said, and seldom make full disclosure of their affairs.

This charge, it needs to be pointed out, is something more than the preceding one, that a foundation is a closed corporation. It could be closed—that is, elitist in its composition—and still practice full disclosure. This criticism has it, however, that, on top of a number of faults of the sort we have already noted, foundations compound their guilt by not telling the public anything significant about themselves. They practice a kind of "privatism" that shows they have no understanding of what it means to be accountable.[54]

How serious is this charge? That it touches a nerve is clear from the statements of foundation people in conferences, annual reports and elsewhere. Our answers are often twofold in nature, consisting in pleas of "not guilty" and "guilty, for justifiable reasons."[55] We no longer brush it aside, and even before the Tax Reform Act of 1969 the world of philanthropy had begun to talk more openly and more frankly about itself.

With the passage of the act, however, many aspects of this criticism are now largely out of date. That act requires full public disclosure. Whether foundations want to or not, they are now required to make available to the public a complete statement of their organization, resources and activities.

It is in respect to the activities of foundations, at least as much as their structure and finance, that this thrust draws blood. For this reason, therefore, further discussion of whether foundations are accountable will take place in the following chapter on program and operating policy, in the section dealing with whether they are secretive. It is enough now to conclude that the direction in which things are going is good, thanks partly to the Tax Reform Act. The arrangements and behavior of foundations are not as mysterious as was once the case, and more of them now realize the importance of speaking out. But there is still room for improvement.

C. SUMMARY: BASTIONS OF SPECIAL PRIVILEGE?

The criticisms noted thus far add up to one overarching accusation: foundations are bastions of special privilege and bul-

54. See, for example, Report of Peterson Commission, *op. cit.*, pp. 70–71, 154–156; Reeves, *op. cit.*, pp. 7–12; Goulden, *op. cit.*, pp. 74–79.
55. See, for example, Andrews, *op. cit.*, chap. 12; Weaver, *op. cit.*, pp. 130–135; Raymond B. Fosdick, *A Philosophy for a Foundation, on the Fiftieth Anniversary of the Rockefeller Foundation, 1913–1963,* New York, Rockefeller Foundation, pp. 20–21; Alan Pifer, "Foundations at the Service of the Public," reprint from *Annual Report, Carnegie Corporation of New York, 1968.*

warks of the established order. Whether the point of complaint is tax dodge, business advantage, inordinate power, close-knit management or something else, the thread of resentment running through all these items is that foundations, in their structure, management and financial affairs, bestow favors on those already favored. The rich get richer, the powerful get more power, and the Establishment gets capitalized. No matter that they do some good, they are wrong for America on balance, for they favor the few against the many, the rich against the poor, the haves against the have-nots. If America is a land of promise, of equal opportunity, of "liberty and justice for all," then foundations run against the grain.

Is this the case? Is this the conclusion to which honest, impartial men must come?

If we were to add up the balance sheet of each of the six criticisms discussed above, we might be forced to the position that, on balance, foundations were irredeemably pointed toward special privilege.

In respect to number one, foundations themselves are not tax dodges, but their donors did receive various legal tax privileges in their establishment, privileges not available in the same measure to those of lesser financial substance.

In respect to number two, donors have undoubtedly benefited in many ways from their having set up foundations. Their families and their businesses have received advantages. In the main these have not been characterized by self-dealing or conflict of interest, though until the new legal requirements, such results were possible and sometimes actual. In any event, it is almost impossible to imagine that a donor, a family or a business would not receive at least some atmospheric benefit from a foundation whose activity was well-managed and generally admired.

As for number three, criminal mismanagement of a foundation's assets has seldom taken place, but unimaginative management has been the norm. Foundations have tended to keep their portfolios close to the interests of founding families, and have practiced very conservative investment policies in contrast with other types of tax-exempt agencies that seek optimal safe returns for the cause of the charity they serve. Accordingly, foundations

84

have been characterized by a very low pay-out to charity. The Tax Reform Act will effect an improvement in the management of foundation assets, which simply means that the record foundations have voluntarily written in this regard is not good.

In respect to number four, that a foundation is a center of power, how could it possibly be denied that foundations do indeed have some influence? It is not as great as is often charged. It does not turn on size, for foundations are not in fact as large a benefit or a financial threat as either protagonist or antagonist often imagines. The foundation's influence is not necessarily a product of its perpetuity, though there is of course a relationship. Power and influence are present, to be sure, but whether foundations deserve to be criticized therefore turns on what they do, not simply on their possession of some measure of power.

Consider number five: in some regard a foundation cannot escape being a closed corporation, but it is so in larger measure than the nature of its activity requires. It has given the impression of being elitist, and so it is, in part inescapably.

As for number six, foundations have not practiced public accountability as they should. But they are beginning to tell their stories more candidly, and to realize the large desirability that they do so.

Everyone of these charges, with the possible exception of the first, has to be answered, therefore, with a yes-but style of reply. The buts are of considerable heft and deserve a careful hearing from any who want to arrive at balanced judgments. But the awkwardness of having to begin an answer with Yes, even if modifications and exceptions are then to follow, can simply not be gainsaid. "Yes-but" is no way to win friends and influence people.

Yet the admission that there are things wrong in the areas of structure and finance should itself not be exaggerated or taken out of context. There is enough truth in the charge that foundations are bulwarks of special privilege to make the good ones apologetic for the bad ones, enough truth to suggest that improvement in foundation management should take place all up and down the line. But in the size of their philanthropy, we must remember, the good ones far outnumber the bad ones. That is,

85

the overwhelming amount of organized philanthropy is on the side of good management, no special privilege, high accountability.

If one were to express a judgment on the basis of simply a head count of all foundations one by one, then the answer would probably have to be that the numerical majority of all foundations were probably guilty of practicing special privilege or were, at the least, insensitive to the extent to which they allowed it to happen. But a judgment expressed on such a basis would be patently unfair, for it would equate a large, public-spirited, professionally-run foundation with a tiny family fund whose only existence, apart from the privilege it bestows on its donor, is in the occasional check it dispenses to a respectful donee.

This is not to say that all large foundations are well run and all small ones are bulwarks of special privilege, for neither of these positions is true. It is to say, however, that judgment should be expressed on the basis of the proportion of the total philanthropic resources that are in the hands of reputable foundations. The question is: Are the philanthropic funds of the United States serving as bastions of special privilege? The answer, on balance, is No.

Foundation people should take little comfort from the fact that the answer, on balance, is No. Government regulation has brought this about more than their own efforts, for if the whole matter of proper behavior in the areas of foundation structure and finance had been left in the hands of the foundations themselves, the answer to the question would still have to be Yes. Even with Government regulation, there are still many improvements that foundations are not legally required to institute but which are highly advisable. As we shall note in more detail in Chapter VI, foundations have got a lot of internal-management homework to do in order to justify a better reputation in the mind of the public. The margin by which they escape the charge that they are bastions of special privilege is not sufficiently large to justify their self-esteem or to quell the complaints of their detractors.

But the direction of development is right. Helped on by the law, foundations have developed an increasing sensitivity to

86

criticisms of the sort we have noted; and there is hardly a foundation, large or small, that is not less subject to such criticisms today than was true some years ago. It will not be long before the denial of the validity of charges noted in this chapter can be made more ringing, because the charges themselves will have even less substance than they have already begun to possess today.

III

Attack and Defense:
Program and Operating Policy

A. INTRODUCTION: PROBLEMS IN
MEETING THE ATTACK

THE second broad sweep of charges against foundations is concerned with their programs and the accompanying operational procedures. Critics often dislike what foundations do or the way they do it. These may be the same ones who criticize the structure and fiscal management of foundations, or they may be an entirely different breed.

The last thing the critics achieve is unanimity. The chief elements of their attack seem to be contradictory as often as they are complementary. Foundations are both too big and too little. They are open-handed and tight-fisted. They want revolution and repression. Thus nearly every item of criticism has its counterpoise.

Criticism has to do with priorities among fields of activity. Foundations spend, depending on the critic's taste, either too much or too little on education, either too little or too much on overseas programs, etc., etc. It is not easy to discover the actual breakdown of foundation expenditures by field or area, for no one has ever added up the charitable giving of all foundations by categories, nor would the facts be available. Refutation of the critic's position, therefore, like the criticism itself, is bound to be subjective.

The most reliable estimate seems to be the survey published in successive editions of the *Foundation Directory*. No claim is made for completeness, for the tabulation is based on information only about grants of $10,000 or more that are recorded in the grants index published periodically in *Foundation News.* This information is perhaps sufficient, however, to indicate proportions and, over a period of years, trends. The American Association of Fund-Raising Counsel accepts the *Directory's* figures as being the best available.[1]

Here are the percentages for foundation expenditures by major fields in 1970: "Education," somewhat narrowly defined —36 percent; "Welfare," which the AAF-RC calls "Human Resources"—17 percent; "Health"—15 percent; "Sciences" and scientific research—12 percent; "International Activities"—7 percent; "Humanities"—7 percent; and "Religion"—6 percent. Slightly over 50 percent of the spending for "Education" went to higher education. As for "Welfare's" total, 39 percent was directed to community funds. Hospitals got 60 percent of the "Health" total. The term "International Activities" is somewhat misleading, for much of this expenditure does not go abroad, being assigned to programs and students in American universities. "Religion" still attracts between 40 and 50 percent of all philanthropy, "but most of this giving is done personally rather than through a foundation." These 1970 percentages, in comparison with ten-year averages, are up slightly for "Education" and "Welfare," down rather sharply for "International Activities" (from 15 percent to 7 percent), and steady for the other categories. At best, these figures are only educated guesses.[2]

Whatever the actual breakdown, however, it would please no one, including foundation people themselves. No foundation's own proportion of grants follows the pattern for the field as a whole and thus no foundation is likely to be happy with the total figures. Critics may sometimes seem to be doing no more than foundation people themselves do, that is, debate among themselves as to what fields should be supported and where the needs are largest. It will always be the case, therefore, that at-

1. See "Introduction" to FD-1, -2, -3 and -4; *Giving USA, op. cit.*
2. FD-4, pp. xv-xvii; *Giving USA, op. cit.,* p. 21. See similar breakdown in Report of Peterson Commission, *op. cit.,* pp. 79–80. Figures for 1971 are comparable with those for 1970; see *Foundation News,* January–February, 1972, pp. 4–6.

tacks on foundation programs will inevitably be contradictory in nature, and some small comfort can be gained from the realization that each criticism will probably have its antidote.

Simply to comfort oneself that criticisms of a foundation's program are bound to be contradictory does not go very far, however, in analyzing the nature of the criticisms and in providing convincing response. Criticisms should not be ruled out or ignored merely because their opposites are also voiced. Moreover, certain charges, even when they have their built-in contradictions, are recurrent over periods of years or are highly explosive at certain times in the national life. They deserve analysis, therefore, and detailed rebuttal. Prior to our taking specific notice of the main charges in this area, let us pause to consider some of the problems that foundations face when they defend themselves against attack on their programs.

The first thing to note is the complexity of the fields in which foundations work. It is always tempting to be a one-field kind of operation, for in that direction lies simplicity and clarity. Family funds can often achieve such a sharp focus, especially if they are small. But when a foundation grows in size to the point where one limited area of activity seems to be inappropriate, or when, no matter the size of the foundation, its donor has a multitude of interests to which he would like to see the foundation contribute, then the problem begins to be inescapable. What are the priorities of need? What organizations in the field of activity are best equipped to meet the needs? How can the decisions be most wisely arrived at?

Soon the foundation discovers that one of the most difficult problems connected with its chosen fields of activity, whatever they are, is the identification of reliable consultants in that field. The overwhelming majority of foundations are run by amateurs and laymen. Often they suffer not just one, but two serious shortcomings: first, the inability to recognize that they need competent advice in fields or on matters chosen for the foundation's activity, and second, when and if counsel is sought, the ignorance as to who reputable consultants are and where they are to be found.

A small foundation is almost inevitably a local foundation. If

90

the activity of the foundation is circumscribed geographically, the donor or manager is hardly likely to give himself airs by wanting to go far afield for advice. Thus he calls upon local talent or leans on his own understanding. In either case, and in many an instance, the result often redounds to the advantage of the community and the credit of the foundation. But in many another instance one suspects that a donor's or a manager's insights are seriously limited, or the advisors he calls upon are no better; and the inevitable result is that the foundation's work suffers from narrow horizons.

That a foundation is large, however, is no guarantee that its horizons are broad. The problem of the adequacy of advice that a foundation receives is present whether it is large or small. Most national foundations, by location and bias, are largely Eastern in their orientation. Their Trustees and their professional staffs, as was noted earlier, are likely to come from Ivy colleges and Establishment backgrounds. The consultants they choose may possess the same limitations of background and understanding. By and large, however, national foundations have the desire as well as the capability to secure the best possible advice on any matter in the orbit of their interests. Most of the time they do so, and the people that foundations call upon for counsel are the best that flattery and modest consultants' fees can buy. But foundations, like other private and governmental agencies, can make mistakes, and the problem of knowing where good counsel is to come from is one that foundations must always face.

It is in respect to this matter of competent advice that a foundation, by nature, runs into one of its most awkward problems. Everybody knows how to run a foundation. That is, everybody knows better how to spend somebody else's money than the person who bears the responsibility. Many times these various everybodies are eager to advise foundations directly, and thus foundations have to suffer through an ironic kind of relationship with some of their friends as well as with their critics.

There is hardly a foundation, I daresay, that does not now and again, and perhaps fairly often, make a grant that it knows is not going to amount to much. It is caught by its own circle

91

of friends, and the circumstances of its institutional existence seem to require it to participate in the support of some project in which, it knows beforehand, the likelihood of substantial results is small. Not only do foundations sometimes find it difficult to identify a reliable consultant; there are other times when it may know better than the best advice it can get from outside. Either way it decides to act, trouble is its lot: it may disappoint its friends, or it may please its friends at the price of doing less well than it could.

This difficulty is related to the fact that, whereas a foundation may appear to the public to be an initiating agency, it is often likely to be merely a responding one. To be sure, foundations do initiate a broad host of projects and activities, as we shall see in the next chapter. In the main, however, their being a source of support for various projects means that the first overture is necessarily the suppliant's, and the foundation's role is in the form of reaction or reply.

Because appeals have grown so numerous and importunate in recent years, a foundation's chief response is unhappily a negative one. No other institution in our society is so practiced in performing rejection. The most prestigious or select private school or college in the land does not have to turn down the proportion of eager candidates for admission that the overwhelming majority of foundations have to decline from among their applicants. As an illustration, a dozen years ago the Danforth Foundation was able to respond in some affirmative fashion to perhaps as many as 20 percent of the total number of proposals received, but times have changed. In the intervening years, the Foundation has come to be better known, applicants conversely pay even less attention than formerly to the Foundation's announced areas of interest, and money is much tighter. Accordingly, at the present time we are responding to no more than perhaps 1 or at the most 2 percent of the requests that are made to us, even though our annual expenditures have increased threefold.

This means, unfortunately, that the stock-in-trade that most foundations have to offer most people is rebuff. There simply is no way around the fact that rejection is much more likely to be

92

the order of the day than acceptance. Because this is the case, many of the critics' charges and much of the virulence back of them stem from rejections that foundations have had to make and serious disappointments that petitioners have thereby suffered.

Cut open the heart of many a critic and you find the unsatisfied suitor. Foundations could easily take too much comfort from this fact, and their critics could readily condemn such self-serving defense. But the actuality remains: every foundation runs the continual risk of making more enemies than friends. And even some friends can be unhappy, if they don't get all they want. Much of the criticism of foundations comes from those who once had an axe that they did not get ground, and thus who now have a second one. Let it be understood that such criticism still deserves to be heard and examined on its merits. But the anomalous position of many critics as unrequited lovers needs to be noted as one of the difficulties that foundations face in responding to attack.

Saying No is harder than saying Yes. Traditionally foundations have not said it as well. Often they are mealy-mouthed or apologetic. They may not give the real reason, or only part of it, out of a desire to be kind and perhaps a mistaken idea as to what kindness consists in. Or they may be curt and completely uninformative in respect to why the answer has to be no. At least a few foundations, it is sometimes charged, don't even answer their mail.[3] When ninety-eight out of one hundred answers must be No, foundations sometimes find it difficult to order their own methods of operation in ways that will receive the approbation of the public.

Another area of difficulty is the evaluation of results. Since this has been an item of large criticism, comment will be made on it below. Let it suffice now to say that this too poses a problem for foundations, for if they were ever to adopt ruthless honesty in the evaluation of institutions or projects they have supported, they might well provoke more rather than less criticism.

Finally, as a difficulty that foundations face in responding to

3. See Goulden, *op. cit.*, p. 79.

attacks on their activities, let us call to mind, again, the fact that a philanthropic fund has no ready-made constituency on which to draw for support. Critics sometimes assume that they are being very brave in blasting out against these massive, all-powerful agencies, the foundations. Actually, if one is worried about reprisal from the victim's friends, to take a potshot at a foundation is a remarkably safe occupation, and thus hardly merits the accolade of courage.

Recipients do not constitute a constituency, for they are much too diverse and concerned about their own institutional interests. When Congress was debating the pros and cons of organized philanthropy in 1969, many foundations naively thought that various recipient institutions would spring quickly to their defense, and were somewhat hurt when this did not happen. The fact is, however, that when some organization receives a grant from a foundation, it does not thereby assume that it has joined the foundation's constituency. There is really no such thing; and the lack of a constituency represents one more problem a foundation faces in seeking to make persuasive answer to the attacks that come its way.

B. Criticism and Response

1. *Inadequate Spending?*

As we noticed in the previous chapter, it has been widely charged that foundations do not spend a sufficient amount of their resources. Since the size of a foundation's annual expenditures is inescapably tied to its income, this question was discussed as part of the criticism of the investment policy of foundations. The new Tax Reform Act's requirements on pay-out will take care of the matter, for henceforth foundations will be required to spend at a considerably higher level than has been the custom for many of them in recent years. Though this topic needs no further discussion at this point, it is mentioned here because spending is concerned with program as much as with fiscal management.

94

2. Secretiveness?

Another criticism of program closely related to a charge concerning management is the oft-stated complaint that foundations are guilty of a lack of communication with the public. In the previous chapter the question of public accountability was raised, to be more fully explored here.

Foundations are widely thought to be secretive. They cherish their status as private entities, their freedom from outside restraint. But their independence, say the critics, is not merely of the innocent variety, namely, an organic separation from some controlling authority. Rather, theirs is a public-be-damned kind of independence that runs against the grain of a democratic society. They are cosey. Whenever they can get away with it, they hide.[4]

We have already noted, above, that the Tax Reform Act has changed all this, that even before the act foundations themselves were becoming more informative, but that further improvement is still possible and desirable. It remains now to make response in more detail, as the charge affects the program and operating policy of foundations.

First to note is that in making response foundations face a different kind of problem from what any other non-profit institution faces. The work of every other type of tax-exempt agency possesses a built-in degree of visibility greater than that of foundations. Anybody who wants to do so can learn a great deal about what goes on inside a church, a school, a hospital, a university, a museum or a symphony hall. Even if he does nothing more than drive by or wander through, he comes to understand that they have buildings and grounds, and that certain kinds of people inhabit or frequent them. Almost casually he sees that this, that or the other sort of activity, causing this, that or the other sort of public notice or traffic jam, takes place under their auspices. If anyone expresses an interest in understanding more of what goes on than he can readily see, the managers of church-school-hospital-etc., are usually delighted to inform him. He

4. See Lundberg, *op. cit.*, pp. 493–496; Patman Reports, *op. cit., passim;* Goulden, *op. cit.*, pp. 74–79; Reeves, *op. cit.*, pp. 8–10.

95

won't learn everything, but he can easily learn enough to convince him that this is an aboveboard organization, devoted to its part of the public welfare.

But foundations have a difficult time giving visible evidence of their own discrete nature. Moody can show off its ranches, but they are simply its resources, *vice* stocks and bonds. Longwood can display its gardens, but they are simply objects of its affection, *vice* programs and grants. To disclose something of its essential nature a foundation has no visual equivalent of a college campus or a church sanctuary.

All it has is an office, A few are worth seeing, to be sure: the Ford Foundation's building in New York City; Kellogg's offices in Battle Creek; Rockefeller's Overseas Conference Center, the Villa Serbelloni at Bellagio on Lake Como, Italy, a gift to the Foundation; "Wingspread," the Frank Lloyd Wright home of the Johnson Foundation in Racine, Wisconsin; Ford's headquarters in New Delhi. These and perhaps a few other offices are just about all that would repay a visit. If the public is to understand what a foundation is, as distinct from what it owns or supports, the foundation will probably have to tell the story in the printed word.

The second thing to say is that, even prior to the new requirement of the Tax Reform Act, information about foundations' activities was never unavailable; it could be secured by anyone who took the trouble. The 990-A forms on which foundations submitted their annual reports to the Internal Revenue Service were, and are, public property and could/can be inspected by anyone who wishes. The difficulty is, the 990-A's are often hard to get hold of.

The Foundation Center has helped considerably in spreading such information, for it has secured copies of 990-A returns from the Internal Revenue Service and made them available in its main offices in New York and Washington and in some of its regional depositories. For example, in the Danforth Foundation's library in St. Louis we keep on file the 990-A's for a large number of foundations in our part of the Midwest, and hundreds of people use them to find out what local and regional foundations are doing. Since any 990-A is available somewhere,

96

the charge that it is not possible to discover what some foundation does is largely without substance. The charge stands up only if a foundation has not submitted a 990-A, or if its submission gives inadequate information.

But whether information is available to the public is a different matter from whether a foundation wants that information known and makes it easy for the public to get it. One way or another, people can find out; but the charge is still made that a lot of foundations try to conceal as much as possible. The record of foundation behavior on this point is not reassuring. In 1968 the Foundation Center estimated that only one hundred and forty foundations followed the practice of issuing annual or biennial reports, a disreputably low figure. Thanks to the Tax Reform Act, the number is now around two hundred and steadily increasing.[5]

The worst offenders appear to be the small foundations, but it is they also for whom there may be most excuse. When a foundation's resources are quite modest, and when its annual dollar activity amounts, even with Federal encouragement, to only 6 percent of that modest capital, then a published report seems to be a waste of money. If a small foundation that is simply the reflection of an individual donor's beneficence puts forth some printed statement of its grants, it looks like personal boasting. Since the great majority of foundations do not have professional staffs, and an immense number do not have even so much as a secretary, the issuing of an annual report, however brief, is an added chore for some volunteer, who probably gets a good bit of satisfaction out of making grants but is bored with the necessary housekeeping.

Moreover, to do more than the bare minimum in issuing reports—that is, to go one step beyond reporting on the necessary forms to the Internal Revenue Service and printing a tiny personal in the local want-ads once a year—is to invite a large number of requests, with no way of processing them and no

5. See Richard Magat, "Compliance vs. Information: The 990–AR," *Foundation News,* January–February, 1972, pp. 14–18. For a considerable listing, though now incomplete, see J. Richard Taft, *Understanding Foundations,* New York, McGraw-Hill Book Co., 1967, pp. 158–164.

chance of responding favorably to them. For all sorts of reasons, therefore, many of which have little or nothing to do with a desire to operate in secret, the great majority of small foundations make modicum effort to tell the public about their work.

The large foundations have less excuse. Most of them do in fact issue periodic reports, but among those over $100 million in market value of assets, the following were not doing so when the latest *Foundation Directory* was published: Alcoa, Brown, both E. McC. Clarks, Longwood, Pew, Sid Richardson, Surdna and Woodruff.[6] If these foundations deserve the criticism that they are not keeping the public informed, then the critics themselves ought to discriminate enough to note that the large majority of the foundations of substantial size do issue carefully prepared, informative reports. In nearly every case, all that any person needs to do in order to find out about the activities of any of the large foundations except those just mentioned— and some of them will issue reports soon—is to write directly to their offices requesting an annual report.

At the least, annual reports tell the basic story of what a foundation does and why. Many reports are carefully edited, appropriately illustrated and interestingly written. Occasionally the complaint is made that they are luxurious in style, but only a very few are properly subject to any such charge. The annual reports of the leading foundations are considerably less costly than the annual reports of leading business corporations, than even the catalogues of many colleges and universities. For content, style, taste and general informativeness, the best of them rank very high. Alongside the annual statements, a number of foundations with extensive programs are now issuing supplemental reports on various projects or special brochures that give more detailed information on some matter of current interest.

Seldom has it been charged that the secretiveness supposedly characteristic of foundations was practiced among themselves as well as vis-à-vis the general public. Such a charge, however,

6. See entries for named foundations in FD-4. The *Foundation Directory* notes "Report published annually" for all foundations that do so.

might have been substantiated—though most critics would have hailed rather than deplored a lack of communication among foundations, lest their sharing too much with each other suggest collusion inimical to the general welfare. In any event, foundations have hardly been more communicative with each other than with the general public, and until some degree of misery began to love company, they seldom cooperated with each other in common projects or even in exchanges of information. A foundation was usually a fiercely independent entity, separate from all others of its type and engaged therefore in what amounted to unilateral action.

But this too is coming to a close, as will be described in more detail in Chapter VI. The secretiveness that many small and a few large foundations have practiced on the general public and even among themselves is fast ending, and the goldfish bowl has replaced the dark corner or the back pocket as the locus of a foundation's life.

3. Inconsequential work?

One of the favorite criticisms is that the work of foundations is unimaginative, inconsequential and safe. It is charged that foundations don't look very far, don't do very much and don't rock any boats.

These are the critics that foundations ought to cherish. In contrast with those to be mentioned in the two following sections, these are usually gentle complainers who speak more out of sadness than of anger. They have a theory that foundations, with their power, prestige and resources, ought to make a difference in the quality of life; and they look around them with regret that the difference isn't as great as they think it ought to be. It is critics such as these that encourage a foundation to be about its proper business—but that is to get ahead of our story. The charge itself is not a restraint. Rather, it is a reminder that the constraints a foundation feels are not as large as it imagines. The force of the criticism, therefore, is to urge the foundation to get on with the job. For this reason, therefore, it should be cherished.

But it should also be listened to. The average individual donor, with modest resources, does not allow himself the luxury of pretending that his personal gifts can change the world or even some small portion of it. He simply does his bit to enable the agencies he trusts to perform their proper functions a little better than they would otherwise be able to do. So he gives to his church, his Community Chest, his favorite charity, his alumni fund, his local hospital drive and, if he dares to take a flyer, one "mad money" project. Not much imagination; no large consequence; pretty safe. Yet this is the sort of personal benevolence that gets the ongoing job done.

But a foundation is expected to do better. A body of money has been set aside for the improvement of some part of the social fabric. Imagination in its use is in order. As for results, though illusions of grand accomplishment are to be eschewed, something of larger consequence than support of the annual budget is anticipated. And always to play it safe is scandalous. The Peterson Commission's most serious criticism of foundations may well rest in the finding that "only 1 percent of all foundations viewed any of their grants as controversial."[7] If this is a fair estimate—and there may be some legitimate doubt, to be noted below—then this could be a more devastating charge than either of the sharper, but more answerable, criticisms in the section to follow.

Before responding to the charge of timidity, let us give the critics their inning:

—Merle Curti, in a 1962 article in *Foundation News:* "Philanthropy on the whole has avoided controversial issues, the very issues, perhaps, that offer the greatest challenge and that point to the greatest need."[8]

—George Kirstein, in *The Nation* for September 16, 1968: "The influence of the rich in philanthropy focuses on the established institution, tends to maintain the *status quo.* It is rare, indeed, that major donations are made to encourage basic

7. Report of Peterson Commission, *op. cit.,* p. 84.
8. Merle Curti, "Creative Giving: Slogan or Reality?" *Foundation News,* November, 1962, p. 8, quoted in Reeves, *op. cit.,* p. 13.

change, or even minor dislocation of any aspect of established society."[9]

—Taylor Branch, in the July, 1971, issue of *The Washington Monthly:* "One need not be a Marxist, or even a Democrat, to deduce that foundations are unlikely to be restless with the world ... foundations are by nature pretty tame social kittens."[10]

—Joseph C. Goulden in *The Money Givers:* "... foundations are ... quiet billions ... administered by philanthropoids who build cuckoo clocks and try to pass them off as cathedrals ... simply another of the many flawed institutions in America ... building their childish sand castles on their private beaches ..."[11]

So the work of foundations is inconsequential? A personal word may not be amiss. Whatever may be true of other outfits, critics can't justifiably say those things about the Danforth Foundation! Just the other day our office received successive telephone calls from a suburban white, complaining about a grant we had made to an inner-city organization working to good purpose in the ghetto, and from a militant black, complaining that by that same grant we were trying to buy off the indigenous leadership he and others had so painfully developed. From opposite points of the social and political spectrum the two critics agreed: the Danforth Foundation was trying to make a difference and they didn't like it. The aim was community reconciliation, and each critic in his own way rejected such a purpose. Both of those telephone callers, therefore, were paying the Foundation an unintentional compliment; it would not have occurred to either of them to say that what the Foundation was doing was innocuous.

All well and good—and if this book were about the Danforth Foundation, it could be filled with illustrations of grants and programs representing the exploration of fresh ideas, the innovation of new projects and the trial runs of quite debatable

9. George G. Kirstein, "Philanthropy: The Golden Crowbar," *The Nation,* September 16, 1968, p. 239, quoted in Reeves, *op. cit.,* p. 14.
10. Branch, *op. cit.,* pp. 3, 14.
11. Goulden, *op. cit.,* pp. 317–318.

propositions. But the Danforth Foundation, even in the prejudiced eyes of its admirers, is not the only innovative and effective philanthropy. The next chapter will refer to hosts of other foundations whose programs are a standing denial of the charge that they engage only in what is unimaginative, inconsequential and safe.

The Report of the Peterson Commission furnishes its own partial rebuttal to the 1 percent canard, noted above, which received wide circulation. Often unmentioned was the significant breakdown by size of foundation. The question was, "Have any of the projects supported by your foundation's grants or gifts in the past three years been considered controversial or particularly unpopular?" Whereas "only 1 percent of all foundations" said Yes, 38 percent of "foundations with assets over $100 million" said Yes[12]—reminding us, incidentally, of the huge proportion of foundations that are minuscule in size as well as timid in program.

Is this to say, then, that the charge, at least for large foundations, has no substance?

The answer is No. Still other foundations remain to be heard from. Of the scores of foundation officers of my acquaintance, I know of none who would admit that his own foundation was guilty of this charge—though there might be some ex-officers who would grant the point. Nearly every foundation executive, however, knows some *other* foundation whose work is pretty namby-pamby and insignificant.

The point is, if one looks for foundation activities to disparage, one can readily find them. It is somewhat like the parlor game of laymen in respect to the titles of doctoral dissertations. Sooner or later anybody can find some subject that a university has honored, or some grant that a foundation has perpetrated, so outlandish and preposterous as to delight the detractors and embarrass the admirers of that university or foundation. Mr. Patman horrified the House Ways and Means Committee with word about the Bollingen Foundation's grant for research on "the origin and significance of the decorative

12. Report of Peterson Commission, *op. cit.,* p. 84.

types of medieval tombstones in Bosnia and Herzegovina."[13]

Even dissertation topics that sound absurd to a layman can often be justified by experts in the field. This is not to suggest that the parallel should hold, that many foundation grants that seem soft-headed are actually quite sound. It is to suggest, rather, that the parallel doesn't hold. Most of those who play the parlor game would believe that silly dissertation topics are an aberration, indicative only that the university is not always on its toes, rather than that the university is a basically disreputable institution and research a dishonorable enterprise. But many who criticize the inconsequentiality of foundations believe this to be the central characteristic of its work, not abnormal but the norm. Foundations, they say, don't just occasionally do something that is bland or useless. This is what they do all the time. This is all they do. Are there any grounds at all for such an amazing charge?

A proposition of this sort can hardly be proved or disproved. It can only be examined from and by all sides, and then the predilections and biases of those doing the examining can be examined in turn. What, for example, does "inconsequential" mean? One man's meat is, at the least, another man's cottage cheese. If a person thinks parks are important, he may direct his foundation to provide green spaces and plant trees. If another person thinks safety is important, he may feel that growing flowers is fiddling while the city burns, and so he may direct *his* foundation to strengthen the local police department. If still another person thinks equal opportunity is important, he may bypass both grass and cops, and center his foundation's attention on improved schooling for disadvantaged youngsters. So who is to judge?

This is not to say that it is six of one and half a dozen of the other. It is not even to say that he who pays his money has the right to take his choice. Some things are indeed more significant than others, more related to human welfare than others, more designed to improve the physical or spiritual condition of man than others. But the perspective from which one judges these matters is all-important; and all of us, I dare-

13. Ways and Means Committee Hearings, *op. cit.,* Part I, pp. 16–17.

say, get tired of the critic who sets himself up as automatically a better judge than the institution or agency against which he is complaining.

The Charles A. Dana Foundation, together with some criticism it has received, is a case in point. In his muckraking volume, *The Money Givers,* Joseph C. Goulden makes great sport of this foundation's "edifice complex," for it likes to build buildings and to have Mr. Dana's name on them. Goulden cites at least fifteen colleges and other institutions that have a Dana Hall, a Dana Auditorium or a Dana Laboratory.[14]

Here then we have at least two perspectives on what is or is not worthwhile. The Dana Foundation believes that its providing various colleges and other institutions with the buildings they need is an important service.[15] Goulden believes, however, that "the construction of conspicuous marble monuments," in which Dana has widely engaged, is one among a group of "non-altruistic motives" that characterize and debase foundation behavior.

Let there be a third perspective that does not buy either the prideful line of the foundation or the iconoclastic slant of the muckraker. This position would hold that erecting buildings is often a very good thing to do, and the various ones that the Charles A. Dana Foundation helped to build were probably all needed by the receiving institutions and represented a considerable benefit to their budgets. As decisions by the Foundation, can they be said to have been imaginative? Hardly. Were they safe? In all likelihood—including even "Dana House in mid-Manhattan," which Goulden points out was "for 'unwed mothers and other troubled girls'."[16]

Does this mean, then, that the Dana Foundation's program is inconsequential? Such an opinion would be absurd. Even if one might himself have spent the money differently, he would be hard pressed to justify the position that he would have spent it better. Either he or the Foundation might have spent it

14. Goulden, *op. cit.,* pp. 24–25.
15. *Charles A. Dana Foundation: A Review, 1963–67,* cited by Goulden, *op. cit.,* p. 326.
16. *Ibid.,* p. 25.

104

worse. If some foundations are going to do nothing more exciting than simply build some needed buildings here and there across the country, this may well be cause for deploring their lack of imagination or courage, or cause for rejoicing, by contrast, that other foundations are doing more imaginative and courageous things; but it is no cause for saying that the work of *all* foundations is unimaginative, inconsequential and safe. The known facts hardly support any such conclusion except for those who start out with the intention so to conclude.

4. *Extremism?*

The next major charge is that foundations are instruments of extremism in American society. They won't leave things alone. They are always stirring things up. Moreover, they don't want an ordinary, garden-variety brand of evolutionary development; they want a massive change.

Foundations support all kinds of inquiries into hallowed institutions and customs, these critics point out, and are continually publishing reports that purport to show what is wrong. Then they compound the problem by underwriting action programs as well as research. Somebody who simply wants to keep things as they are doesn't have a chance to get a grant from a foundation. But let a fellow advocate extremist policies in one direction or another, and some foundation will be sure to come along and pick up the tab.

Let us note, in passing, that this general criticism runs almost directly counter to the preceding one that foundations don't do anything significant and play it too safe. The contradiction doesn't really bother the critics. Both positions are widely argued, sometimes by the same person. One has to grant, moreover, that it is at least theoretically possible for both charges to be true about the same foundation. Some woolly-headed outfit might well want to see the existing order overthrown in one direction or another, and might get so fouled up in its own operations that they come literally to naught. Illustrations, however, would have to be largely imaginary; and

105

when these two contradictory charges are made, critics are thinking about one group of foundations for the charge of inconsequentiality, and an entirely different group for the charge of extremism.

To be precise, the latter is composed of two groups. Extremists, as they are usually labeled, are of both the left and the right. One group is revolutionary, the other reactionary. Seldom is any individual foundation charged with being both, though again it is at least theoretically possible.

Prior to responding to each of these extremist charges in turn, it is important to note that both do in fact exist, that neither is simply the figment of a defensive imagination trying to balance off the charge from the opposite direction. Anybody who feels that there is at least some small measure of justice in one of these complaints is likely to pooh-pooh the other. How absurd to think that foundations are revolutionary/reactionary when "everyone knows" that they are reactionary/revolutionary! But the morning mail of almost any executive of a large foundation could dissipate such a one-sided notion. Both points of view are held by a considerable number of people.

Granting the philosophic position of complainers founda- tions are bound to be in their line of fire. That is, an extreme right-winger would be happy only if all foundations espoused extreme right-wing policies. But unless America loses its char- acter as a pluralistic society, such a thing is not going to be. The extreme right-winger, therefore, is going to be unhappy with most foundation behavior, and is undoubtedly going to say so. Ditto exactly for the extreme left-winger. There is no way around it.

Yet foundations should beware of the conclusion, You can't win. Inviting as such a shrug-off may be, the fact remains that the charge about extremism does not come only from one or another brand of extremists, outraged that the foundations don't support his position. Middle-of-the-road critics voice this complaint from time to time, especially with regard to founda- tions in particular rather than in general. Many Americans, relatively balanced in their political, economic and social opinions, and conscientious in their effort to look at the facts,

have come to believe that the actions of at least a few foundations are often ill-advised, tending toward the undesirable
extremes of fostering either revolution or reaction. It is important, then, to ask whether and to what extent either or both
of these criticisms, contradictory as they are, seem to be true.
One of the reasons that this blanket charge of extremism has
got so far is that foundations have not sufficiently analyzed and
responded to it.

4a. *Reaction?*

First in point of time was the charge that foundations were
much too conservative, even reactionary. This was the under-
lying theme of the first Congressional investigation, that of the
Walsh Commission in 1915.[17] But even though its opposite number has come to be popular, this charge is not out of date, for
those who argue that foundations are the playthings of "the
rich and the super rich" are attracted to the notion that they
resist change and try to turn the clock back.[18] A genuinely
new idea or fresh approach has got little or no chance, so these
critics say. It was in some pristine time back yonder, fifty, a
hundred, two hundred years ago, that America was right or
strong or good; and, practicing ancestor worship, these reactionary foundations mean to recreate it.

This line of thought is congenial with many of the criticisms
noted in the preceding chapter, all adding up to the general
position that foundations are bulwarks of the established order.
To the extent to which foundations are used by the wealthy and
powerful to buttress up their own favored position, it is logical
for the critic to extend the argument to the effect that the
alleged charity of privileged people is thereby directed against
the grain of social advance.

What are the facts? Is there any evidence to support such a
charge?

The summary answer is, Some but not much. Some sections

17. See Weaver, *op. cit.*, pp. 170–171; Kiger, *op. cit.*, pp. 85–88;
Keele, *op. cit.*, pp. 7–9; Fremont-Smith, *op. cit.*, pp. 51–52.
18. See Lundberg, *op. cit.*, chap. 10; Lindeman, *op. cit.*

of the liberal press and some left-wing journalists have been eager to reveal any reactionary foundation behavior they could find, and they have succeeded in finding and giving publicity to some juicy examples. But the case that reaction is the norm has simply not been made, for the total body of reliable information about foundations does not support it.

Let us look at some of the alleged examples. Several small foundations seem to have, or have had, ties with the John Birch Society and similar far-right groups. Among those mentioned are the Chance Foundation of Centralia, Missouri, and the Grede and Harnischfeger Foundations, both of Milwaukee. Others that have consistently supported right-wing causes are the O'Donnell Foundation of Dallas, the soon-to-be-liquidated Volker Fund of Burlingame, California, and the Relm Foundation of Ann Arbor, Michigan. All of these are of sufficient size to win listing in the *Foundation Directory;* many others not so large are undoubtedly enrolled among the supporters of reactionary agencies, but seldom receive public notice. The super-wealthy Texan, H. L. Hunt, is widely known for his ultra-conversatism, but his Life Line Foundation lost its tax exemption when its right-wing propaganda got too blatant; and his H. L. Hunt Foundation is quite small. The Freedoms Foundation of Valley Forge is rightist enough to deserve mention, but it isn't a foundation in the endowed sense. A number of foundations, including a few large ones, have made occasional grants to such far-right heroes as Fred Schwarz of the Christian Anti-Communism Crusade and George S. Benson of Harding College. Only one large foundation, the Pew Memorial Trust, seems to follow a consistently reactionary line.[19]

Anyone who cherishes the good name of foundations is bound to feel that this catalogue is a sorry story. But the thing not to be overlooked is that it is also a quite limited story. The various waves of far-right sentiment that sweep across the body

19. See Arnold Forster and Benjamin R. Epstein, *Danger on the Right,* New York, Random House, 1964, pp. 272–277; quoted by Reeves, *op. cit.,* pp. 120–127; Cook, *op. cit.;* Goulden *op. cit.,* pp. 163–175.

politic from time to time do not seem to have received any major portion of their financial support from established foundations. With only an occasional exception foundations have steered clear of such reactionary movements as McCarthyism, Ku Kluxism and John Birchism. In spite of a few illustrations that support the notion, the position that foundations as a field are agents of fascism is simply laughable.

4b. *Revolution?*

The other side of the extremist coin is that foundations have been captured by the radic-libs or worse. They help hippies, or foment campus revolt, or pander to the demands of the militant blacks. They meddle with the legislative process and undertake to influence government officials. They are tearing down the very fabric of our society and are engaging in all sorts of controversial activities. If the mainstream of American citizenry doesn't rise up to stop them, so these critics say, the supposedly virtuous foundations will despoil us of our time-honored values and change beyond recall our present way of life.[20]

This notion is contradictory not merely to the preceding complaint that foundations are reactionary but also to the charge noted in Chapter II that foundations are bastions of special privilege. But this does not seem to worry the critics. Logical consistency is no ideal. They think they can have it both ways. Their contradictory position runs to this wise: Though foundations are monuments to the success of the capitalistic system, they subvert our way of life with socialistic ventures. Products of society based on law and order, they give support to those who flout the law and disrupt the order. So the critics conclude that foundations question, and probe and meddle—and it all adds up to revolution.

Perhaps this is a good moment to note, parenthetically, that many who do not go so far as to charge foundations with being

20. See references to Cox and Reece investigations in chap. I, above, and footnotes 24 and 25 of chap. I.

revolutionary or destructive are still caught in something of the same contradiction of viewpoint. One of the popular positions in Washington in 1969, during the debates on the Tax Reform Act, was that foundations were both too privileged and too independent, and ought to be made to pay for their paradoxical condition. As holders of high status, foundations were suspected of using their preferred position to subvert the lesser status of others. Many of the same critics who wanted to impose taxes on the foundations wanted also to limit their freedom of movement by keeping them from making grants to individuals, or having any contact with Government officials, or trying to affect public opinion on issues of the day. Most contradictory of all is that many who criticized foundations fiercely were the same ones who deplored big Government, seemingly unaware that if foundation grants are reduced, Government will have to get bigger in order to fill the gap. Whatever else one feels about the critics of foundations, it is clearly not fair to charge them with consistency.

The supportive evidence for the charge of revolution is even more meager than for its contradictory partner, the charge of reaction, noted above, A few cases of foundation behavior that could perhaps be described as far-left have been turned up. Just about the only endowed fund that such a word might fit is the Louis M. Rabinowitz Foundation of New York City, whose "affinity for left-wing causes" has recently been re-marked. Individual grants of otherwise reputable foundations have now and then gone to allegedly, perhaps actually, sub-versive groups.[21]

But whenever any dust-up about the supposed leftist lean-ings of foundations has come along, it turns out that the dusting is being done by the self-styled "anti-Communists" whose charges are soon shown to be ludicrous. Robert M. Hutchins said that "the Reece investigation in its inception and execution was a fraud."[22] When the Reece Committee's counsel, René A. Wormser, wrote a book to display the "Communist penetration of foundations," he proved nothing except that Hutchins was

21. See Goulden, *op. cit.*, pp. 162–163.
22. Hutchins, *op. cit.*, p. 117.

110

correct.[23] Under Hutchins' leadership the Fund for the Republic, a spin-off from Ford, suffered more extreme vilification than perhaps any other foundation has ever known, but as Thomas C. Reeves has ably documented, it merited none of the slanders of the super-patriots.[24] Those were the fifties, and Joe McCarthy is now dead. Left-wing subversion is still occasionally charged against foundations by right-wing fanatics, but the credibility they once produced has gone.

When the full count is in, therefore, the poverty of this preposterous notion is revealed. Nobody but an extremist of the opposite stripe could take seriously the proposition that foundations are out to subvert or overthrow the society.

5. Partisan Political Activity?

To say that foundations are not guilty of the charge of extremism, however, is not to say that they have refrained from participating in partisan political activity. The charge that foundations are either reactionary or revolutionary is separate from the charge that they play politics. It is quite conceivable that, escaping the former, they may have succumbed to the latter.

Once the bugaboos of fascism and communism have been buried, we must ask the crucial question: Is it true that foundations have abused their non-profit, tax-exempt status by taking sides on public issues, lobbying and working for legislative changes? If so, what, how, when and where? If not, why all the hullabaloo? The complaint of extremism is insignificant in comparison with this block-buster charge of political maneuvering, for if the facts support any such attack, the foundations are indeed in grave peril and ought to be.

Since much of this charge has lodged in Congress, it is appropriate to call upon the *Congressional Quarterly* for its sum-

23. See René A. Wormser, *Foundations: Their Power and Influence,* New York, Devin-Adair, 1958, quoted in Reeves, *op. cit.,* pp. 97–112.
24. See Thomas C. Reeves, *Freedom and the Foundation: The Fund for the Republic in the Era of McCarthyism,* New York, Alfred A. Knopf, 1969.

111

mary statement: "An era of war, crusades for human rights and changing priorities spurred non-profit groups and tax-free foundations to move from eleemosynary grants to gifts with legislative and political goals . . . Such activities attracted the concern of Congress, particularly after charges of impropriety by some foundations in 1968 and 1969. Members termed some foundations 'holding companies' for out-of-power government officials, and charged that the influence of powerful foundations constituted a sub-government that swayed the thinking of legislators and executive branch officials."[25]

Instances given for this alleged misbehavior of foundations are surprisingly few in number. One of the favorites cited in Washington is the case of Congressman Rooney and the Frederick W. Richmond Foundation. mentioned in the preceding chapter as an instance of a donor's getting personal advantage from his philanthropic fund. Both Mr. Richmond and Mr. Rooney tried to use the behavior of the Foundation to advance personal political ambition, and Mr. Rooney won the contest.[26] Broader political causes, however, were not at stake. and thus this episode is not really an illustration of the problem we are here considering.

Most of the widely publicized illustrations of meddlesome political activity on the part of foundations have been grants by the Ford Foundation. Perhaps the first to get large attention was the grant to the Cleveland Chapter of the Congress of Racial Equality (CORE), announced in June, 1967. Joseph C. Goulden, who has little good to say about foundations, though much of that is in bemused admiration of Ford, writes that "the CORE grant was at once the bravest and the most naive action

25. This long statement, of which the quotation is only a brief excerpt, was given a remarkably broad circulation in scores of small city newspapers across the country, though hardly noticed in the big metropolitan press. See, for example, the *Tulsa, Okla., Tribune,* June 10, 1971, the *Ft. Lauderdale, Fla., News,* June 13, 1971, and the *Flint, Mich., Journal,* July 5, 1971. In each instance the source was stated as "By Congressional Quarterly." See *Congressional Quarterly,* June 11, 1971, pp. 1251–1256.

26. Ways and Means Committee Hearings, *op. cit.,* Part I, pp. 213–237.

ever taken by a major foundation."[27] Quibble with the superlatives as you will—for a number of other foundation grants as candidates for those adjectival categories could be mentioned—there is little doubt that this grant has drawn more widespread and sharp-tongued censure for being politically partisan than any other single foundation action.

Briefly told, the grant to CORE was for a voter registration drive in parts of Cleveland populated by blacks. Carl Stokes, a black man, was running for mayor. When he got elected, Ford was widely accused of having been responsible. Wright Patman raised the question that was occurring to many others: "Have the giant foundations made or do they plan to make grants that will aid certain candidates to run for National, State and local office. Does the Ford Foundation have a grandiose design to bring vast political, economic, and social changes to the Nation in the 1970's?"[28]

A second Ford activity that was widely condemned as being politically motivated was the series of travel-study grants given to eight aides of Senator Robert F. Kennedy soon after his assassination in 1968. Short-term subsidies of individuals for generous amounts—the largest was for $22,200 for a six-month period—these grants grew out of a burst of sympathy for men who had suffered grievous loss in the death of their leader and whose own careers had thereby been seriously dislocated. But this was not the way Congress and the general public saw it. Rather, this was politics. At its best, these grants were "severance pay"; at worst, this was "sub rosa financing for a shadow Kennedy political machine."[29]

Other Ford activities received lesser national attention for their supposed political implications, but in their own parts of the country and to the extent to which they were generally known, they added fuel to the charge. One of these was the

27. Goulden, *op. cit.*, p. 262.
28. Ways and Means Committee Hearings, *op. cit.*, Part I, p. 15.
29. Goulden, *op. cit.*, p. 278. See Wright Patman's comments on the grants to Kennedy's aides, in Ways and Means Committee Hearings, *op. cit.*, Part I, pp. 15–16.

Ocean Hill-Brownsville School dispute in New York City that ran roughly from 1967 to 1969. The Ford Foundation gave fiscal and moral encouragement to the effort at decentralization of the public schools, and, for its pains, it was charged by various participants in the confused struggle with having engaged in a variety of political efforts.

Another illustration was Ford's support in the late sixties of projects on behalf of Chicanos in the San Antonio region of Texas. Ford made grants to the Mexican-American Youth Organization (MAYO) and the Mexican-American Legal Defense Fund (MALD), and soon these groups offended not only right-wing Texas whites but old line Mexican-American politicians. Both the Ocean Hill-Brownsville and the South Texas excursions, along with the grants to CORE and to Kennedy's aides, received the attention of Congress, and it all seemed to add up to the hypothesis that Ford was embarked on a course of political partisanship.

What Congress did about it will be discussed in Chapter V. Now we need to ask whether such an interpretation of the Ford actions is fair either to the intent or to the result. Answers are bound to be varied, for the available facts are not fully determinative, and the standpoint from which any commentator views the activities of the Ford Foundation comes close to predetermining what his conclusions will be. All I claim is that, admiring much but not all that Ford has done, and owing nothing to and wanting nothing from Ford, I have developed a completely objective view of the matter!

The central response to the charge is quickly stated: though Ford made mistakes in procedures and timing, it is not guilty of either wanting to be, or in fact being, a partisan political agency. The CORE grant was amateurishly handled, and because the voter registration part of it was focused on black districts rather than aimed at enlisting all unregistered voters, it had the look of being partisan no matter what the press releases claimed. As for the grants to Kennedy's aides, Ford had been providing subventions to individuals of this general sort for some time. Other foundations have also made such grants on occasion. A majority of the Ford trustees, as is probably true for the boards of all other large foundations, are Republicans. That foundations like Ford are involved in political machinations on behalf of some aspiring Kennedy or any other Democrat is nonsense.

Ford's visibility hurts. Its visibility is of two sorts: one, sheer size, and two, McGeorge Bundy. Many of Mr. Bundy's colleagues and assistants are also men of national reputation, but by virtue of the role he played in national affairs some years ago, opinions about Mr. Bundy, especially in Washington, are likely to be sharper and more pronounced, whether they consist in admiration or dislike. It is a strange circumstance that, whereas criticism of smaller operations is seldom couched in personal terms, the criticism of the largest foundation is often made to seem highly personal. Perhaps the opposite is also true, that it is sometimes made to appear impersonal, when in fact it is personally motivated. In either case it is probably not fair to Mr. Bundy or to the Ford Foundation.

Those who for any reason are unfriendly to foundations in general cannot ignore Ford, and obviously don't want to. Yet it is extremely difficult to make really stick against Ford any of the charges thus far considered in this and the previous chapter. If confidence in Ford is to be successfully undermined, thus throwing suspicion on all foundations, it will have to be done through some kind of attack on what this giant does that is presumably not in the public interest. Inadequate spending? Secretiveness? Inconsequential work? None of these can be convincingly charged against Ford. Extremism, whether of a reactionary or a revolutionary cast? The defense could make mincemeat of any such suggestion.

But Ford's indiscretions, whether attributable corporately or personally, gave room for making the charge that the Ford Foundation was engaged in partisan political activity. When the mistakes, or for that matter accomplishments, of other foundations go unreported, headlines can always be made by or about Ford. A school dispute in New York City or a Chicano fuss in South Texas or any of a number of lively community interests in which Ford might get involved, can furnish the spark for further charges of partisanship by someone on the other side,

115

whatever the other side is. As would be expected, Ford pleads not guilty. In spite of all the public ranting and congressional raving, the case has not been proved. The alleged facts don't add up to support the charge.

But Ford is not the whole show. In respect to political partisanship, what other foundations besides Ford have supposedly misbehaved?

Just about the time this general charge was gathering steam it was revealed that Mr. Justice Abe Fortas had accepted a continuing consultant's relationship with the Wolfson Family Foundation, at a handsome annual stipend, and that Mr. Justice William Douglas was serving as the President of the Parvin Foundation, also with generous honorarium. Since both of these foundations were thought to be connected with some shady characters, and since even or especially Supreme Court Justices are felt to be political figures, the publicity left the impression that here was further support for the proposition that foundations were political instruments. One or both foundations and one or both Justices may have acted unwisely. In fact, Mr. Fortas was forced to resign his seat on the Supreme Court. But only in the heated critical atmosphere of Washington in 1969 could these cases have been thought to have been indicative of more widespread sinister behavior by foundations.[30]

Yet sinister may be the right word for the disclosure, first made by *Ramparts* magazine in 1967, that the Central Intelligence Agency had used foundations as fronts and conduits for the channeling of Federal support to various kinds of groups whose activities seemed to the CIA to be in the public interest even though they couldn't be advertised. The CIA, it seems, used some small foundations already established and set up a few new ones. Some of the foundations, it appeared, did not know they were being used. Since all of this was hush-hush, its revelation produced cries of outrage from many points of the political compass.[31]

30. See Goulden, *op. cit.,* pp. 297–305; Reeves, *Foundations Under Fire, op. cit.,* p. 21.
31. See Weaver, *op. cit.,* pp. 193–194; Lundberg, *op. cit.,* pp. 498, 504–505; Robert G. Sherrill, "Foundation Pipe Lines: The Beneficent CIA," *The Nation,* May 9, 1966, quoted in Reeves, *op. cit.,* pp. 133–141.

Unfortunately the high dudgeon did not last very long. There has been no assurance from the CIA that the practice of using foundations or other groups as covers for secret governmental operations has in fact been stopped. While attention was still being given to this cloak-and-dagger act, it looked to some as if this were one more sign that foundations have strong political proclivities. But apart from its distressing implications about Government, the very most that this episode could demonstrate in regard to foundations is that a few small ones are politically naive and uncritically susceptible to outside suggestion.

Some critics have held that the evidence for foundations' political activity lies in the large number of persons who have had dual relationships: at one time or another in their lives they have been connected with both foundations and Government agencies. McGeorge Bundy not only went from the White House to Ford; he has carried a number of other high government officials with him: David Bell, formerly Director of the Budget, Harold Howe, formerly U.S. Commissioner of Education and others.

Traffic is heavy both ways. Didn't Dean Rusk go from Rockefeller to the State Department, and John Gardner from Carnegie to HEW? Compiling such a list can be a pleasant indoor sport, and the more people having dual relationships that one can think of, the more conspiratorial the whole business appears.[32]

But if this is the evidence on which the charge must rest, it is a pretty insubstantial reed. As much or more could be charged against business corporations or universities. All that such evidence really shows is that large foundations, like leading institutions of any category, try to employ the most able leadership they can put their hands on; and as long as business, education, Government or any other field is doing the same thing, there is bound to be traffic to and fro.

The absurdity of this guilt-by-association-with-Government was brought home to us in the Danforth Foundation in the spring of 1970, when one of my staff colleagues and my wife ran for separate local school boards. Each of them had to put

32. See, for example, Lundberg, *op. cit.*, pp. 482–483.

up with the opponent's charge that the Danforth Foundation was obviously trying to take over the school systems of the area. I was advised by a friend that if I used this illustration it would be wise not to report that both of them had won!

These are the instances and bits of behavior cited. Nothing more. The charge against the whole foundation field, therefore, breaks down. Once it is granted that a few foundations have been indiscreet or naive or even narrowly partisan, the widespread slashing charge of political misbehavior can be categorically denied. There is simply no body of reputable evidence to support any such preposterous proposition; there are only individual, gossipy incidents here and there.

But are foundations concerned about matters that have political implications? This is a quite different question, and the answer to it is, increasingly, Yes. Some people are convinced that to be politically aware is to be politically partisan; and if this were the case, then the plea to the earlier charge would have to be guilty. As it is, however, it is important to make the distinction that, whereas foundations are innocent of the sweeping suggestion that they engage in partisan politics, more and more of them are becoming active in problem areas of American society, areas that must inevitably receive governmental, and thus political, attention.

Goulden believes that the Ford Foundation got charged with political partisanship simply because it was coming to be increasingly concerned about social problems. It was when Ford "boldly moved . . . to activism" in 1966 that the die was cast. It is his view that in becoming socially active Ford led the procession and thus drew the fire of those who feel that social concern and political manipulation are synonymous.[33]

Ford deserves great credit for its social awareness through recent years, and McGeorge Bundy has led the Foundation into new areas of useful service. But even as Goulden recognizes at one point, "activism was not new among foundations," though among the hosts of names that might have been noted, Goulden mentions only three: "The Stern Family Fund, the Field

33. Goulden, *op. cit.,* p. 240. See his chap. 8, "Activism and Acrimony," pp. 239–282.

Foundation, the New World Foundation."[34] Arguing that Ford led the way, Goulden writes: "At the beginning of 1969, other foundations, tentatively, hesitantly, began to follow Ford's example and find community action projects." Then he mentions, as illustrations, "the ultra cautious Rockefeller Foundation," the Carnegie Corporation and the Rockefeller Brothers Fund. That is all. [35]

All these foundations do indeed merit such recognition, and many others besides. Moreover, careful inspection of their activities through the years suggests that they weren't as hesitant or as frightened as Goulden seems to think. The work of many of them predated Ford's interest, and even Ford's activity predated 1966. Goulden's justified admiration of Ford's social conscience and his relative lack of knowledge of other foundations combine to produce a more limited picture of the community action programs of various foundations than the facts justify.

For example, back in 1963, the Danforth Foundation invited Ford, along with eighteen or twenty other foundations, to attend a two-day conference at which the Southern Association of Colleges and Schools would present plans for an ambitious program to upgrade educational opportunities for blacks in Southern cities. Though several of the foundations, including Danforth, had been working for many years with the Southern Association and with individual Negro colleges, the Ford Foundation during the preceding ten years had spent only about $35,000 in this field. As an outgrowth of that meeting, however, the Ford Foundation has made grants to that one program of the Southern Association totalling around $19 million, and millions more to other such programs. Goulden rightly praises "Bundy's declaration that 'full equality for all American Negroes is now the most urgent domestic concern of this country'."[36] But the full story is that Ford was at work on this problem before Bundy came along, and that many other foundations were at work on it before Ford began to take it seriously.

34. *Ibid.*, p. 240.
35. *Ibid.*, pp. 279–280.
36. *Ibid.*, p. 262.

No such work can fail to have some kind of political repercussion. The area of application for that statement is no longer limited to the South. As will be discussed in the next chapter, foundations are widely involved all across the country and around the world in matters of pressing social concern and in urgent community problems. To the extent to which this makes them political, then they are inevitably related to the political scene. But only in this sense, and not in the sense that they are engaged in partisan politics, can the charge be upheld that they are politically active.

6. *Monitoring and Evaluation?*

The last major criticism to be noted in this chapter is one that, strangely, is not widely voiced but perhaps ought to be. This is the charge that foundations do not monitor and evaluate their own work.

The only systematic effort that has been made to determine foundation practice in this regard is the work of the Peterson Commission. The following sentences from their Report summarize their findings: ". . . the Commission's data on present policies among foundations underlines a need facing many foundations themselves to reassess their own follow-up procedures . . . 41 percent of all foundations . . . never take any steps to monitor their grantees or follow up their grants . . . over half of the foundations never make field visits or use any other device for periodic personal checks on grantee activities; 72 percent never require periodic reports as a requirement for payment of installments of the grants; 91 percent never require independent auditing of the grantee's expenditures."[37]

To put these findings into proper perspective, several things need to be remembered. First, the percentages are for foundations of all sorts and sizes, and the situation as to monitoring is not nearly so bleak for "the larger foundations with their full complement of professional staffs," as the Peterson Commission discovered.[38]

37. Report of Peterson Commission, *op. cit.,* p. 91.
38. *Ibid.*

Secondly, it must be not assumed that monitoring and evaluation are always sound practices. On the contrary, certain types of recipients do not need foundation inspection and would be understandably offended if they were to get it. When an endowment grant is made to a major university, the foundation would simply look silly if it were to institute some automatic monitoring process as to what happened to the money. Close and rigid supervision of grants would change radically the nature of the relationship between grantor and grantee, and if foundations were to undertake any such task on an all-inclusive basis, they would have to add substantially to their staffs and shift markedly their style of work.

Finally, many grants, especially those made by large foundations, simply cannot be evaluated. As the Peterson Report says: "The Commission realized that there are many kinds of innovative social programs which, by their very nature, seem to defy an evaluation even by the most sophisticated and talked-about cost-benefit analytical technique."[39] Evaluations of any grants having to do with intangibles of mood and temper are likely to be pretentious and preposterous. Time, too, is a factor, and whereas the success of some program might be estimated after, say, a twenty-year period, such a judgment after only one or two years would be immature.

Foundations must not be let off the hook, however, simply because appropriate follow-up of their activities is difficult. Take the Danforth Foundation again as an illustration. We probably do as much monitoring and evaluation as any foundation, proportionate to our size. When we recently suffered through a friendly seven-month audit by the Internal Revenue Service, we were pleased that they took occasion to compliment our staff on the surprising amount and character of the reports and evaluations in the Foundation's program and grant files. Like most other large foundations, Danforth makes numbers of grants to recipient institutions in the two fields of its special interest, education and urban affairs; unlike most other large foundations, Danforth also sponsors programs that are administered by members of its own professional staff. On nearly every grant

39. *Ibid.*

121

there will be multiple reports and progress statements. Every foundation-administered program is evaluated periodically, with an eye to the question as to whether it has served its purpose and should be discontinued, or whether it should be maintained or enlarged. Much time and effort go into this part of our work, and in conversations with other foundation officials, I have come to realize that Danforth gives more attention to this task than perhaps all but two or three other foundations.

The point of such immodesty, however, is to say how poorly we perform in this regard. We know that our follow-up work is not as good as it ought to be, and further, is not good enough. In respect to grants, sometimes we know only what the grantee wants us to know. In respect to our own programs, we are not always as harsh on ourselves as some outside critics might be. For the size of the operation we run, both grants and programs, ours is a small staff, unable to get everything done that ought to be done. The immediacies of administration take precedence over postponable items, and monitoring and evaluation are always postponable.

Similar laments and confessions are made, at least privately, by other foundation executives. The sad truth is, in this respect, the best of us are none too good. The facts about foundation practice in monitoring and evaluation do not give cause for questioning the Peterson Commission's conclusion "that most foundations apparently find the process of conceiving or making grants more satisfying and more worthy of their time and resources than evaluating the success or failure of these grants, what was learned by means of them, and the extent to which the results were disseminated to interested publics."[40]

D. SUMMARY: AGENTS OF CONSTRUCTIVE CHANGE?

The attack on the programs and operating policies of foundations is widespread and diverse. It is, moreover, sharp and substantial. Not least, it is contradictory.

40. *Ibid.*, p. 92.

The attack's being all these things does not prevent it from also being simple and remarkably consistent in the central question it raises about foundation programs. The question is: Do foundations serve as major instruments of change in American society? Whether by friend or foe of change, this is the heart of the challenge that is today being directed at foundations' programs and operating policies.

The particular criticisms that have been noted, and the necessary responses to them, contribute a partial answer to this summary question. Noted, first, was that foundations as a whole have been guilty of inadequate spending, but the pay-out requirements of the Tax Reform Act of 1969 will pretty well take care of this fault.

Secondly, we took note that foundations have not communicated well with the public or even with each other, but that this inadequacy was also in process of repair. These two are matters of structure and management as much as of program and policy, and thus were also mentioned in Chapter II.

Coming then to items that apply more specifically to the programs of foundations, we noted the charge that foundation work is often unimaginative, inconsequential and safe. True in part, it is not as true as some critics would maintain; and the very existence of the following charges is its partial denial.

The fourth criticism is that foundations are widely engaged in extremism of one sort or another, either revolutionary or reactionary in character. Once a handful of foundations engaged in such disreputable behavior has been called to account, the charge is nonsense.

Much more serious, but hardly more substantial, is the charge that foundations are engaged in partisan political activity. They are indeed engaged in activities that have political implications, but except for a few well-publicized indiscretions, the charge that foundations are politically partisan simply does not stand up.

Finally, foundations do not follow up their work very well. The criticism that foundations are guilty of poor monitoring and evaluative procedures is not often made, but it is true.

What, then, does this amount to in toto? One way and another, the various criticisms turn around the question as to

123

whether and in what regards foundations are change agents. Some critics want them to be, some do not. Some critics think they are too much so now; others think they are not so at all. But whatever the limitations of understanding and the biases from which the critics speak, this question of change is the central line of attack that has to do with foundation programs. It takes its place, alongside the charge that foundations are bulwarks of special privilege, as one of the two major charges against foundations.

The overall answer that must be given here, however, is quite different from what had to be said in the previous charge. In respect to structure and finance, the answer in the preceding chapter to the charge of special privilege was that, on balance, it is not borne out by the facts.

But to the charge that foundations in their programs are major instruments of change in American society, the reply must be, again on balance, Yes.

As far as one can tell, no foundation makes grants in the hope that nothing will happen. Such an intention would be preposterous. A foundation may indeed make grants in the hope that very little will happen, and that that much will not ruffle any feathers. But if a foundation does nothing more than make automatic contributions to safe and dignified agencies, it is hoping that at the least their safety and dignity will thereby be enhanced.

For the large foundations, their very size prevents them from doing nothing. Most of them have defined purposes, announced programs and priorities of action; and the easily ascertained knowledge of what they do makes it clear that they are intent upon bringing changes to pass in the field of their chosen activity. Even those few large foundations that do not like to tell the public what they do are still intent on causing some change in the society around them, as their activities, which they can no longer successfully hide, convincingly show. The next chapter will detail some of the many kinds of changes that foundations of various sorts and sizes are trying to bring about.

To argue that a foundation is not, or conversely, is but ought not to be, an instrument of change, is a two-sided absurdity. Foundations stand midway between these conflicting groups of

124

critics, taking the position that they both do and ought to cause change in the society around them.

This is not to say that they always succeed. Every foundation knows the disappointment of having made grants that seem to produce no beneficial results. But however often or seldom it misses, its purpose is still to make a difference. This means improvement, substitution of one goal or one action for another, change. The nature of the change, by virtue of the nature of man himself, is more likely to be in the direction of the exploration of the new than of the recovery of the past. To those who suspect or resist any forward-looking change, the activities of most foundations are bound to be unsettling.

Moreover, given the character of our society, changes in certain areas are always going to be more needed and more upsetting than in others. When most urgent, then almost assuredly most controversial. Does this mean, then, that foundations are interested not alone in change but in controversy, and are really conspirators against the American Way? Nonsense. The likelihood, as many students of foundation behavior have observed, is in the opposite direction. Though foundations do support change, they are more likely to be timid than bold, overly safe rather than highly experimental, following the procession of change, rather than leading it. Exceptions catch the headlines because that is what they are, proving the rule. And the rule is this: Foundations try to change things, but not too fast and not too much.

One critic says "subversion." Another says "sand-castles." In some specific case each might be correct. But neither knows in general what he is talking about. Granted that, as in any other area of human endeavor, there is room indeed for improvement in the programs of foundations. Yet, though they could do more, they are doing a great deal. The answer to the charge that they are major instruments of change in society is a glad and clarion Yes, on balance this is true.

IV

Counter-Attack: The Record of Achievement

A. INTRODUCTION

THE two previous chapters have paid attention to negative factors that allegedly characterize foundations and to elements of the attack on them. To respond to these criticisms is necessarily to take, in at least some part, a defensive posture. But after attacks have been answered, something more affirmative must be said.

It is time, therefore, to attend to the positive side of the picture. The record of achievement of foundations is broad, and deep, and, in many of its specific parts, genuinely exciting. Yet it is not generally known, and it badly needs to be stated factually and persuasively. Because of the limitations of the author and his space, this is not the encyclopedic and persuasive statement that is needed; but it is at least a foreword.

The place to begin is to complain about where most such discussions begin. Whenever anybody wants to say an appreciative word about the fine contributions of foundations to American society, he is quite likely to start out, "Abraham Flexner's study of medical schools . . ." or "The eradication of hookworm in the South . . ." or "Miracle rice . . ." If he is really up to date he is likely to say "Sesame Street. . . ."

It is indeed true that foundations were and are responsible for these worthy achievements. The only trouble is, there is much more to be said, and thus it is extremely unfortunate when the overly familiar and tired illustrations are given.

Of a piece with the mention of Flexner, hookworm, et al., is

126

the limited listing of names. The impression is often given that only Carnegie, Ford and Rockefeller, to be quite alphabetical, are really busy, or if a few others get into the act now and again, these three are the ones that bear the main burden. Let it quickly be said that each of these three has a superb record of accomplishment, and that each deserves all the plaudits it receives and more. The problem is that there are many others equally deserving, and to let it appear that only a few foundations are writing the positive record, or just that they are doing most of the writing, is to falsify the record.

Sometimes the critic will contribute to this strange game of limited recognition. Starting from pretty much the same premise that most of what matters is done by these three, Carnegie, Ford and Rockefeller, he may then go on to point out that each of them is flawed in some regard or other. The impression is allowed to develop, therefore, that if these well-known foundations have made mistakes or are less admirable than they appear to be, how much more must this then be true of the host of anonymous others. In other words, the best of them are none too good.

The point is, C., F. and R. don't deserve to be the sole objects of opprobrium any more than they merit being the sole recipients of praise. The fault, of course, is that most of those who comment about foundations and their work, whether to honor or to blame, know only a very small part of the story.

It is my contention, therefore, that all the reviews of foundation achievements are inadequate, including this one. A large number of foundations have done very many fine things, and yet few are ever called to the attention of the public. Limitations of space always apply, of course, and thus the name-dropping to follow will also be incomplete. Illustrations must always be selective, but they can at least go further afield than taking note of the activities of the big three, or the big ten or the big thirty, whoever they are.

Perhaps the most comprehensive effort yet made to state the important contributions of foundations to American life was Warren Weaver's in his book, *U.S. Philanthropic Foundations: Their History, Structure, Management, and Record.* Over half of the volume, totaling over 230 pages, consisted in "Part II, Judgments Concerning the Value of Foundation Aid." Rather than writing this section himself, Weaver called upon experts in eighteen different fields "to write a short critical summary, based on his own direct, intimate, and extensive experience, of the ways in which philanthropic aid appears to have been fruitful, and the ways in which it may have failed."[1] In his own concluding word Weaver noted that the "favorable opinions . . . are overwhelmingly in the majority."[2] His summary statement of the matter, which served as the final paragraph of his study, is reproduced in the Preface of this volume.

Those whom Weaver chose to write on subjects of their expertise were indeed first-rate people, and many though not all of the major areas of foundation activity were represented in the eighteen articles. For example, Lee Dubridge wrote on foundation contributions in the field of physics, Erwin Griswold on law, Whitney Oates on the humanities and Brooks Atkinson on the theater. As is true for all symposia, however, the chapters were quite uneven, and the knowledge of the respective authors about foundations distressingly spotty.

For example, Fred Hechinger, long the education editor of the *New York Times,* wrote knowledgeably about that field. He gave full marks, of course, to the contributions of Carnegie, Ford and Rockefeller, but in the course of the seventeen pages of his chapter he managed to mention over twenty foundations altogether, including two or three whose offices are not in New York City.[3]

Contrast his treatment, however, with the immediately preceding chapter by George M. Beckmann, "The Role of the Foundation in Non-Western Studies." Beckmann took fourteen pages to tell about his much more limited subject, but in the course of his discussion he mentioned the work of only three foundations. You guessed them! He can't be excused on the ground that only those three were active in the field, for he himself called attention to "two recent reports" that have encouraged

1. Weaver, *op. cit.,* pp. 221–457.
2. *Ibid.,* p. 444.
3. *Ibid.,* chap. 31, pp. 410–427.

128

American universities and colleges to increase the international aspects of their programs, *The University and World Affairs* and *The College and World Affairs*. A footnote indicated that the former was a Ford Foundation publication, but neither in the text nor in the footnote was it mentioned that the Hazen Foundation was responsible for the latter.[4]

In a summary word at the end of the eighteen chapters Warren Weaver wrote, "No sensible person would think of rating the foundations on the basis of the number of times the names turn up in favorable context; but it is nevertheless interesting to observe that the Rockefeller Foundation is mentioned well over 150 times, and the much younger Ford Foundation over 100 times."[5] Interesting perhaps, but not altogether reassuring as to the objectivity or breadth of coverage. Though some of the chapters did indeed mention the work of many smaller foundations, the unfortunate impression was left that when one talks of the contributions of foundations to American life, he can safely center attention on only a very few.

Even more subject to the charge of incompleteness, because less lengthy, was the Peterson Commission's treatment of foundations' achievements. Two brief chapters, totalling twenty-four pages, gave small chance for breadth of reference, though the names of around forty foundations were at least mentioned. One of the two chapters was spent almost completely in praise of the work of Ford and Carnegie in the field of non-commercial television, a truly superb achievement, and in the other chapter those two plus Rockefeller came in for repeated reference for work in medicine, scientific research, education and the arts. A couple of paragraphs on the activity of a few Chicago foundations helped to relieve somewhat the New York orientation. But the "overview" of foundation achievements that the Peterson Commission meant to present turned out to be a once-over-lightly and a hop-skip-and-jump.[6]

Throughout its history the Foundation Center has tried in various ways to call attention to the significant work of founda-

4. *Ibid.*, chap. 30, pp. 395–409.
5. *Ibid.*, pp. 440–441.
6. Report of Peterson Commission, *op. cit.*, pp. 93–116.

tions. The long-time president, F. Emerson Andrews, has done more extensive writing in this field than any other one scholar, and though he has made no recent surveys, his earlier volumes represent the widest-ranging and best-informed material of this kind that is available.[7] Moreover, for many years the Foundation Center sponsored the publication of *Foundation News,* now under the aegis of the Council on Foundations. This journal regularly carries large sections reporting the various grants that foundations across the country are making in diverse fields of interest. It is not easy to collect such information, and even the voluminous listings of *Foundation News* are admittedly incomplete. If one is to be disabused of the notion that nearly all foundation activity is conducted by a few super-large outfits in New York City, all he needs to do is to look at the regular Grants Index in *Foundation News.*

Shorter treatments of the accomplishments of foundations appear from time to time, and some of them have been helpful. For example, when foundations testified before Congress, many statements of admiration and appreciation were inserted in the record. Such public figures as Dr. John Cooper of the Association of American Medical Schools, Theodore M. Hesburgh of Notre Dame, Felix Robb of the Southern Association of Colleges and Schools, Dr. Jonas Salk of polio vaccine fame and the late Whitney Young of the Urban League stated their views of the value of foundation work, and many of their comments were printed in the brochure, *Foundations and the Tax Bill,* produced by the Foundations' Coordinated Testimony Group.[8]

The trouble with any one of these statements, however, is

7. Andrews, *Philanthropic Foundations* and other volumes, *op. cit.* Yet even a man as broad-gauged as Andrews can fall into the Carnegie-Ford-Rockefeller syndrome. In an article, "Foundation Influence on Education," in *Educational Record,* Winter, 1972, he mentioned by name the work of Ford-related agencies (the Foundation, the Fund for Adult Education and the Fund for the Advancement of Education) twenty times, Carnegie-related agencies (the Corporation, the Carnegie Endowment for Peace and the Carnegie Foundation for the Advancement of Teaching) sixteen times and Rockefeller-related agencies (the Foundation, the General Education Board) ten times. Though he also named twelve others, none is mentioned more than once, except the long-deceased Peabody Fund—twice.

8. See *Foundations and the Tax Bill, op. cit.*

130

that in the nature of the case it could be nothing more than it pretends to be, namely, the grateful word of one who knows only a small part of the total story. The things that get mentioned are the ones that have most often caught the headlines, and the unfortunate impression is given that only those things exist.

To broaden the scope of the story the Council on Foundations began the practice in its Annual Report of 1970 of printing a "brief review of some members' 1970 grants," so as to illustrate the remarkable variety and usefulness of the work of foundations that do not easily catch the public eye. In the space of only four or five pages, the report calls attention, with pictures, to the work of approximately forty foundations, big and little. This section will undoubtedly be expanded in future reports.[9]

Added to these various reviews are the brief references to foundation achievements that one can find in the works of the chief critics. To try to persuade his readers that he is looking at the subject objectively, nearly every self-respecting critic will throw into his discussion some such comment as, "Of course the foundations have done some good things," or, "Not everything that foundations do is radical," or "conservative" or "softheaded" or "self-serving." Then there will follow a few references to Flexner, hookworm or whatever that particular critic may have heard of and approved. These treatments don't go very far, of course, and add little to the effort to understand the genuine accomplishments of foundations.[10]

So much for what the surveys, whether by admirers or critics, usually provide. Yet it is easier to complain about the incomplete treatments of others than it is to remedy the fault. How best can the achievements of foundations be told? An obvious approach is to take note of the various fields in which foundations work and then to list some foundation names for each field in turn. But an ambitious job of this sort is already being done, namely, the Foundation Grants Index, noted above, that

9. Council on Foundations, *Annual Report for 1970.* See also the Council's *Annual Report for 1971.*

10. See Lundberg, *op. cit.,* p. 522; Branch, *op. cit.,* pp. 5–7; Goulden, *op. cit.,* chaps. 5 and 8, *passim.*

is "a record of foundation grants of $10,000 or more . . . about which the [Foundation] Center receives information from the donor, the recipient, news reports, or public records."[11] It would not be possible to compete with this valuable running account, or with other summary listings that appear from time to time for individual fields.

B. Tangible Accomplishments

Let us take a different tack. In the following sections we shall look at the chief accomplishments of many foundations one by one. Since attention will be focussed on each foundation rather than on the field of activity, the listing within each section or sub-section will be largely in alphabetical order, by the main word in the foundation's name. We shall refer briefly to grants and philanthropic projects that seem to have contributed to some chosen segment of the general welfare.

If any reader were to be so impolite as to ask, Whose definition of the general welfare? the confession would need to be made: Mine. So far as I am aware, there is no such thing as perfect impartiality in the realm of attitudes toward foundations, any more than there is in any other realm; and my likes and dislikes will be only partially, and unsuccessfully, hid.

Even as there is no pretense to complete objectivity of portrayal, so no effort is being made to be exhaustive. We must name more than ten foundations, of course, or even twenty-five; else we don't get beyond the giants. Yet trying to rival the *Foundation Directory* would be as foolish as competing with the Grants Index. The presentation, then, will consist in enough names, I hope, to support the thesis that useful and important philanthropic activity is being practiced by many more than just a handful of foundations in some one part of the country. Since the catalogue cannot be comprehensive, let it be recognized that

11. See "The Foundation Grants Index" (Mrs. Lee Noe, Grants Editor), a regular feature in *Foundation News;* the quotation is from the introductory explanation of the Index. See also Mrs. Lee Noe, ed., *The Foundation Grants Index, 1970–71,* New York, Columbia University Press, 1972.

what follows is a series of impressions as to some of the foundations that have substantial achievements in their records.

So to any reader's taste there will be unfortunate omissions. Absences from the lists may be explained by one or more of the following reasons:

—because sufficient information was not available; or

—because space ran out; or

—because the omitted foundation has given the public to understand that it does not want its work to become known; or

—because its work is meager in comparison with its resources, or poor in quality, or inimical to the public good; or

—because its work, while creditable enough in itself, is simply routine and unimaginative, and scarcely represents an achievement or accomplishment to the credit of the field of philanthropy.

In light of the warning that this chapter will be judgmental in character, perhaps "achievement" and "accomplishment" should be more clearly defined. Some foundations work hard at their job; they are *active* in the pursuit of the charitable purposes they have set for themselves. Other foundations are essentially *passive;* they merely respond to the overtures that outsiders make to them. Some are innovative, others simply reactive.

The two broad categories, almost but not quite mutually exclusive—for occasionally a foundation can be both, showing one face in one part of its work, another in a different part— constitute two forms of self-conception as well as two styles of action. A foundation can see itself as a reservoir of dollars, to be drawn upon by the successful applicant, or as a catalyst on behalf of some humane purpose, to which cause its dollars are devoted. Of these two types, it is much more likely that the active, innovative catalyst will "achieve" something. The passive, respondent reservoir will undoubtedly do some good, but that is what it is supposed to do; and if a foundation's work is altogether routine and predictable, it need hardly be called an "accomplishment."

Time and again the *Foundation Directory* uses two phrases in its descriptions, neither of which, needless to say, is meant to be disparaging. "Broad purposes" has a complimentary ring about it, and "primarily local giving" is merely descriptive. But these phrases often denote the foundation that is only an exercise in preferential check-writing, of the same sort that a benevolent person would do. To earn kudos for thoughtful and effective philanthropy requires something more than sending assorted checks to the duly certified charities of the community.

Does this mean, then, that only the large and/or non-family and/or professionally staffed foundation can qualify? Not at all. The active-passive dichotomy is not the same as professional-amateur, both of which may be bad words when applied to a foundation. "Professional" sounds heartless and tough-as-nails, and "amateur" sounds sloppy and misguided; whereas a reputable foundation must not be either. Size may have something to do with it, to be sure, but even quite small foundations can be creative.

The family character of a foundation can sometimes be a problem. Donald R. Young, former President of the Russell Sage Foundation, used the terms, "proprietary" and "institutional," to describe the two types; and said, "Perhaps a third category should be recognized, those that have some characteristics of the two prime categories, mainly large foundations in transition from proprietary to institutional form. . . ." The "impersonal, institutionalized foundations" are "relatively few in number, but mostly among the largest." The proprietary foundations, alternatively called "personal convenience" or "donor-controlled" or "family conduit" foundations, are in the overwhelming majority. It is Young's position that, whereas "the measures of success or failure of proprietary foundations are measures of the proprietors rather than of the foundations as such . . . institutionalized foundations, free of obligations to their donors and responsible only to the public, properly are subject to more stringent measures of worth."[12]

It may be, as Young and others contend, that it would be better for all concerned if his distinction could be embodied in the law, putting different requirements and expectations upon

12. Donald R. Young and Wilbert E. Moore, *Trusteeship and the Management of Foundations,* New York, Rusell Sage Foundation, 1969, pp. 149, 151.

the two types of foundations. In any event, the active-passive dichotomy is not synonymous, as I see it, with the institutional-proprietary one; and I do not believe that the family fund is unable to attain high standards of philanthropic achievement. Any foundation, family or otherwise, ought to be judged on the merits of its work, and nothing automatically disqualifies a family fund from the list of foundations of large accomplishment. Again, any foundation, family or otherwise, may have special handicaps to overcome—minute size, temptation to provide special treatment, tendency to want to do the safe and easy thing, etc.; but as long as it keeps its eye alertly on the target of public service it can make a productive contribution to the general welfare.

1. *The Work of Large Foundations:*

For the purposes of this book "large," as already noted, means over one hundred million in market value of assets. If one were to compare the entries to follow with the tables on pages 65–66 and 67, he would discover that not all of the large foundations are included here, for one or more of the reasons cited above. Surely there is very little that any of the large foundations, listed or unlisted, is doing that is downright bad; but when and if its activity is of the order of a check for the local United Fund (as important as that is for the United Fund), there is no call to blow the trumpet, no matter how handsome the amount. The following list is limited, with a few exceptions for special reasons, to those that seem to fit in the category of active, innovative catalyst.

(Most of the foundations, in this and the sections to follow, issue periodic reports; so that any reader who wishes to get a full picture of their activities, which these impressionistic vignettes obviously cannot give, may write to the foundations for further information.)

It is appropriate that the first one alphabetically is the *Carnegie Corporation* of New York City, which comes close to being everybody's favorite. The maturity of its administration has long been remarked, and currently it probably gets, and deserves, a better press than any other foundation. Its chief attention is higher education; it takes large interest also in pre-school education, governmental affairs, education for minority groups, urban problems and related concerns, mainly in the United States, secondarily in parts of the British Commonwealth. Down the years it has sponsored hosts of significant studies, such as Gunnar Myrdal's *An American Dilemma* and James B. Conant's series on American education. Through the related *Carnegie Foundation for the Advancement of Teaching* the Corporation is providing support for the research projects of the Carnegie Commission on Higher Education, of which Clark Kerr is Chairman. It supports action as well as reflection; for example, "Sesame Street" is one of its recent triumphs.

The *Commonwealth Fund* of New York City has long concentrated its work on medical education and community health, always with an eye to the support of the fresh approach rather than simply the status quo. Its grants demonstrate its belief in the importance of research, experimentation and institutional cooperation. Through the medium of fellowships to senior medical and bio-medical students the Fund has encouraged a great deal of important study and publication. The Harkness Fellowships, named for the donor family, have gone to potential leaders from Western Europe and parts of the British Commonwealth.

The *Danforth Foundation* of St. Louis has centered its efforts in higher education, with recent expansions into secondary education and urban affairs, the latter largely in the St. Louis area. It was during the fifties, under the leadership of Kenneth I. Brown, that this foundation grew from the status of a regional family fund to that of a national educational agency, providing large numbers of fellowships for graduate students, and workshops and conferences for faculty people, as well as an assortment of grants in its areas of interest. Since Brown's retirement in 1961 I have had major responsibility for minding the store. Thus you'd better ask somebody else how Danforth is doing.

Because of the widespread impression that the *Duke Endowment* is part of Duke University (which it is not), and makes substantial grants to the University (which it does), it has failed to receive as large a measure of national recognition as its size

136

and annual expenditures would justify. This may be due, however, to the fact that though its offices are in New York City its work is limited chiefly to North and South Carolina. Grants go normally to Davidson, Furman and Johnson C. Smith as well as to Duke, and to hospitals, medical schools, orphanages and Methodist religious agencies. In the continuing debate as to the advisability of a foundation's imposing geographical limitation on its activity, the experience of the Duke Endowment shows that much can be accomplished by focussing on a restricted area.

In Dwight Macdonald's well-known bon mot, the *Ford Foundation* "is a large body of money completely surrounded by people who want some."[13] Listing the areas in which Ford does not work would be quicker than noting all the places and things in which it does get involved. Vast and visible, it is especially concerned, under McGeorge Bundy's leadership, to throw its weight into efforts to solve the most pressing social problems in America and around the world. Ford has been the main support of Woodrow Wilson Fellows and National Merit Scholars; of ballet companies, repertory theaters and symphony orchestras; of street academies, improvements of criminal justice procedures and legal-aid programs—to mention only a few outstanding efforts at home and none at all from the immense activity overseas. Big enough to go it alone most of the time if it should so choose, it has believed in and practiced cooperation with public and private groups, including governments and foundations—with Rockefeller, for instance, on high-yielding rice; with Carnegie on non-commercial television; with Danforth on citizenship education; and with a host of smaller foundations on black entrepreneurship. A statement twice as long would be equally incomplete.

The elusive man-in-the-street is not likely to know, if asked, that the *John A. Hartford Foundation* is one of the largest and most single-minded funds in the country. Those who do know it admire its intensive work in the field of bio-medical research; and whereas laymen may not be able to appreciate the value of research on the laser, hyperbaric oxygenation and cryosurgery, everybody knows something about transplants. The first success-

13. Macdonald, *op. cit.,* p. 3

ful human organ transplantation, a kidney graft, was performed back in 1954 with financial assistance from this foundation. It continues to support significant research in its chosen field of concentration.

Among Texas foundations the *Houston Endowment* is distinguished because it makes a few grants to other parts of the country as well. Most of its subventions are in response to appeals for institutional aid from schools and colleges. It has long supported scholarship programs, mostly undergraduate, administered by the recipient institutions. In line with the plan of its donor, Jesse H. Jones, as expressed at its founding in 1937, the Endowment will be liquidated by 1987.

The *Robert Wood Johnson Foundation* of New Brunswick, New Jersey, is in process of sharp transformation. From having been listed as possessing only $6.8 million in assets at the beginning of 1962, it achieved the rarefied status of owning something over a billion dollars of assets at the beginning of 1972. As its new President, Dr. David Rogers, formerly Dean of the Johns Hopkins Medical School, is primarily responsible for the development of the expanded program. Its chief interests will probably continue to be medicine, medical and dental education and health care.[14]

Every now and then a foundation manages to put its stamp upon a major development. In the case of the *W. K. Kellogg Foundation* of Battle Creek, Michigan, the field is "lifelong learning" or "continuing education," for across this country and even at Oxford can be found Residential Centers for Continuing Education on leading university campuses. Its work has been decisive in other important fields as well: agriculture, community colleges, higher education for the disadvantaged, nursing education, hospital administration and other philanthropic work abroad as well as in this country. In its various fields of operation its style has been to favor action programs as distinct from research.

The *Kresge Foundation* of Detroit likes to build buildings. It bestows its grants for construction or renovation on colleges,

14. FD-2, p. 405; *Foundation News,* January–February, 1972, p. 39 and May–June, 1972, pp. 10, 17–23.

seminaries, medical schools and other educational and cultural agencies throughout the country.

The Lilly Endowment gives considerable but not exclusive attention to its home base, Indianapolis, and to the state as a whole. It proclaims as its chief interests the three fields of education, religion and community services. The program of unrestricted grants to all the private colleges and universities of Indiana is a good example of Lilly's important regional work. Its support of the valuable Administrative Consultant Service of the Association of American Colleges is indicative of its national activity.

The *Avalon* and *Old Dominion Foundations* were combined in 1969 to form the *Andrew W. Mellon Foundation,* with offices in New York City. Even prior to merger, the two Mellon-established funds (by Mrs. Ailsa Mellon Bruce and Paul Mellon, respectively) had worked together in a number of ways, notably on behalf of conserving natural resources, fostering the liberal arts and preserving historic sites. For example, they strengthened the National Trust for Historic Preservation, endowed fourteen university chairs in the humanities and aided in the acquisition of the Cape Hatteras and Cape Lookout National Seashores. The combined operation, with considerably enlarged resources from the estate of Mrs. Bruce, has begun to concentrate heavily in institutional aid for private liberal arts colleges, private universities, predominantly black institutions, theological and medical schools and special institutions such as the Navajo Community College in Arizona. As its new President, Nathan M. Pusey is bringing his Harvard experience to bear on responding to the needs of higher education.

Pittsburgh's *Richard King Mellon Foundation,* not organically related to A. W. Mellon, has also developed a special concern for colleges in the private sector; and its Administrative Trustee, Joseph D. Hughes, has forcefully called to the attention of other foundations the plight of the independent liberal arts institution.[15] Once having contributed heavily to the National Gallery of Art, it now gives preference though not exclusive attention

15. Joseph D. Hughes, "The Little Man: A Forgotten Cause," *Foundation News,* July–August, 1970.

139

to educational, environmental and social service projects in its own metropolitan area. It has played a major role in the "Pittsburgh Renaissance," helping to set up prototypes in city planning, slum clearance, industrial development, public school rejuvenation and other aspects of urban renewal.

The *Moody Foundation* of Galveston limits its activities strictly to the state of Texas. When and if it can shake loose from the widely publicized toils of litigation in which it has long been enmeshed, it will be able to give undivided attention to the development of a systematic program of philanthropy for its region. The rudiments of such a program are already present in the wide-spreading charity that Moody is now practicing.[16] Another over-$100 million Texas fund making local general-support grants is the *Brown Foundation* of Houston.

Flint, Michigan, will never be the same again, for the *Charles Stewart Mott Foundation* has taken a particular interest in its own hometown, especially in regard to education, health services, recreation and other civic needs. "Its intent is to make Flint a laboratory or proving ground for new concepts in enrichment of living," chief of which is the "Community School Concept" to which Mott has given strong support since 1935.[17] That the community school movement is receiving wide and favorable attention around the country is due primarily to its work. This, in turn, is persuading Mott to be more active outside Flint; for example, through programs of leadership training in community education, strategically located at eleven college or university regional centers. The beaten paths that develop as the result of better mousetraps go in two directions.

Any family fund as large as the *Pew Memorial Trust* of Philadelphia can hardly be omitted from this listing, even though *Fortune* magazine, no enemy of large-scale philanthropy, notes it is "amazingly hostile to public scrutiny."[18] Grants have gone to educational, religious, medical and other charitable agencies

16. See "The Texas Hearings and the Moody Foundation," *Non-Profit Report,* May, 1971, pp. 9–12; *Grants 1942–1971,* Moody Foundation, Galveston, Texas.
17. *Annual Report,* The Mott Foundation, 1970.
18. Irwin Ross, *op. cit.,* p. 172.

that received the approval of J. Howard Pew, now deceased.

A family foundation such as the *Rockefeller Brothers Fund* redeems the term from becoming a pejorative. Though its board is heavy with Rockefellers, they have shown through its program their capacity for impartial and effective contribution to the general welfare. Its grants cover the map of major social problems in most parts of the country, with a few going abroad—international affairs, urban problems, the arts, religion, equal rights, conservation and a good bit else. It plays the role of good local citizen by supporting a wide variety of charitable agencies in New York City.

Long used to being No. 1 in size, and then No. 2, the *Rockefeller Foundation* has not allowed its diminution in rank (now perhaps fourth though still No. 2 in annual expenditures) to affect its leadership in wise and productive philanthropy. To its five main program areas—"the conquest of hunger," "problems of population," "university development," "equal opportunity for all," and "cultural development"—it has recently added a sixth, "quality of the environment." The first three are international interests, the latter three largely American. In every one Rockefeller has major accomplishments to its credit. Consider, for instance, that it is more responsible than any other one agency, public or private, for bringing about the "Green Revolution," the continuing successful attack on world hunger through the development of high-yielding grains, rice, wheat and maize. A believer in research as much as in application, Rockefeller has strings of Nobel Prize winners to its credit, as well as having aided many other distinguished scientists in their work. It works both through grants to other groups and operations of its own. Its important projects are many too numerous to be mentioned. Suffice it to say, if you search for significant effort on hepatitis and lead poisoning, or on the revival of music and the dance, or on safe and simple birth control, or on training for inner-city black leadership, there you will find the Rockefeller Foundation at work.[19]

19. For discussions of the "Green Revolution" and new program areas, see The Rockefeller Foundation, *President's Review and Annual Report, 1969* and *Ibid., 1970.*

The *Sarah Mellon Scaife Foundation* of Pittsburgh and the *Surdna Foundation* of New York City—Mellon-in-the-middle and Andrus-backwards indicate the sources of these funds, respectively—are both over $100 million in size, and make general support grants largely to local educational and charitable organizations.

It seems fitting that a major foundation established by a General Motors magnate should center its interests in technology, the physical sciences, business management and economics. Not quite so expected but equally serious is the involvement of the *Alfred P. Sloan Foundation* in various problems in the fields of higher education and urban affairs. Though based in New York City, its activity is spread nation-wide. Along with pursuit of the various parts of its "general program" Sloan has recently developed what it calls "particular programs," to which it will give large attention for a season, with marked emphasis on evaluation, before passing on to other special demands. Two of these particular programs are the expansion of professional opportunities for blacks and other minorities, and support for "the emerging scientific discipline of neuroscience." Thus Sloan seeks to combine continuity, freshness and careful assessment of results into its ongoing work.[20]

In spite of its preference for anonymity, the *Emily and Ernest Woodruff Foundation* of Atlanta has not been able to hide all knowledge of its useful benefactions from citizens in Georgia and the Southeast generally. Sooner or later almost any regional need is recognized by a grant: orphan homes, traffic safety, preservation of historical monuments, schools, hospitals, churches and museums.

2. *Accomplishments of Selected Middle-sized Foundations:*

"Middle-sized" is both imprecise and comparative. Wherever the lines of division were to be drawn, those in the category would still seem awfully big in assets and very few in number, in comparison with the thousands of tiny founda-

20. *Alfred P. Sloan Foundation Report for 1969,* pp. 6–10.

tions that are hardly more than personal benevolent accounts. In the first chapter the large-medium-small breakdown mentioned boundaries of $100 million and $10 million for the second group, but for the purposes of this section the lower cut-off for middle-sized foundations will be at approximately $25 million. Even then, we will split the discussion into several sub-sections, to keep comparable groups in closer relationship.

The entries to follow are by no means all the foundations in the $25–100-million range. That there are omissions means that there are foundations whose work is essentially routine—helpful, to be sure, but achieving little except giving sustenance on a fairly regular basis to well-established worthy agencies. There is nothing wrong with that, let it be repeated; but such work does not make a foundation eligible for special plaudits.

First, let us note some of the near-large foundations, close to $100 million in size, which might soon move over that line or may already have done so since the last figures were released. It is always difficult to get reliable information on some funds. For example, who knows anything about *De Rancé* of Milwaukee, reported to have had assets of $97 million at the beginning of 1970? What happened to a few that moved over the line in a downward direction: to the *William R. Kenan, Jr., Charitable Trust* of New York that went from $110.7 million in 1969 to $83.1 million in 1970; to *Edwin H.–Helen M. Land, Inc.* of Cambridge, Massachusetts, that went from $139.4 million in 1969 to $75.4 million in 1970? But these are atypical, whereas information about the following is more readily available:

The *Vincent Astor Foundation* is chiefly interested in children, and is currently giving special attention to the prevention of juvenile delinquency in New York City.

Though the office of the *Claude Worthington Benedum Foundation* is in Pittsburgh, its first concern is with West Virginia, then with the Tri-State area (including western Pennsylvania and Ohio). It provides scholarship funds to

143

every college in West Virginia and to selected institutions in the rest of its region; and makes grants also to churches, hospitals and social agencies.

A merger of two earlier trusts the *Booth Ferris Foundation* of New York City has achieved an unusual diversity in its grant-making: to theological education, opera, hospitals, college opportunities for minorities, the Travelers Aid Society, the YMCA, and a school for the deaf.

The various Callaway philanthropies, the largest of which in the *Callaway Foundation* of LaGrange, have made a considerable difference in the health, education and religious life of the citizens of Georgia. Baptists may have benefitted more than others, but there are of course more of them.

In Chapter III mention was made of the interest of the *Charles A. Dana Foundation* (Greenwich, Connecticut), in buildings. Dana does much else as well, making grants for scholarships and professorships, and for health and welfare purposes, such as children's cancer research.

The *El Pomar Foundation* of Colorado Springs is single-minded in its devotion to the state but multi-purposed in the expression of it. The diverse recipients of its grants have included boys' clubs, the Colorado Springs Symphony, medical research, educational scholarships and even municipalities for specific projects.

It is intended that the *Max C. Fleishmann Foundation* of Reno be liquidated by 1980. About half its support has gone to Nevada, the other half widely dispersed in place and purpose. In late years increasing attention has been given to the needs of disadvantaged students of various colors and disciplines. It has also contributed substantially to buildings and equipment, and to research in the medical and biological sciences.

The *Grant Foundation* of New York City deserves to be much better known by the general public for its deep-grounded interest in the psychological development of children and youth. It sponsors broad-ranging research and some demonstration projects in various aspects of emotional maturity, and announces that "preference [is] given to the

144

support of younger and less well-established investigators, and to new research programs in their initial stages of development."[21]

The *Phoebe Waterman Foundation* of Philadelphia has recently changed its name to the *Haas Community Fund,* and has fallen below $100 million is size, having once been as high as $133.9 million. Little known outside its chosen area of work in eastern Pennsylvania, it has engaged in general support grants in such fields as education, health, conservation and social welfare.

Boys in New York and Boston are the special concern of the *Charles Hayden Foundation,* of the former city. Grants normally go for physical facilities to boys' clubs, camps, settlement houses and the Boy Scouts.

The *Howard Heinz Endowment* has found at least fifty-seven ways to be of help to worthy institutions in the Pittsburgh area. Among primary interests are music and the arts, community planning and local colleges.

The *Louis W. and Maud Hill Family Foundation* of St. Paul has staked out the northwest quadrant of the United States as its area of activity. Its distinction, however, lies not in its geographical but in its programmatic focus: it specializes in pioneering work, in fields as diverse as agriculture, law enforcement, the medical sciences, social welfare, the arts and humanities. Its effort is to bridge the gap between research and practice, to encourage the better use of existing knowledge and the development of new knowledge.

Another just-under-$100-million fund that is not afraid of the new and the different is the *Charles F. Kettering Foundation* of Dayton. Matter of fact, it makes so bold as to announce that it "supports only innovative, high-risk programs which do not receive sufficient attention from other sources."[22] Some of its recent enthusiasms are photosynthesis, constructive change in education, the cause and cure of cancer and the role of the citizen in the formation of public policy. Through the years Kettering has spun off a number of satel-

21. FD-4, p. 284.
22. *Ibid.,* p. 392.

lite institutions for research and/or action in fields of its concern; among these have been the highly regarded Sloan-Kettering Institute for Cancer Research (which the Sloan Foundation also supports), the Institute for Development of Educational Activities (I/D/E/A) and the Charles F. Kettering Research Laboratory, with its own offspring, Kettering Scientific Research, Inc., for current work in nitrogen fixation, photobiology and cell specialization and control.

The *Olin Foundation* of New York City makes bricks-and-mortar grants for the construction and equipment of college and university buildings, and takes delight in financing the total cost of its projects.

The *Z. Smith Reynolds Foundation,* late of Sapelo Island, Georgia, but now of Winston-Salem, has been devoted all along to North Carolina: its schools, colleges, hospitals, libraries, parks and playgrounds; and such unusual cultural assets as the North Carolina School for the Performing Arts.

The *Sid W. Richardson Foundation* of Fort Worth and the *Smith Richardson Foundation* of Greensboro are not to be confused, even though they are roughly on a par in size of assets, amount of annual disbursements and preferential treatment in their programs to respective home states. But there are differences: Sid stays strictly in Texas, whereas Smith sometimes goes outside North Carolina; Sid makes general grants to the usual broad assortment, with special interest in aid to the handicapped, whereas Smith is an operating as well as grant-making agency, and emphasizes research toward the development of creative leadership and the improvement of living conditions.

The latest (fourth) edition of the *Foundation Directory* lists two Chicago funds, the *Spencer Foundation* and the *W. Clement and Jessie V. Stone Foundation,* as possessing assets of only $1.0-and $1.3-million respectively, whereas because of recent sizeable acquisitions each may now belong in the just-under-$100-million category or possibly larger. The program of both are necessarily undergoing considerable expansion. Spencer is interested in research in behavioral science and educational process, and in the application of it.

146

Stone is concerned with the development of positive mental attitudes in education, religion and other fields.

One more pair will complete the alphabetical listing of this sub-group. The *William K. Warren Foundation* of Tulsa and the *Robert A. Welch Foundation* of Houston, both between $85- and $90-million in size, are indicative of the growing wealth and philanthropic disposition of the Southwest. As with the Richardsons above, the non-Texan is less parochial, giving preference but not exclusive attention to Oklahoma; Warren's emphasis is in grants to hospitals and Roman Catholic religious groups. Welch, the Texan, has had a sharp focus in program as well as in region, its passion and achievement being research in chemistry, together with supporting activities; but recently it has begun to broaden its fields of work.

From the foundations to which we have already attended, it is abundantly clear that New York City, by any normal head count, possesses more than its numerical share. It is a further fact, perhaps not surprising, that much of the creative leadership for the foundation field provided by the middle-sized foundations comes from New York. To demonstrate the point, the lower half of the middle-sized group, those from roughly $25 million to roughly $60 million in size, will be presented in two parts. First, the lower-half middle-sized group that are all in New York City:

The *Association for the Aid of Crippled Children* is indeed a foundation and does just what its title says. By way of research programs and conferences the Association investigates "the causes and consequences of handicapping," especially facets that are "relatively unexplored."

Another fund whose name reflects its single-minded purpose is the *Carnegie Endowment for International Peace.* Founded by Andrew Carnegie, of course, it predated by one year the establishment of the Carnegie Corporation in 1911, to which it is not organically related. Mainly an operating foundation, the Endowment's work of research, conferences, publications and other educational activities on behalf of

147

world peace and international order are well known and widely admired.

Proclaiming its special interest in "programs for young people in disadvantaged neighborhoods," the *Louis Calder Foundation* has not hesitated to do the unusual. At one time or another it has supported research, scholarships, building funds and operating budgets, but its emphasis is on experimental grants.[23]

In this $25- to $60-million range are many "special purpose foundations" whose contributions to the public weal may be all greater because of their sharper aim, providing their purpose is not trivial or allowed to become obsolete.[24] The next entry of this sort is the *China Medical Board of New York,* which, when mainland China went Communist, adjusted its program so as to provide support for medical and nursing schools in other countries of the Far East.

The *William H. Donner Foundation* eschews the usual form and content: no automatic support grants to charities' campaigns. Instead, it sets its well-aimed sights on target areas to which insufficient firepower of other foundations seems to have been directed. For example, Donner is concerned about the American Indian's education and economic health. For another example: Canada, that the United States come to a better understanding and appreciation of its neighbor. For still another: the provision of expanded opportunities for disadvantaged young people. To break both the alphabetical and New-York-City patterns of presentation, it is of interest to note that another William H. Donner philanthropy of roughly the same size, the *Independence Foundation* of Philadelphia, also follows special bents to good purpose. In its case, two of these are support for independent secondary education and for radiology and cancer research.

Like Welch in Texas, the *Camille and Henry Dreyfus Foundation* is a specialist in chemistry, supporting fellow-

23. *Ibid.,* p. 258.
24. Weaver, *op. cit.,* pp. 44–46.

ships, research projects, professorial chairs, summer institutes, laboratories and other ways to foster chemical and related investigations.

The maker rather than the boarder of bandwagons, the *Field Foundation* was active in child welfare and interracial relations long before they became popular areas for philanthropic work. It is in respect to the increase of opportunities for blacks that Field has achieved its greatest recognition: civil rights, legal problems, student exchange, voter registration and similar courageous and constructive activities. On occasion it sponsors some work in intercultural relations, outside the bounds of the United States.

The *Helene Fuld Health Trust* is dedicated to the nation-wide health and welfare of student nurses.

Guggenheim is a long and widely honored name in philanthropy, which can be attributed to the beneficent and imaginative work of not one but at least four New York foundations, each of which is independent of the others. The largest is the *John Simon Guggenheim Memorial Foundation,* whose forte is fellowships for advanced study in all fields to citizens of this and other countries of the Western Hemisphere. The list of Guggenheim Fellows is virtually a catalogue of a large proportion of the outstanding scientists and creative artists of the United States. Next in size is the *Solomon R. Guggenheim Foundation,* whose field is modern art. Its chief concern is the prestigious Guggenheim Museum, designed by Frank Lloyd Wright. The remaining two, on the basis of assets, belong in the next section, but better to note them now so as to distinguish among the four. The *Murry and Leonie Guggenheim Foundation* has perhaps the broadest agenda, but it too has its specialization: dentistry and dental education. The *Daniel and Florence Guggenheim Foundation* is the oldest as well as the smallest. Except when it supports the Guggenheim Memorial Band Concerts, it concentrates on aviation; and any knowledgeable person in the fields of airplane design, rocketry or jet propulsion could tell of the decisive role that this fund and family have played, all the way

149

from support of the pioneering experiments of Robert God-
dard through space exploration to current studies of the
peaceful applications of aeronautical science.

The *Jackson Hole Preserve* is not quite as specialized as
its name suggests, for its interest in conservation has led it to
broaden its activity beyond the bounds of the Grand Tetons.
Besides this and the two large Rockefeller agencies already
noted, several other small foundations owe their existence to
one or another branch of this philanthropic family. Among
these may be mentioned now the *JDR 3rd Fund* and the
Sealantic Fund, though in size they fall in a smaller category.
The former is interested in arts and art education, both in Asia
and in the United States; and the latter's notable contribution
has been (for it is now in the final stages of liquidation) in
the field of theological education, whose neglect by other
foundations Sealantic has helped to repair.

Alphabetically the next sizeable New York fund is the *W.
Alton Jones Foundation,* whose widespread and varied grants
to worthy institutions and charitable agencies happen not to
catch much of the public eye or to take on distinctive colora-
tion. In this regard it may be typical of a number of other
New York foundations in this bracket, whose "broad purposes" make special identification difficult: the *Altman Foundation,* the *Robert Sterling Clark Foundation,* the *Edward E.
Ford Foundation* and the *Ambrose Monell Foundation.*

The *Juilliard Musical Foundation,* it will be no surprise,
takes a large interest in the Juilliard School of Music, and
practices other musical charities as well.

Painting is the next of the arts that comes in for special
attention, this time from the *Samuel H. Kress Foundation.*
Studies in art history, restorations of works of art, gifts to
museums, fellowships, support of scholarly publications—
these are some of the ways in which Kress contributes to its
primary purpose.

The *Henry Luce Foundation* deserves better than to be
described as the dedication of a *Fortune* to the *Life* of our
Time. Its range is vast, yet selective: higher education in this

150

country and Asia, urban problems, theological education, race relations and other aspects of public affairs.

The next two foundations have long been interested in the same field, medicine, but with a difference. The *Josiah Macy, Jr., Foundation* specializes in support for research and medical education, and its highly professional work has resulted in important scientific advance. No less is this true, in general, of the *John and Mary R. Markle Foundation,* whose best-known activity has been the Scholar in Medical Science program, to prepare young medical school teachers, known as Markle Scholars, for positions of leadership in academic medicine. Recently, however, Markle "has shifted from medical education to the educational uses of mass media and communications technology," and is now making grants "to foster better understanding of the media and improve their educational service."[25]

Still another foundation interested in some aspects of medicine is the *Milbank Memorial Fund,* which dates all the way back to 1905. Its emphasis has been in public health and preventive medicine, and it has supported pioneering work in such crucial and occasionally controversial fields as nutrition, birth control and population studies.

The *Research Corporation* is another time-honored foundation, having been established in 1912. Through the years it has been true to its title, for its practice is to support fundamental research across a broad spectrum of the natural sciences, all the way from biology and medicine to mathematics and engineering; and to underwrite the cost of projects implementing that basic research.

A third straight senior citizen, whose birthdate was 1907, is the *Russell Sage Foundation,* occupying a unique position as elder statesman for the field of philanthropy. That is, its numerous studies and publications on foundations are widely respected, for it has done more than any other single foundation to encourage the field to develop a sense of its own identity and to adopt sound procedures in fiscal and program

25. FD-4, p. 310.

151

affairs. Its interest, however, is much broader than simply the field of philanthropy, for it has conducted or encouraged both research and publication in many areas of the social sciences, including such topics as the relationship of law to social science, the formation of government policy, the development of human resources and the improvement of the mass media.

The *Teagle Foundation* was once aimed narrowly at helping employees of the Standard Oil Co. of New Jersey, but as its resources have grown it has expanded its human circle and sharpened its program. It now takes special interest in religious education and in recruitment and training for the ministry.

The rough and artificial bracket, $25 million to $60 million, provides some examples of outstanding foundations outside of New York City as well as in. Falling in this category are the following:

The *M. D. Anderson Foundation* is located in Houston and devoted to Texas. Making grants to a variety of institutions, it has concentrated support on a superb medical center in its hometown and on other agencies that serve the handicapped and the ill.

To possess and act on a conscience about the serious problems of its state and region is not always an easy thing for a foundation, especially a family fund with strong local ties, to do. But this is, in fact, the accomplishment of the *Mary Reynolds Babcock Foundation* of Winston-Salem, whose grants have gone for the upgrading of education, welfare, social service and equal opportunity, both in North Carolina and outside.

The *Boettcher Foundation* of Denver confines its grantmaking to Colorado organizations in a wide variety of fields: educational institutions, cultural agencies, hospitals, community funds, welfare programs, parks and gardens, etc. It is a good example of a philanthropy that concentrates not so much on solving problems as on being of steady, substantial help to worthy non-profit enterprises, usually local or regional. Other foundations of similar size that fit this general

152

description are the *Annenberg Fund* of Philadelphia; the *Cannon Foundation* (Concord, North Carolinia); the *Amon G. Carter Foundation* of Fort Worth; the *Herbert H. and Grace A. Dow Foundation* (Midland, Michigan); the *Lettie Pate Evans Foundation* of Atlanta; the *William Randolph Hearst Foundation* of Los Angeles (special interest: journalism education); the *Hoblitzelle Foundation* of Dallas; the *Godfrey M. Hyams Trust* of Boston; the *J. E. and L. E. Mabee Foundation* of Tulsa; the *Raskob Foundation for Catholic Activities* (Wilmington, Delaware); the *Florence and John Schumann Foundation* (Montclair, New Jersey); and the *Amherst H. Wilder Foundation* of St. Paul (an operating foundation providing community services for local needy people).

Like the various Callaway funds, above, Atlanta's *John Bulow Campbell Foundation* is devoted to Georgia, but its religious allegiance is to Southern Presbyterians. In pursuit of that and other commitments it works on occasion throughout the Southeast, with capital grants to colleges and universities. Its activity is often unknown, for it prefers anonymity.

The *Clayton Foundation for Research,* in Houston, has made its reputation by sponsoring research for agriculture, biochemistry and the prevention and cure of disease in farm livestock.

The *Arthur Vining Davis Foundations,* operating out of Miami, are three related trusts with a central organization to facilitate their philanthropic activtiy. Medicine, religion (Protestant) and education, especially private schools and colleges, are among their interests.

Medicine, religion and education sum it up pretty well also for the *Carrie Estelle Doheny Foundation* of Los Angeles, but this time the religious loyality is Catholic. Research in ophthalmology is a specialty.

Upstate New York has two general purpose foundations in this size category the *Fred L. Emerson Foundation* of Auburn and the *Charles E. Merrill Trust* of Ithaca.

The *George Gund Foundation* of Cleveland has recently re-

153

ceived large new money through the will of its donor, and has adopted large new goals of social consciousness. Limiting its work mainly to Ohio, it announces it is prepared to give "priority to education projects, with emphasis on new concepts and methods of teaching and learning and on increasing educational opportunities for the disadvantaged; to social programs, including improved services, economic opportunities and housing for minority and low-income groups, and drug abuse; support also for ecology, principally in the Lake Erie Basin area, medicine and public health, and cultural affairs."[26]

The *Irwin-Sweeney-Miller Foundation* is administered in conjunction with the *Cummins Engine Foundation,* both of Columbus, Indiana. Whereas numbers of foundations working in the field of religion are handicapped by the narrow denominational attachment and fundamentalist orientation of their donors, these two funds reflect a breadth and sophistication about religious interests that would be expected of their widely known officer, J. Irwin Miller, formerly lay President of the National Council of Churches. Among other areas of activity they are deeply concerned about race, making grants for both integration and the strengthening of black consciousness. Significant for the whole foundation field was the recent appointment of an able young black activist, James A. Joseph, to be their Executive Director.

Limiting its interest largely to Michigan, the *McGregor Fund* of Detroit has worked on a wide variety of community problems: the aging, delinquency, mental health, minority groups. Its emphasis is on higher education, providing scholarships and gift-loans through a fund of its creation, the *Student Aid Foundation* of Michigan.

The *Edward John Noble Foundation* of Washington Depot, Connecticut, is not related to the *Samuel Roberts Noble Foundation* of Ardmore, Oklahoma. Each is about $45- $50-million in size, and attends first to its own region. The Connecticut Noble has broad interests, which include fellowship programs that emphasize the development of leadership and advanced training in international affairs. The Oklahoma Noble is largely

26. *Ibid.,* p. 388.

an operating agency, engaged in medical and agricultural research.

Care of aged women is a quite special concern of the *Fannie E. Rippel Foundation* of Newark. Its work embraces other interests as well, such as aid to hospitals and research on cancer and heart disease.

Another New Jersey foundation, the *Turrell Fund* of East Orange, centers its attention on underprivileged children and spreads its grants among camps, clinics, settlement houses and other similar agencies.

The *Woods Charitable Fund,* with offices in both Chicago and Lincoln, Nebraska, serves general interests but with an eye to special needs. For example, it makes much of community organization and planning in the field of health and welfare; in education it has sought to strengthen regional college associations, and has provided scholarships in the humanities, fine arts and social work.

3. *An Incomplete Honor Roll of Smaller Foundations:*

The word is "smaller," not "small." For though the entries in this section are less large than those above, they are still sizeable, running from approximately $25 million down to $3- or $4-million, with only one or two less than that. Foundations of this size are big enough to undertake important tasks if they have a mind to do so.

Those whose names are listed can be said to be out of the ordinary, performing some unusually valuable service for society. They are often the pace setters for the big foundations; they tend to be streamlined, non-bureaucratic and capable of quick action. Time and again they get the creative idea first, and try it out first. It is this group as much as their larger colleagues in philanthropy who redeem the field from charges of being innocuous and safe.

Even rigorous selection makes for a plethora of names; and the author is aware that he will undoubtedly perpetrate some unwarranted omission. The aim, however, is simply to be suggestive. Once again we shall divide the section into various

155

groupings, this time four in number, to relieve the boredom of a long unsorted parade. We shall consider, first, those roughly between $12- and $25-million in assets, and then those below $12; and within each of these divisions we shall note in turn the foundations in New York City, followed by those outside. In most instances comments will necessarily be quite brief.

The *Bodman Foundation* is geared to the needs of young people: education of minorities, schools for the handicapped, a children's psychiatric center, youth agencies of various sorts.

The *Cleveland H. Dodge Foundation* has to do with religious agencies, educational institutions especially in the Near East, and war and relief funds.

The *Edwin Gould Foundation for Children* is both an operating and a grant-making agency, whose singleness of purpose is matched by the variety of ways in which it promotes the welfare of boys and girls.

Rebelling against the usual areas to which foundation grants are assigned, the *J. M. Kaplan Fund* announces an interest in "selected experimental programs in architecture, arts, city planning and design, local community activity, and music."[27]

If something frankly labelled the *New World Foundation* were to devote its efforts simply to the perpetuation of the old, its name might be an embarrassment. No danger. Its two major thrusts are on the growing edge: innovative education for children, and mutual understanding among peoples and nations. These two themes, especially the latter, put New World in the midst of the sharpest tensions of our time, such as race and war, and its influence has consistently and courageously been on the side of eliminating intergroup and international conflicts.

The *New York Foundation*'s major interests—health and welfare, the arts and education—are not as pedestrian as they sound. In each area this private foundation (which is not a community fund) looks for the especially needy and neglected program; such as: rehabilitation of the disabled, prevention of juvenile delinquency, educational opportunities for blacks and Puerto Ricans.

27. *Ibid.*, p. 297.

156

The *Jessie Smith Noyes Foundation* goes in big for scholarships, fellowships and internships on both the undergraduate and graduate levels, carefully chosen to foster leadership and meet needs of special groups.

The emphasis of the *Twentieth Century Fund* is on research and publication, specializing in studies of economic, political and social problems. A largely operating foundation that is almost a research institute, it has sponsored treatises on such important and varied subjects as *Reapportionment* (by Robert B. McKay), *Performing Arts: The Economic Dilemma* (by William J. Baumol and William G. Bowen), *Megalopolis* (by Jean Gottman), the poverty of Southeast Asia (a Gunnar Myrdal volume, *Asian Drama*), and the behavior of large foundations. (At the time of writing, the latter study, by Waldemar Nielsen, had not yet been published; but based on recent oral remarks of his, it is expected to be critical.)[28]

Recently moved from Cleveland to New York City, the *Weatherhead Foundation* owns to a special interest in, confusingly, the Southwest. Its other major field is the government of cities.

The *Wenner-Gren Foundation for Anthropological Research* tells part of its story in its name. The rest is that it does many useful things besides research, such as grants-in-aid, conferences and publications.

Research and related activities are also the chief stock-in-trade of the *Helen Hay Whitney Foundation,* with the important difference that its focus is rheumatic fever and rheumatic heart disease.

Now for some honorees in the $12- to $25-million category whose offices are not in New York City:

The *Louis D. Beaumont Foundation* says it is in Cleveland but often acts, happily, as if it were in St. Louis. Unhappily, it will bring its program of broad grant-making to a close in 1977.

To support music education, and especially the Curtis Institute of Music, is the main endeavor of the *Mary Louise Curtis Bok Foundation* of Philadelphia.

28. See *Non-Profit Report,* September, 1971, p. 9.

The *Buhl Foundation* of Pittsburgh is a good example of those funds that stay close to home, making a marked difference in the life of a variety of worthy local institutions. In its case, the Buhl Planetarium and the University of Pittsburgh have been among major beneficiaries. Other funds of similar size that fit this general description are: the *S. H. Cowell Foundation* of San Francisco; the *Eugene C. Eppley Foundation* of Omaha; the *Lillia Babbitt Hyde Foundation* of Elizabeth, New Jersey; the *Kerr Foundation* of Oklahoma City; the *LeTourneau Foundation* of Longview, Texas; the *A. W. Mellon Educational and Charitable Trust* of Pittsburgh (*not* the A. W. Mellon Foundation); the *Self Foundation* of Greenwood, South Carolina; the *Trexler Foundation* of Allentown, Pennsylvania; and the *George F. Baker Trust,* the *Charles A. Frueauff Foundation,* the *William T. Morris Foundation,* the *Samuel Rubin Foundation,* the *Scriven Foundation,* the *Seth Sprague Educational and Charitable Foundation* and the *Whitehall Foundation,* all of New York.

The *Maurice Falk Medical Fund* is another Pittsburgh philanthropy, established by the *Maurice and Laura Falk Foundation,* now dissolved. Whereas some of the Foundation's chief interests were citizenship education, economic research and the law, the Fund's emphasis, as its name suggests, is in medicine, especially mental health.

Another Pennsylvania foundation, this one in Philadelphia, is the *Samuel S. Fels Fund,* whose characteristic behavior is the continuing support of important projects and institutions that the Fund itself has established. Chief examples are the Fels Research Institute for the Study of Human Development, the Fels Institute at the Temple University Medical School, and the Fels Center of Government at the University of Pennsylvania.

The *Kansas City Association of Trusts and Foundations* is not the usual private foundation, community trust or family fund. It is not the usual anything, for it has an effective form and style all its own. Through the imaginative leadership of its President, Homer C. Wadsworth, it acts like a private foundation engaging in a variety of grants and projects for the betterment of its city and region. In reality it is a cooperative agency for the more effective administration of *Funds* bearing the names

158

of *Carrie J. Loose, Jacob L. Loose, Ella C. Loose* (dissolved), *Ralph L. Smith* (dissolved) and *Edward F. Swinney*, whose total resources put them in this bracket, and which retain some measure of their autonomy but coordinate their work for the larger good.[29]

Because of the prominence of the family, it is widely but still insufficiently known that the *Joseph P. Kennedy, Jr., Foundation*, late of New York but now of Washington, is especially interested in mental retardation and the problems of handicapped children.

The *Eugene and Agnes E. Meyer Foundation* is also based in Washington. It is interested in a variety of community services, and while Agnes Meyer was still alive was of great sustenance to the National Committee for Support of the Public Schools.

Medical and surgical research, and hospital management and administration are among the special interests of the *Elisabeth Severance Prentiss Foundation* of Cleveland.

The *W. E. Upjohn Unemployment Trustee Corporation* of Kalamazoo supports the W. E. Upjohn Institute for Employment Research.

Two New Jersey agencies, the *Victoria Foundation* of Montclair and the *Wallace-Eljabar Fund* of East Orange, are especially concerned with pilot projects to meet the urgent problems of central cities.

The *T. B. Walker Foundation* of Minneapolis directs much of its attention to the arts, especially the Walker Art Center and, far away, the San Francisco Museum of Art.

After having supported a variety of educational and other projects in earlier years, the *Thomas J. Watson Foundation* of Providence began in 1968 to concentrate on an unusual fellowship program for graduates of thirty-five selected colleges of national reputation. Each of the seventy annual winners is given a *Wanderjahr* of independent study and travel abroad.

Next is a group each of which has less than $12 million in assets. First, for some New Yorkers:

29. See *Foundations and the Tax Bill, op. cit.,* pp. 81–88; *Foundation News,* January–February, 1972, pp. 20–21.

It is almost a shame that the *Abelard Foundation* must lead off, for its rare combination of sharp conscience, large imagination and a thin purse makes the work of almost any other philanthropy look second-rate. Among its achievements are help to such diverse organizations as the Appalachian Volunteers in Eastern Kentucky, the Bay Area Educational TV Association in San Francisco, an integrated community-run nursery school in Albany, Georgia, the restored Old Sturbridge Village in Massachusetts, the East Harlem Block Schools, the Congress of American Indians for Cherokee language radio broadcasts, and the Southern Regional Council for the first Conference of Black Elected Officials in American political history. One more: through its aid to the Worcester Foundation for Experimental Biology, Abelard had a part in the development of the oral contraceptive. At last report its assets were less than $2 million.

The *Aquinas Fund,* also just under $2 million, finances research having to do with "medico-psychological science."

The *Marion R. Ascoli Fund* is interested in, among other things, the rehabilitation of refugees, and the *Max Ascoli Fund* emphasizes international cultural relations.

The chief activity of the *David and Minnie Berk Foundation* is "its sponsorship of the Max Berk Award, presented each year for 'a major achievement in prolonging or improving the quality of human life.' "[30] Though winners have been such well-known people as Michael DeBakey, Ralph Nader and George Wald, few would know about the foundation's good works if David Berk hadn't died recently. The *New York Times* took notice, and reported how "lesser known people also benefitted from the Foundation": Andrew Angioletti, seventy-two, a fruit vendor of Brooklyn, received a new horse when his old one dropped dead.

Like the Duke Endowment, its older and larger cousin, the *Mary Duke Biddle Foundation* has its office in New York City but commits a large part of its income to Duke University. Its other work is directed to the support of programs in the arts

30. "David Berk, 75, Led Foundation," *New York Times,* February 8, 1972.

and to welfare and rehabilitation agencies, mainly in North Carolina.

The *Compton Trust* is a cousin of the Danforth Foundation, for the two families are kin and the two funds share some trustees. It is through the Trust that the Compton family exercises its informed concern for, among other things, equal opportunity for all races, population control and peace.

When the question arises as to whether small foundations can accomplish anything worthwhile, F. Emerson Andrews delights to tell about the *Dorr Foundation* (recently moved from the City to Bedford, New York), which was responsible for having white lines painted on the sides of roads and thus reducing traffic accidents.[31] Highway safety, however, is only one of this family fund's continuing interests, which also include "intensifying precollege science education" and the "development of better understanding of America in foreign lands."[32]

The *Ittleson Family Foundation* has sponsored important sociological studies in intercultural relations—for example, conscious and unconscious racial and religious prejudice in Sunday-school lessons—and is currently putting emphasis on mental health and psychiatric research.[33]

The improvement of low- and middle-income housing and of neighborhood planning, to make the city more human and humane, is the high, hard goal of the *Fred L. Lavanburg Foundation*.

The *Norman Foundation,* formerly the Aaron E. Norman Fund, is not interested unless a program is "innovative or demonstrative." It aims to work for "the protection of civil rights and civil liberties, and in general, broadening and improving the quality of citizen participation in the political, economic and social processes of American life."[34]

The *Gustavus and Louise Pfeiffer Research Foundation* is for medicine, with particular consideration for public health and pharmacy.

31. Ways and Means Committee Hearings, *op. cit.,* Part I, p. 98.
32. FD-4, p. 269.
33. See *Selective Giving: An Account of the Ittleson Family Foundation,* New York, Mental Health Materials Center, 1971.
34. FD-4, p. 322.

161

The *Christopher D. Smithers Foundation,* spreading its support across a broad front of activities, is especially interested in treatment and research in the field of alcoholism.

It should come as no surprise that the *Statler Foundation* makes grants to universities that offer training programs for hotel management.

The plethora of Stern-named foundations—there were seventeen listed in the second edition of the *Foundation Directory*—makes differentiation tricky. The largest is the *Max Stern Foundation,* formerly called the Stern Family Foundation, which gives mainly to Jewish welfare funds. But the palm will have to go to the *Stern Fund,* formerly the Stern Family Fund, formerly the Edgar Stern Family Fund—you can see how hard it is. This foundation has long been noted for its adherence to liberal causes and its strong support of pilot projects in areas that other foundations have been slower to enter, if at all: workshops for civil rights in the Deep South, campus activist groups, anti-poverty programs, ghetto business opportunities, anti-war organizations. In "An Open Letter to the Ford Foundation," published in *Harper's Magazine,* January, 1966, Philip M. Stern describes the philosophy of giving that his own Fund has demonstrated.

The *Taconic Foundation,* like the Stern Fund and many another we have noted, is deeply immersed in difficult social problems. Its special attention is directed toward programs that aim to provide equality of opportunity in education, housing and employment. It has led the way in coordination of activity among foundations, to the end that concerted attack may achieve what individual efforts fail to accomplish.

Finally, the following are some noteworthy less-than-$12-million foundations located elsewhere than in New York City:

The donor of Philadelphia's *American Foundation* was Edward W. Bok, whose *Americanization* inspired an earlier generation and explains the title he gave to his philanthropic fund. Its program consists in maintenance of Bok's delight, the Singing Tower at Lake Wales, Florida, and in sponsorship of

162

substantial research on international law and, currently, corrections and the problems of offenders.

CFK Ltd. of Denver was developing an imaginative program "on improving the learning environment at the elementary and secondary school level," including an "annual Gallup Poll on how the nation views the public schools";[35] but its founder, Charles F. Kettering II, was recently killed by an automobile.

The *Trustees Under the Will of Lotta M. Crabtree,* of Boston, make grants for the aid of, among others, World War I veterans, needy actors, discharged convicts and "dumb animals." Also interested in animals, especially "to provide a home for old, worn out, or disabled horses," is another Massachusetts charity, the *Red Acre Farm, Inc.*[36]

Gerontology is the preserve of the *Forest Park Foundation* of Peoria Heights, Illinois. Research and pilot programs in care for the aged are among its interests.

The highly publicized Glide Memorial Methodist Church of San Francisco is the home and chief beneficiary of the *Glide Foundation,* an operating fund "for experimenting in social and organizational change and . . . the training of churchmen for mission in urban culture, and the encouragement of indigenous leadership among minority groups and groups with specialized need."[37]

In Chicago, the *Graham Foundation for Advanced Studies in the Fine Arts* provides fellowships for just what its title says.

The *Stanley W. Hayes Research Foundation* of Richmond, Indiana, is deeply interested in ecology. Among other work in this field it maintains the Hayes Regional Arboretum as a laboratory for research.

Perhaps the most remarkable thing about the *Edward W. Hazen Foundation* of New Haven is not its own long record of useful work in counseling, religion in higher education and intercultural cooperation, as unusual and valuable as that has been.

35. "A CFK Ltd. Occasional Paper," Denver, n.d.
36. FD-4, pp. 158–159, 169.
37. *Ibid.,* p. 17. See also Louie Robinson, "Glide To Glory," *Ebony,* July, 1971, pp. 44–52.

It is, rather, the influence it has had on many of the large foundations, persuading them of the importance of taking up some of its own causes. (The Danforth Foundation is a case in point.) Indicative of Hazen's leadership is its agenda for the seventies, in "four major areas: 1) the humanizing of an educational system which becomes increasingly monolithic and impersonal; 2) the opening of new opportunities to a large segment of youth challenged by careers which entail service and promotion of fundamental changes in the system; 3) the encouragement of interest in moral values and internalized religion; [and] 4) the achievement of cultural parity among the world's peoples, making partnership in problem solving not only possible but mandatory."[38] Without giving itself airs Hazen has already accomplished much in these four fields, and in the years ahead the big foundations will undoubtedly adopt many of its concerns.

The *M. S. Hershey Foundation,* whose office is appropriately located on West Chocolate Avenue in Hershey, Pennsylvania, was once a much larger fund, but it now belongs in this size bracket because in 1969 it gave well over $40 million of its capital to build a new medical school and medical center under public auspices, thus guaranteeing increased public expenditures for such purposes in the future. Hershey itself has now turned its attention to elementary and secondary schools, and to adult education.

The catalytic effect of the *Johnson Foundation* of Racine, Wisconsin, is of a different order from that of Hazen or Hershey, though no less pronounced. Its limited resources go a long way because its characteristic style is to hold high-level conferences, usually at its conference center, "Wingspread," on behalf of its broad areas of interest: "international understanding, educational excellence, intellectual and cultural growth, and improvement of the human environment."[39]

The *Lalor Foundation* of Wilmington, Delaware, limits its

38. "The Hazen Foundation, General Information," New Haven, n.d.
39. FD-4, p. 509. See also "Summer 1971, Wingspread: Report on Activities", The Johnson Foundation Conference Center, Racine, Wisconsin.

post-doctoral research grants to studies in fertility, reproduction and pregnancy termination.

The *Elsa U. Pardee Foundation* of Midland, Michigan, has two main interests: the Starr Commonwealth for Boys, and cancer research, which has produced useful radioactive drugs.

The program of the *Albert Parvin Foundation* never deserved the notoriety it received because Justice William O. Douglas was once its salaried President.[40] Its support has gone chiefly to fellowships for students from developing nations, for study at Princeton and UCLA.

So far as is known, the *Ellis L. Phillips Foundation* of Ithaca, New York, and the *Frank Phillips Foundation* of Bartlesville, Oklahoma, have nothing in common but their last name and their being out of the ordinary. Having phased out the intriguing program of Phillips Internships in college administration, Ellis now makes support available for such groups as minority businessmen; while Frank takes interest in, among other things, Midwest youth agencies and the Woolaroc Wildlife Refuge and Museum.

The *Minnie Stevens Piper Foundation* of San Antonio is determined to improve higher education in Texas, both by providing such customary things as scholarships and loans and by undertaking the difficult task of choosing, and awarding $1,000 each to, ten outstanding Piper Professors per year.

Equally elusive is the effort to improve the objective reporting of the news, which is the ambitious aim of the *Poynter Fund* of St. Petersburg, Florida.

The *Rosenberg Foundation* takes on the temper of its own home city. Surely San Francisco, whatever else it is, is both sentimental and tough, and persons of every background feel welcome. So the Foundation's chosen fields of activity embrace the enrichment of community life, especially for minority groups, and the improvement of education and recreation, especially for children and youth. The mode is frankly experimental: Rosenberg tends to support projects that are not already proved but need testing.

40. See Goulden, *op. cit.,* pp. 300–301.

The *Southern Education Foundation* of Atlanta is heir to all of the idealism and some of the money of the *Peabody Education Fund,* the *John F. Slater Fund* (both philanthropic pioneers of the nineteenth century), the *Jeanes Fund* and the *Virginia Randolph Fund.* All these had worked in a variety of ways for equal educational opportunity in the South, and their moral suasion far outweighed their modest support.[41] The Southern Education Foundation has continued much of their activity and established important programs of its own: grants for teachers' salaries, graduate fellowships, teaching internships, inter-institutional cooperation, accreditation for black colleges, and pre-school education.

Concord is the office locale and New Hampshire the chief program arena for the soon-to-be-dissolved *Spaulding-Potter Charitable Trust,* whose tried-and-true method is a combination of carrot and goad. By carefully devised challenge grants the Trust has brought to maturity such diverse state-wide programs as community mental-health clinics, consolidated school districts, cooperation of cities through the New Hampshire Municipal Association, cooperation of small foundations in the New Hampshire Charitable Fund, community conservation commissions, and the student-aid Dollars-for-Scholars program.

The *Alexander and Margaret Stewart Trust* of Washington focusses its attention on cancer, to help both those who suffer from it and those who study its cause and cure.

Along with regular charitable giving in its own home town of St. Louis, the *Sunnen Foundation* expresses special interest in problems of population control and race relations.

The *Wieboldt Foundation* of Chicago is a good example of a philanthropic fund that has refused to give up on the inner city, even when it means working in ways of which, and with groups of whom, the suburbs don't always approve. Among its concerns are human welfare, especially of children, and community stabilization and development.

An operating fund for research publication in international affairs, the *World Peace Foundation* of Boston has had a con-

41. See Weaver, *op. cit.,* pp. 24–25, 435–436.

tinuing influence since 1910, far outstripping its meager resources.

The *Zale Foundation* of Dallas has transcended Texas by
making grants to Brandeis University and a high school in Is-
rael. It would be a mistake, however, to conclude that its operative allegiance was Jewry, for its prevailing work has been on
behalf of the urban poor and disadvantaged, especially the
blacks, to improve opportunities and resolve conflicts.

4. *Community Funds, Company Foundations and Clusters:*

Although community funds are not the concern of this volume, their work is often of a piece, in content, method and
effect, with the privately endowed single-source-of-origin foundations that we have been considering. The Tax Reform Act
confuses things by putting them in a separate category,[42] but
apart from differences of structure and related matters they make
much the same kind of contribution to the general welfare.

The normal pattern of receiving funds from several sources
and making grants to a variety of objects could easily mean that
community funds would find it difficult to take on a character
of their own, or concentrate on any one thing long enough to
make a difference. The surprise, then, is that they are often
planners and innovators, not just quiescent moneybags. The
recognition that hosts of foundations deserve because they are
effectively on the side of a better nation and a better world
should be widespreading enough to include many of the community funds, whose carefully considered subventions add lustre
to the field of philanthropy.[43]

42. See TRA, *op. cit.*, Code Section 509; note on IRS's ruling of the
Cleveland Foundation as "a 509(a)(1) Public Charity," *Foundation
News*, March–April, 1972, p. 2.

43. See Weaver, *op. cit.*, pp. 41–42; Report of Peterson Commission,
op. cit., pp. 51–52; *Giving USA, op. cit.*, p. 21; *Community Foundations
in the United States and Canada*, published annually by the Council on
Foundations, New York; Russell T. Foster, "Big Frog in a Small Pud-
dle," *Foundation News*, July–August, 1971; James P. Heron, "Building a
New Community Foundation," *Ibid.*, March–April, 1972; *The Story of
Modern Giving*, The Williamsport Foundation, 1967.

The first and still the largest community fund is the *Cleveland Foundation,* whose assets are well over $100 million and whose annual expenditures run above $6 million. Its program is exactly what one has come to expect of any well-ordered community fund, and it is itself largely responsible for that high expectation: grants for education, cultural affairs, health and welfare, urban problems, recreation and other civic interests, with special attention to urgent human need. As pace setter in its field, the Cleveland Foundation continues to serve as a worthy model for the growing number of community funds existing across the country.

Next to Cleveland the largest community funds are, in rank, the *New York Community Trust,* the *Chicago Community Trust* and the *Committee of the Permanent Charity Fund* of Boston. While no other big city funds challenge these first four in size of assets, several have begun to exceed $1 million in amount of annual expenditures: in order, the *Winston-Salem Foundation,* the *San Francisco Foundation,* the *Kalamazoo Foundation,* the *California Community Foundation* of Los Angeles, the *Vancouver Foundation* in British Columbia, the *Hartford Foundation for Public Giving* and two Pennsylvania funds: the *Philadelphia Foundation* and the *Pittsburgh Foundation.*

If we had time for a full examination of available figures, it would quickly become evident that, in the field of community funds, the factor of size is illusory in several ways. Size of active capital is no reliable indicator of size of annual disbursement, for funds for grant-making may come at any time from special gifts rather than from endowment. (Such a thing may happen to privately endowed non-operating foundations, of course, but is much rarer.) Special gifts may skew the rankings from year to year, so that annual listings are notoriously unreliable. As is also true for other kinds of foundations, the amount of annual dollar activity tells nothing about the quality or effectiveness of the work. Finally, the size of the parent city has almost nothing to do with the case.

Note, for example, the presence of such smaller cities as Winston-Salem, Kalamazoo and Hartford in the list above. Any thoughtful honor roll of outstanding community funds would

168

have to include, at the risk of some unjustified omissions, the foundations of the following smaller cities and towns, now ordered alphabetically: the *Aurora Foundation* of Illinois, the *Beloit Foundation* in Wisconsin, the *Grand Rapids Foundation,* the *Hawaiian Foundation* of Honolulu, the *Mount Vernon Community Trust* of Ohio, the *New Haven Foundation,* the *Norfolk Foundation,* the *Quincy Foundation* of Illinois, the *Rhode Island Foundation* of Providence, the *Richland County Foundation of Mansfield, Ohio,* the *Foundations* of both *Riverside* and *Santa Barbara* in California, the *Savannah Foundation,* the *Williamsport Foundation* of Pennsylvania, and the *Winnipeg Foundation* in Manitoba.

Nor are the charitable trusts of business and industrial corporations the concern of this book. Even as with community funds, however, so with company foundations, some passing mention of the chief benevolences seems called for. When companies spend thought as well as money in their charitable giving, it redounds to the credit of philanthropy generally. This is now true in the practice of a considerable number of large firms, enough to justify our taking note of it.

The motivations back of company funds are as mixed as for family endowments. Escape from excess-profits taxes, repair of a bad image, public relations, a genuine desire to be helpful in worthy causes—all these things and more have gone into, first, the practice of philanthropy on a somewhat episodic basis, and later, the establishment of this practice in a systematic program and, often, a legally separate corporation. Gifts fluctuate greatly from year to year, even though many companies have set aside some capital so as to make any year's grants more stable in amount, less subject to the vagaries of profit-and-loss. At best, however, the endowment of company funds tells little about the size of the annual charitable activity.

And tells nothing at all about its nature and quality. The spectrum is vast, all the way from the bland purchase of local goodwill by handouts to approved agencies, to innovative programs in areas of major social need as carefully designed as those of the leading private foundations. Education, mainly col-

169

leges and universities, is getting the largest share of corporation giving, followed closely by health and welfare agencies. Though still small in proportion to the whole, the arts, urban problems and opportunities for minorities seem to be increasingly popular categories.[44]

The *Alcoa Foundation* of Pittsburgh is the only company fund over $100 million in assets, but it lacks by at least half a dozen places being first in annual expenditures. No. 1 in grants is the *Ford Motor Company Fund* of Detroit, with the *Sears-Roebuck Foundation* of Chicago and the *United States Steel Foundation* of Pittsburgh competing for no. 2. The Ford Fund spends well over $10 million per year, and the other two over $5 million each.

Two of the largest are generally considered to be among the most imaginative in program and best administered: the *Esso Education Foundation* of New York City, whose Executive Director is Frederick deW. Bolman; and the *Shell Companies Foundation,* soon forsaking New York for Houston, built to its present stature by W. M. Upchurch, Jr. Several other oil companies have also established first-rate corporation trusts: the *Atlantic Richfield Foundation* and the *Mobil Foundation,* both of New York City, the *Gulf Oil Foundation* of Houston, and the *Standard Oil (Indiana) Foundation* of Chicago.

Oil is not the only eleemosynary industry. Yet I mask my ignorance of the corporation charities in other fields by saying that elaboration of this subject is not part of this essay's purpose. Let it suffice simply to note that the number of companies practicing careful philanthropy is large and growing. And let there be an end to the matter by the naming of a few assorted funds that are no better, to be sure, than many others that might be listed, but that have come to some prominence in the field and are, I trust, representative: the *Burlington Industries Foundation* of Greensboro, the *Chrysler Corporation Fund* in Detroit, the

44. See Weaver, *op. cit.,* pp. 42–43; Rembrandt C. Hiller, Jr., "The Company-Sponsored Foundation," in F. Emerson Andrews, ed., *Foundations—20 Viewpoints,* New York, Russell Sage Foundation, 1965; *Giving USA, op. cit.,* pp. 22–24; *Handbook of Aid to Higher Education,* New York, Council for Financial Aid to Education, 1972, pp. A-1 to A-50; Taft, *op. cit.,* pp. 5–6 and *passim.*

Crown Zellerbach Foundation of San Francisco, the *Eastman Kodak Charitable Trust* of Rochester, the *Firestone Foundation* of Akron, the *General Electric Foundation* of Bridgeport, the *Inland Steel-Ryerson Foundation* of Chicago, the *Monsanto Fund* of St. Louis, the *PPG Industries Foundation* (which stands for Pittsburgh Plate Glass) of Pittsburgh, the *Proctor and Gamble Fund* of Cincinnati, the *Republic Steel Corporation Educational and Charitable Trust* of Cleveland, the *Smith Kline and French Foundation* of Philadelphia, the *Western Electric Fund* of New York City, and two *Westinghouse* agencies in Pittsburgh, one the *Educational Foundation* and the other the *Electric Fund.*

To have traversed the ground over which we have just come in this chapter is to be made aware that the map of American philanthropy is an unbalanced, spotty picture. Foundations have gathered in a number of large or middling clusters here and there, and certain cities or relatively circumscribed regions are well endowed, at least comparatively, with grant-making institutions. As has already been noticed, New York City easily leads the list of favored places, but a few others are fairly close behind in possessing a concentration of funds.

In the first rank are Atlanta, Houston, the states of Michigan and North Carolina, and the two Pennsylvania cities, Philadelphia and Pittsburgh. In a second echelon of less well-supplied centers are Chicago, Cleveland, the Dallas-Fort Worth area, Denver-Colorado Springs, Minneapolis-St. Paul, Oklahoma City-Tulsa, and the San Francisco Bay areas. Even some of these are named on the basis of potential rather than because the foundations located there are already caring fully for local needs. Several of these cities or regions are starving for sustenance from private philanthropy, and would undoubtedly resist being classified as specially fortunate.

But this *is* a comparative matter; and the seriousness of the situation for other parts of the country is fully exposed when we take note of cities and regions not mentioned. It comes as a surprise to most people that Boston, and New England generally (with the possible exception of central Connecticut), are not well furnished in this respect. Nor is there much philanthropic

171

activity at the other end of the country, in the Pacific North-west. Florida has very little, as is the case with most other parts of the South. South of the Tehachapi is also a philanthropic wasteland, for few of the large fortunes of Los Angeles and San Diego have found their way into organized benevolence. As for the broad mid-belt of America, most of the major cities and nearly all the small ones and the rural areas are without large philanthropic resources; and usually only one or two founda-tions, if any at all, have to carry the burden of the load.

This realization, if taken to heart, might easily lead to a further tightening of the local screws. If our city doesn't have as large resources for private giving as some other city—and everybody but the New Yorker can play that game—then obviously we should direct everything we can to the old home-town. Charity begins you-know-where. And if this means that West Virginia, Mississippi, North Dakota and Idaho, to name only four out of a larger number, don't have anywhere to turn except to the Federal Government, then that's just too bad.

It *is* too bad. The heavy concentration of philanthropic funds in New York City is a great pity for the rest of the nation. Moreover, it sometimes seems as if a few of the large New York foundations are encouraging those in the hinterland to become more parochial than is already the case. The head of the Crossroads Symphony goes to the Big Town, and the Gotrocks Trust tells him, "You can't expect us to help you until Lessrocks right there in your own city has come across." But the irony is that Lessrocks has never worked in music and the arts, and Gotrocks knows it. Do the New York foundations really want Flint to stay in Flint, and Texas in Texas? Is that the way to even things up a bit?

Wouldn't it be healthy, instead, if the Mott Foundation—I'm meddling!—decided to work in Texas, and if this annoyed Moody and Brown and some of the other Texas foundations so much that they said, "We'll show you what you need and what we can do; we're coming up to Michigan"? Wouldn't it be even healthier if they all decided to do some work in Arkansas, or Vermont or Wyoming? Or for that matter, some other part of the world?

172

Danforth is the only large foundation in St. Louis, and, in fact, in all of Missouri. The State could use all of Danforth's resources and a great deal more. Does this mean, then, that Danforth should stay at home? If it did, and if similar foundations elsewhere did, the State and all the other states would be the losers. The accident whereby clusters of fat foundations developed in a few places, with lots of lean spots in between, is understandable historically, economically, socially. In and of itself it need be no great danger. Trouble begins to brew only when those pockets of affluence start being geographically particular. Let the physical clustering develop as it will (though it *would* be nice if some of the big ones moved around a bit). What really matters is the outlook. The large foundations need to learn what the great universities learned long ago: that Oxford and Cambridge, Princeton and Oberlin are pretty small towns, but the non-profit institutions that proudly bear their names have other and far horizons.

As a postscript to this section on tangible accomplishments, it may be helpful to note why some names that might have been expected did not appear. One explanation is that they aren't foundations, either that they never quite had that status, or that they once had it but have given it up because of the Tax Reform Act or for some other reason. Philanthropologists are themselves puzzled by borderline organizations; both the second and the third editions of the *Foundation Directory* (noted hereafter as FD-2 and FD-3) list, but not consistently with each other, a number of well-known and often well-heeled agencies that the public have sometimes taken for foundations, but that don't strictly fit, and that the fourth edition now skips.

For example: It never really made sense that the *American International Association for Economic and Social Development,* of New York, and the *American Philosophical Society* of Philadelphia (both in FD-2), should have been listed; for the former is an AID-style private operation in Latin America and the latter, though it goes all the way back to Ben Franklin and makes a few grants, is a membership group. A couple of exotic plants in Honolulu, the *Bishop Estate* (with well over

173

$100 million in assets) and the *Watumull Foundation* (both in FD-3), are no longer the usual kind of foundation; the former is largely a special endowment fund for two local schools, and the latter is mainly a series of projects to promote better relations between the United States and India. Like Bishop, the *Cranbrook Foundation,* outside Detroit (FD-3), exists for the support of special Cranbrook institutions. Both the *Winterthur Corporation* in Delaware (FD-2) and the *Carnegie Institution of Washington* (FD-3) are generously endowed, but are operating agencies for the accomplishment of special purposes, the former for the support of a museum and related activities, and the latter for high-level scientific research.

A brief word will perhaps be useful on four more quite different from each other, whose absence from the earlier listings may have seemed strange. First, the *Phelps-Stokes Fund* of New York (FD-2), established as early as 1911, has a long and distinguished record of achievement on behalf of blacks in this country and Africa, and of North American Indians; but it has now come to be much more of an operating agency, receiving support from other foundations. *Spectemur Agendo,* (FD-3) is the personal photogenic organ of Stewart R. Mott, who engages in direct political activity.[45] Princeton's *Woodrow Wilson National Fellowship Foundation* (FD-3) was always a specialized self-operated program, financed by Ford and other foundations. Finally, the *Hogg Foundation for Mental Health,* which operates very much like a large, well-run philanthropy, is structurally a constituent part of the University of Texas at Austin (and thus is not in FD-2, -3 or -4); its long-time executive, Robert L. Sutherland, who recently retired, is recognized as the most distinguished and influential foundation man in the Southwest.[46]

As already noted, dissolutions explain why some once-known names are missing. A few recent alphabetical examples: the

45. See Betty Baer, "Stewart Mott: Money on the Make," *Look Magazine,* July 28, 1970.
46. See *The Hogg Foundation for Mental Health: The First Three Decades 1940–1970,* Austin, The University of Texas, 1970, *passim.*

Vivian B. Allen Foundation of New York City (FD-3), interested in the Lincoln Center; the New York foundations connected with David Baird (FD-2) and the *Bollingen Foundation,* all Patman targets;[47] Ford's *Fund for the Advancement of Education* (FD-3); the *Greenwood Fund* (FD-2), for the administration of the John Hay Fellows Program; the *Leonard C. Hanna, Jr., Fund* of Cleveland (FD-2); the *Kate Macy Ladd Fund* of Newark (FD-3); and the *William Volker Fund* of Burlingame, California (FD-3).

Would any reader, perhaps, expect to find mention of the Mark Gable Foundation or the Rosewater Foundation, the fictional creations of Leo Szilard and Kurt Vonnegut respectively?[48] But it may come as something of a shock to Mr. Vonnegut to know that there really is a Rosewater Foundation, doing good in ways that perhaps his President Eliot Rosewater would approve.[49]

C. DISAPPOINTMENTS AND FAILURES:

Part of the glory of foundations' work is their record of disappointment and failure.

("How's that again?" But you read it right the first time.)

In any consideration of achievements, some attention should be paid to that part of every foundation's performance that consists in its having tried something that did not succeed, supported something that did not justify the confidence placed in it, bet on something that lost.

This is not to say that every failure is an achievement. On the contrary, most failures are just that and no more; and to doll them up in the language of better-to-have-loved-and-lost is to engage in a self-deceptive exercise. The point of this section is not to try to turn the tables, or to call things by their opposites.

47. For Patman's charges against the Baird foundations, see Patman Reports, *op. cit.,* II, 1963; for his criticism of Bollingen, see Ways and Means Committee Hearings, *op. cit.,* Part I, pp. 16–17.

48. Leo Szilard, *The Voice of the Dolphins and Other Stories,* New York, Simon and Schuster, 1961, story entitled "The Mark Gable Foundation"; Vonnegut, *op. cit.*

49. FD-4, p. 335.

Rather, the point is twofold: first, to note the positive good that is gained when a foundation recognizes a negative item in its record; and second, to argue the actual superiority of at least a few imaginative failures as over against what might have been some dull successes in their place. A disappointment is not a triumph; but then again, and on rare occasion, it just might be. Surely it *is,* when a foundation learns from failure to the benefit of forthcoming grants in that field..

Some critics would have it, however, that foundations won't even admit they have failures. Joseph Goulden wrote: "In going through more than a thousand annual reports [!] ... I found only one foundation which candidly told which of its projects failed and why."[50] The exclamation point is mine. He was undoubtedly so bleary-eyed from having looked at "a thousand annual reports" that he couldn't recognize the tactful admissions of error that occur now and again; or maybe they weren't candid enough for his taste. In any event, let us not take credit away from the one he did find, the Louis W. and Maud Hill Foundation of St. Paul.

The Peterson Commission, supposedly friendly to foundations, opined that

they would bury their mistakes just as quickly as any other human agency. . . . Very few foundations show much willingness to chat with the public at all; even fewer to talk about any of their 'bad experiences.' The foundation world can hardly be blamed for being as success-oriented as the rest of America, though it is ironic that foundations which have initiated so many evaluative projects of other institutions and their programs seem reticent either to evaluate or to talk candidly about their own programs.[51]

There's that word, "candidly," again.

Strictly speaking, maybe the Commission is correct. The phrasing was, ". . . bury their mistakes just as quickly as ... ," not "sooner than. . . ." We need to admit that foundations don't like to fail; and when they do fail, they don't go around patting themselves on the back. In this regard they are indeed like any other human institution.

50. Goulden, *op. cit.,* p. 77.
51. Report of Peterson Commission, *op. cit.,* p. 115.

But the suggestion that foundations try to pretend to themselves or others that they simply don't have disappointments or failures is absurd. When foundation people get together the talk turns as quickly to defeat as is the case with university presidents, or ministers of the gospel, or professional athletes—which is to say, all such groups chew the rag of victory as well as defeat, and expose their own shortcomings as little as possible.

Then how can the impression get abroad that foundations are congenitally incapable of confessing to error? The answer is easy: A foundation's failure is almost inevitably, and universally, the failure of some other organization or person as well. If a foundation is to give chapter and verse as to where, when and how a failure took place, complete candor would require that something or someone else also be labelled as culprit. But who wants to cast aspersions? So foundations do not fill their reports with such explanatory comments as "X University misused the money," or "Y Scholar proved to be a disastrous choice," or "Z Agency was a fraud."

Thus the foundation will sometimes have to cover up, not because it believes and would have the public believe that no mistake has been made, but for the exactly opposite reason, namely, because it knows very well that an error *has* been made and that public knowledge of it might be harmful to an otherwise admirable organization or person. How do I know this is the case? Because I've played this game, and have seen my colleagues in other foundations play it.

Anyone who takes the trouble to learn how to read annual reports can find plenty of evidence that foundations know they suffer disappointments and are involved in failures. This comes to be especially clear when this year's report is compared with last year's and the year's before: Why was the unpaid portion of that grant, noted a year ago, not paid during the past year? Why was some other grant series stopped short? Why was a certain refund recorded? The critic who wants the foundation to bare its soul, and in the process expose the misbehavior of others, is bound to be disappointed; for the annual report won't tell why. But for him who doesn't run while he reads, the evidence of a mistake is there.

177

The Peterson Commission's complaint that foundations "would bury their mistakes" is puzzling in light of the information that the Commission itself asked to be gathered, but then did not use, on the work that foundations "consider disappointing or unproductive." The Commission requested the Foundation Center to send a questionnaire to a small representative group of foundations, to inquire about both "especially significant" and "disappointing" grants; and "replies came from about twenty foundations, including the largest and most prestigious and various smaller ones." The Report spends a couple of sentences on the "unproductive" replies, and concludes, "The answers give no reassurance that the foundations truly look on their failures as being as significant as their successes"; and then follows the sentence about burying mistakes.[52]

The impression is left that the foundations clammed up and didn't want to answer the negative question. This is not the fact. The Foundation Center has been good enough to share those questionnaires with me. Herewith, then, a few quick references to show that the overwhelming majority of those responding to the questionnaire were quite prepared to own to the presence of "disappointing and unproductive" items in their records—and my notes to follow are fewer and less explicit than theirs in mentioning names, dates and places:[53]

Abelard was disappointed because a private school it had helped "made no attempt to change and respond in any creative way to the current needs of our society."

Carnegie admitted it failed in efforts to measure esthetic judgment or predict artistic ability, or to encourage the development of a program of European Studies comparable to concentrations in other area study programs.

(Danforth will be referred to below.)

Duke was unhappy when a child-caring institution it was aiding did not establish a needed "social service staff development program," and again, when one of its recipient colleges did not

52. *Ibid.*, pp. 112, 115.
53. "Survey of Noteworthy Grants," The Foundation Center, New York, MSS (copies in author's possession).

complete plans for "construction of a service center designed to make maintenance operations . . . more efficient."

Esso Education Foundation had high hopes for a regional science laboratory for use by colleges and high schools, but "the money went down the drain"; for a scholarly study of innovations in higher education, but the person trusted to do the job "abandoned the project"; and for a program involving improved classroom utilization, but "nothing of significance resulted."

As was appropriate for the largest, Ford answered for each of its major divisions rather than for just the Foundation as a whole. Thus it had a host of disappointments to note, among which were: efforts to strengthen the quality of teacher education, and of education in the visual arts; to encourage collaboration among painters, sculptors and other artists; to provide "a national program in translation"; to arouse the interest of medical students in careers in reproductive biology; to develop "a productivity center" in an African country and "a teacher-training program in vocational agricultural education" in a South American country; to demonstrate land-use controls in small river basins; to increase the number of blacks in foreign service positions; and to provide air-borne television instruction for the public schools.

Hazen felt badly because an important study of racial discrimination in American law was not sufficiently reported; and deplored, further, the occasional "casual attitude of some scholars and institutions whose view of the appropriate role of foundations appears to be as distributors of funds rather than as interested supporters of significant scholarly and other activities."

The Kansas City Association of Trusts and Foundations was unsuccessful in an inner-city youth employment service, a program to create new careers for the poor, and a multi-college English language institute for their foreign students.

Disappointments were the lot of Kellogg in such diverse efforts as aid to the blind, hospital group purchasing and meeting the special needs of the aged.

Lilly supported a "program to combat juvenile delinquency" that consisted in training high-school dropouts to build houses.

179

But "only seven boys were trained, only two houses were built in three years; and then the director left town and the operation collapsed."

R. K. Mellon has learned that "general lack of community support" can bring to naught a foundation's effort to aid such worthy agencies as a repertory theater, a drama school, a performing arts association and the disadvantaged youth program of a community cultural center.

The New York Community Trust set up a store-front medical facility for hippies, which proved to be a mistake. (Whereupon it substituted a mobile medical unit which was more practicable.)

Rosenberg sponsored an ambitious project "to demonstrate a new approach to teaching ghetto children," that called for the cooperation of public schools with private social agencies and that used both in-school and after-school activities. The coordination and sympathetic atmosphere necessary to its being a success was more than the various participants could muster.

A program of services for prisoners' families and a big-brother project for ghetto youngsters were a couple of good ideas of the San Francisco Foundation that unfortunately did not pan out.

Scaife's trust in some university programs for the development of new sources of food supply in the Caribbean, for repertory theater, and for research into the geophysical and geochemical nature of the oceans, proved to be misplaced.

Smith Kline and French had inner-city woes of several sorts. For example, it supported a plan "to bus disadvantaged children to parks and recreational areas," but the supposedly competent agency in charge did such a poor job that "a program designed to ease racial tensions made them worse."

The high ideals of the Southern Education Fund on behalf of desegregation, quality education and equal opportunity produced, predictably, feelings of defeat and frustration. The surprise is not that the Fund has often failed, and knows it; the surprise is that it has used its failures to such good purpose in writing its record of success.

Spaulding-Potter expressed disappointment over grants to

180

private schools, a conservation agency and programs for the aged, either because the grants didn't turn out as well as hoped or because the projects weren't able to become self-supporting.

Any organization that supports significant exploration is going to dig some dry holes. The Twentieth Century Fund felt dissatisfied about recent studies on America's public environment, the ideology of city planning and the industrialized urban environment.

One of Zale's illustrations was a grant to a junior college, "to recruit and train high-school dropouts," but the program was bungled.

The Foundation Center's questionnaire did not pretend to go very far, for all it seems to have wanted to find out was whether foundations would admit to error, not merely in general but specifically. The answer was clear: foundations in the main are aware that they suffer disappointments and failures. But how deep does this recognition go? Does a foundation ever take its failures to heart? Does it ever learn from them, for similar work in the future; or does it eschew such work entirely, learning only to stay away? Can it ever mount the courage actually to court disaster? Will it on occasion consciously take the riskier path, knowing in advance that success is much less certain? If the answer to such questions as these is on the positive side, then that foundation can speak of its defeats as part of its record of service.

The only example I know well enough to use is Danforth—which is fortunate, since it is the only one I dare use. A public analysis of the faults of others is never a winning gambit. Nor is breast-beating on behalf of one's own outfit. All that is left, therefore, if one is to speak a word on his favorite subject, is to examine Danforth's failures and its attitude toward failure.

There is literally nothing that Danforth touches that isn't tinged with failure. (How hard it is to hide one's pride!) This grows simply out of the strange kind of shop it happens to be. Danforth says, ad nauseam, that it is interested in persons and values, and by so saying it has bought itself endless trouble.

Persons are deceptive and values are slippery. In the service of either it is bound to come a cropper; in the service of both it is often lost.

For example, among the various educational programs that members of the Danforth staff administer are several national fellowship and award programs; and the aim in all of them is to find persons not only of unusual competence, which can be measured in part, but also of unusual temper, which can only be assessed. Small wonder, then, that nary a session of our numerous selection committees goes by without the making of mistakes. Sometimes horrendous ones, to my taste. We have even had to admit, on occasion, that the selection committees themselves were not as well chosen as they should have been. We never get done with examining our selection processes; for they never attain perfection. They only get improved.

Or take the business of grant-making, which was the special interest of the Foundation Center's questionnaire. In answer, Danforth mentioned three disappointing experiences, which are as good or as bad as any number of other illustrations that might have been given. The failures chosen for mention were (1) a series of grants to small, regional colleges in close proximity, to foster their faculty and institutional improvement—but the program on the Foundation's part was neither well planned nor well administered; (2) both regional and national support on behalf of civic education, especially in high schools—but those in whom the Foundation put its trust were incompetent; and (3) a sizeable effort to persuade teacher-training institutions to introduce the study of religion in their regular curricula—but the timing and perhaps the sponsorship of the program were wrong. (If it were pertinent, it could be pointed out that each of these has its encouraging sequel. The Foundation did not abandon any one of the three aims.)

Among a host of other disappointments that could be mentioned, let us note two whose critiques have appeared in print. One of the Foundation's long-time emphases is the improvement of teaching, especially on the undergraduate level. Our twin prevailing interests in people and in values converge in this theme, and their very imprecision makes less precise the ways we choose to pursue it: not only fellowships for graduate study and awards for distinguished teaching but also conferences, workshops and grant series of various kinds. Two of these latter were recently reviewed by members of the staff in our occasional publication, *Danforth News and Notes*. Each was felt to be successful on balance, but each could have been stronger, as the Foundation pointed out to its constituency.

The first was a series called Teaching Improvement Grants, totalling $253,900 to 12 colleges and universities. Among the "weaknesses of the program" the following were mentioned:

The grants should have been made earlier in the year to enable proper planning on the part of the institution and key faculty members. . . . The institutions invited to submit proposals should have been investigated more carefully. . . . The program tended to place too much confidence in one key person on a campus. . . . No plan for disseminating what is learned as a result of the projects was included in the program. . . .

The Director concluded:

. . . it is unlikely that such a grant program will lead to any major break-throughs or new developments in higher education. Were the Foundation to expend all of its resources in this way, it would be involved in only a series of unrelated, small efforts. This limitation of the Teaching Improvement Grants program is therefore a caution: while a limited-size program of this nature would appear to have a significant place among the Foundation's various strategies for change, it should not become the sole instrumentality through which the Foundation operates.[54]

The second was an even more ambitious program called Teaching Internship Grants, stretching over several years to eleven colleges and universities and totalling $3,115,565. Teaching assistants have traditionally been the less able graduate students who failed to get the higher-valued research grants, and who did their menial chores with freshmen and sophomores, without supervision. In order to help break this sorry pattern, the Foundation provided support for programs of "guided apprenticeships" or "teaching internships," whereby the teaching

54. W. David Zimmerman, "Teaching Improvement Grants," *Danforth News and Notes*, October, 1970, pp. 1–4.

183

experience was to be made an integral part of the graduate training, and careful supervision of interns by senior professors was to be provided. One junior college, two senior colleges and graduate departments in various disciplines in eight universities developed such programs.

But when the Foundation came recently to add up the results, it was clear that the verdict had to be mixed. On the one hand: "There can be little question that the teaching internship programs have served as symbols of a renewed emphasis on teaching in the participating universities"; and " . . . almost all of the interns developed a dedication to their teaching." On the other hand, many of the graduate departments were considerably less dedicated to the interns, and the assurance given as to a genuine interest in training for good teaching turned out often to be simply lip service. Other conclusions: " . . . the educational enterprise has underestimated the difficulty of learning to teach well"; " . . . the procedures employed to analyze the problems of teaching were almost completely lacking in imagination"; and " . . . the basic assumptions common to almost all of the programs under discussion here, namely, that graduate students should learn how to emulate their mentors, is partially rejected by a substantial proportion of the interns." "Whether later developments will indicate that the programs initiated new perspectives on the responsibility graduate schools and undergraduate faculties bear for the induction of new faculty into their craft, and whether they will give rise to new structural arrangements for increased support of such responsibilities by universities, is impossible to predict."[55]

The reader will have noted that several of the disappointments mentioned by foundations above had to do with their work on urban problems. Whether the inner city can be saved is, of course, the tragic question being asked these days both by government at various levels and by private agencies. Every foundation that has posed the question seriously has met with setbacks; and to make a short end to what could be a long rehearsal of disappointment, the Danforth Foundation is again a case in point.

55. W. Max Wise, "Teaching Internship Grants," *Ibid.*, pp. 4–7.

The point, though, is that the probability of failure was seen in advance, accepted and, when it came, lived with and learned from. At their meeting in January, 1968, the Danforth Trustees debated whether to institute a modest program in urban affairs. Euphoria and the smell of righteousness were in the air, until one of their number pointed out "possible difficulties" that would have to be faced, such as the semblance of "political involvement, even if we say we are not, . . . the displeasure of city fathers . . . when we take the first action that cuts across . . . customs, . . . the good possibility of a bad press even from a sympathetic publisher," and most of all, "failure," which is "clearly part of the experience" of any agency that undertakes important work in the inner city.[56]

Even though his colleagues almost believed him, they took the step. His predictions came true, of course, for those and other problems were encountered in the succeeding years. It is the response, however, that is significant. The Foundation did not continue to wave its feeble banners when some particular attack was getting nowhere, nor did it retreat in disarray from the field. Rather, it regrouped, changed its strategy and pressed on. This is not the place to tell the story in detail, though it is available for any who might be interested.[57] This is simply the time to say that "ad astra per aspera" is the motto of many a foundation, of whom Danforth is merely an example; and that among their accomplishments should be listed the mistakes from which they and others have profited.

The most common faults of foundations can be quickly catalogued. They are at least eight in number:

1. The basic idea proved to be no good. Sometimes even the smartest are smart only after the fact; and the not-so-smart, of whom foundations have their full share, are usually in character.

2. The institution or person to whom the idea was entrusted was simply a bad choice. A better recipient-agent could

56. Minutes, Danforth Foundation Board of Trustees, January 6–8, 1968, p. 17, MSS (in the files of the Foundation).

57. See William C. Nelsen, "Urban Affairs in St. Louis: The Educational Approach," *Danforth News and Notes,* March, 1971, p. 6; *The Danforth Foundation Annual Report,* 1970–1971, pp. 64–67.

probably have been discovered if a broader or more careful survey had been taken in advance.

3. Even though idea and agent were defensible, the method to be employed was not adequately assessed in comparison with other possible methods.

4. The specific terms of the foundation's action were ill-advised: the amount of support was too much or too little, the conditions were too few or too many, the timing was wrong.

5. Even when the foundation has acted on the basis of a good idea, a worthy institution or person to put it into effect, a sound method and effective terms and circumstances, the performance on the part of the recipient could turn out to be poor, to the dismay and helplessness of the foundation itself whose own part in the episode had been first-rate.

6. Maybe even the recipient's performance was not at fault, but the whole project was unproductive. Some thoroughly admirable efforts can produce negative results, or even no results at all.

7. Then there is the frustration when all has gone well and the results were positive, but nothing happened on the part of those who should then have come forward to take over: no public interest, no community support, no follow-through.

8. Finally, and back to the beginning of the list, the aim was shown to be unachievable, not meanly but magnificently so.

These, then, are the ways of failure, not to be sought or ignored, but to be confessed. And most of all, used. It is when foundations use their mistakes and disappointments, as they often do, that those things become part of the record of achievement by which they contribute to the well-being of the country.

D. Intangible Accomplishments: A Concluding Word

The list of benefits that society gains from the work of foundations is not exhausted by reference to tangible items of frequent profit and occasional loss. The intangibles are real, though by their very nature they often go unrecognized, unmentioned and unappreciated.

What I mean is this: Some of the best things foundations do are never credited to their account, even by the foundations themselves. Such things as listening, advising, criticizing, saying No, exploring and bringing people together.

The penance that a foundation person has to do for his unparalleled chance for affirmative action is being required to listen. He gets good at it—or maybe he doesn't, and gets sent off to some other job. A philanthropoid is, first, a listener. Unless he is to deny the essential nature of the field and organization he serves, he must make himself available to hear the hopes and needs of those around him. Nor is this quite the sedentary role it might first seem to be. To hear is to see, to expose oneself, even to touch. Thus foundation people do a lot of traveling as well as listening in the line of duty, and it all adds up in the impact foundations make on American life.

Quite often the advice of foundation officers is sought. Some of it, of course, is sycophantic, part of a general softening-up campaign. But it can also be sincere, on the justifiable ground that many a foundation manager is one or another kind of expert, and usually he was the expert before he became the manager. In any event, and even when sound advice was not really expected, it has often been supplied; for people who work in foundations, whether donors, trustees or staff, come by that fact to possess a body of experience and a set of perspectives that others find useful.

Criticism, though less often bargained for, can also be part of a foundation's valuable service. The simple arithmetic of any philanthropic fund dictates a negative answer to appeals more often than an affirmative one. Seldom, however, will an uncluttered No suffice. At least some tiny sliver of a reason must be given, and one that can be defended is better than one that can't. This often requires the foundation to tell the truth, or a portion of it. Except when the reason is altogether in house— no money left, no interest in the field or contrary to established policy—the explanation of the foundation's decision may need

187

to include some tactful criticism of the proposal. Whether or not always appreciated at the moment of reception, such criticism has often been of large help to the person, or the institution or the later development of the idea.

No, itself, can be fruitful. It is sometimes naively supposed that the way to get a grant is just to keep at it: the tenth time the answer will be Yes. The odds support no such proposition; the odds say the tenth answer will also be No. When someone successfully bucks the odds, it is because he has taken the earlier No to heart and improved his proposal accordingly. The proper punishment for some benighted critic who doesn't like what foundations do would be to make him read a comparable sheaf of project descriptions that foundations refused to do. Whether or not, as is sometimes claimed, saying No is an art, it is indeed an accomplishment.

All these things point toward exploration. To learn to listen hard enough to understand, to advise and criticize, to say No as well as Yes, require a person or a foundation to ponder. Is this the best way to accomplish the purpose? Are there other ways? Can the purpose itself be refined? Who else is concerned? What are they doing? Can they help us, or we help them? What are the likely consequences, and what will then be the next step? Is the job really worth doing? Will its being done well redound to the genuine benefit of the community? These are some of the questions that foundations ask in the course of their daily work, and the very act of asking moves things forward.

Finally, bringing people together: The Danforth Foundation is sometimes accused of believing in salvation through conferences, for it probably holds more meetings under its own auspices in the course of a year than any other foundation. But this is more a quirk of methodology than a distinctive policy. Most large foundations subscribe to togetherness, though their more usual course is to make a grant to some other agency to convene the meeting. Whether performed by the foundation's staff or by others, the gathering of people for the consideration of common interests is an extra dividend, a piece of philanthropic lagniappe. Some would have it that foundations are well fitted to play this role because they can exercise leverage upon

188

those who ought but might otherwise be reluctant to come. The absence of foundation pressure, however, may be as operative as its application; that is, foundations may succeed in bringing people together because they can more readily be accepted as neutral in the sponsorship of serious discussions than perhaps other public agencies. Whatever the reason, people meet with each other every day at the direct or indirect behest of foundations, by the twos, the scores and the thousands; and the resulting ferment, once full allowance is made for all the noisome chatter, is an inestimable boon to the spread of thought and sensitivity.

Tangibly and intangibly, foundations have done much of which they have cause to be proud. The good record has been made by hundreds, not by just a few. And as foundations themselves gain maturity in the doing of good—for the great majority are still quite young, and inexperienced in their role—the record of the future promises to be even more impressive than that of the past. We shall take a look at the future, and at what foundations must do in order to seize upon its promise; but first we must look at one special part of the immediate past that complicates the future, namely, the Tax Reform Act of 1969.

V

The Tax Reform Act of 1969

A. INTRODUCTION

THE Tax Reform Act is thought to have been a watershed for foundations. Up to that time they had seldom been given peculiar legislative attention, though they were subject, of course, to the same regulations that applied to all other charitable organizations. But in the 1969 Act new sections were added to the Internal Revenue Code to define and regulate "private foundations" and, incidentally, to separate them for the first time from other charitable agencies. It is a new set of ground rules, quite different from those of the past.[1]

Yet the way in which it is a watershed is understood differently both among foundations and in the public generally. Some feel that up to that time foundations were free, or at least possessed a relatively remarkable degree of freedom, whereas with the passage of the Act they became tightly regulated and controlled. Others feel that the difference will really be more psychological than real; that whereas before the Act foundations were pretty much ignored by government, hereafter they will be watched, though something as insidious as restrictive measures will seldom be necessary.

Some feel that the Act will put an end to financial shenanigans or to radical program activities. Others feel that little or no change will be discernible in these areas, either because little change was called for and the foundations were in pretty good

1. See TRA, *op. cit.*, Title I, Subtitle A, Act Section 101, "Private Foundations."

190

shape already, or because much greater change was called for
and the Act itself did not go far enough. For some observers
the Act itself is not the divide; rather, it is the new attitude
among foundations that the Act, its preparation and its follow-
through, have produced.[2]

It should also be noted that, in whatever way the Bill can be
said to be a watershed for foundations, its full effect on them
is still uncertain three years and more after the Congressional
debates and the final passage. Many of the regulations of the
Treasury Department, necessary for the interpretation and enforcement of the Bill, have not yet been issued. Until all Regulations are out, and are themselves clarified by the form and
character of enforcement that the Internal Revenue Service will
institute, an assessment of the effect of the bill on organized
philanthropy cannot fail to be in some part premature. The full
effect obviously cannot be known for quite a long time. One
must go ahead, then, and make the best judgment he can on
the basis of what is seen and known to date.

It may well be that the calendar year, 1969, much more than
the Tax Reform Act that Mr. Nixon signed on Decmber 30,
was the great dividing line for foundations between their past
and their future. That is, the process of debate, and the role
that the foundations themselves played in the ten-and-one-half-
month-long discussions in Congress represented the watershed.

2. For a variety of analyses of, and reactions to, the portion of the
Act dealing with foundations, see: *Foundations and the Tax Reform Act
of 1969, op. cit.,* especially chapters by Laurens Williams, Robert H.
Mulreany, Thomas A. Troyer, and Norman A. Sugarman; Kutner, *op.
cit.,* chap. xii; Report of Peterson Commission, *op. cit., passim;* Thomas
A. Troyer, "Private Foundations and the Tax Reform Act of 1969: New
Program Restrictions; Business Limitations," *Proceedings of the New
York University Twenty-Ninth Annual Institute on Federal Taxation,*
Albany, N.Y., Matthew Bender & Co., 1971, pp. 1909–1977; Homer C.
Wadsworth, "Effects of Tax Reform Act of 1969 on Role of Private
Foundations," Tax Institute of America Symposium, Washington, D.C.,
December 2–3, 1971, MSS; "Foundations on Trial," addresses by Alan
Cranston and Alan Pifer, Council on Foundations Conference, San Fran-
cisco, May 28 & 29, 1970, pamphlet published by Council on Founda-
tions, New York City; Stanley S. Weithorn, "Summary of the Tax Re-
form Act as it Affects Foundations," *Foundation News,* May–June, 1970,
pp. 85–89; Leonard L. Silverstein, "TRA 1969 and the Foundation's
Lawyer," *Non-Profit Report,* June, 1971, pp. 1–5, and July, 1971, pp. 5–7.

In mid-February, 1969, most foundations did not know they were in for serious trouble; in late December, 1969, many foundations were greatly alarmed at what had happened. The story of the intervening months is the story of the change in temper among foundations themselves as well as the sharpening of attitudes in the general public.

The House Ways and Means Committee began taking testimony about foundations on February 18, 1969. The first person to speak was Representative Patman and before any foundation representative got to the stand, a sharply critical mood had been set. Leading off on February 19 was Representative Rooney, to complain about the thinly veiled support that the Frederic W. Richmond Foundation had given to a defeated political rival, Frederic W. Richmond. Mr. Patman asked rhetorically, "Are the giant foundations on the road to becoming political machines?"[3]

There was no coordination in the testimony of foundation representatives. Knowing that Mr. Wilbur Mills, Chairman of the Ways and Means Committee, intended to look into the subject, a number of foundations had offered to testify, and their representatives came as individuals in order to try to present a balanced picture of how foundations were handling their resources and what they were doing on behalf of the general welfare. Nearly every foundation representative, however, felt that he was being treated as a hostile witness, unless his testimony were simply being ignored; and as the records of the hearings show, some foundation people were given an unfriendly grilling.[4]

How far the House Ways and Means Committee was prepared to go in its proposed legislation was not revealed until the announcement in May of the tentative bill. The relations of Justices Douglas and Fortas to foundations, noted in Chapter III above, had recently been spread in the newspapers, and the line of Committee questioning to which McGeorge Bundy and others were subjected had been widely reported. Even then, foundations were hardly prepared for the revelation on May 27 that, among other restrictive or even punitive measures, foundations

---

3. Ways and Means Committee Hearings, *op. cit.,* Part I, pp. 12–78 (Patman) and 213–237 (Rooney). Quotation from Patman is on p. 15.
4. *Ibid., passim.*

would not be allowed henceforth to make fellowship or scholarship grants directly to any individuals.[5]

One of the useful results of the Ways and Means announcement was that it alerted foundations to the danger of highly restrictive legislation and thus to the desirability of coordinating their efforts so as to keep this from happening. For several years the executive officers of a dozen or so large foundations had held informal discussions of subjects of mutual interest. This Foundation Executives' Group, which was not formally organized and had always taken the position that it was really a non-group, began to meet more frequently in the summer of 1969, in order to prepare coordinated testimony for the Senate Finance Committee, when its hearings on the tax bill were to be held later in the fall. Not all the foundations in the group decided to participate. Most vigorous in the coordination of their positions were, alphabetically, Carnegie, Danforth, Ford and Rockefeller. Participation was not limited to these, however, for persons from Duke, R. K. Mellon, Rockefeller Brothers, Sloan and occasionally one or two others lent their advice. Representatives from smaller funds such as the Irwin-Sweeney-Miller and the Cummins Engine Foundations of Columbus, Indiana, and from the Council on Foundations played a large and useful part. Staff members and lawyers of the cooperating foundations worked together in developing constructive positions on the various ideas and proposals then being considered in Congress.

Accordingly, when the Senate Finance Committee began hearings in the fall, this group of cooperating foundation people was able to present a much more cogent and constructive position. The statements of what came to be called the Foundations' Coordinated Testimony Group were subsequently published by the Foundation Center under the title, *Foundations and the Tax Bill*. Though only a few foundations participated in this activity, their joint testimony was widely hailed as a sound position and a constructive effort on behalf of philanthropy in general.[6]

In the meantime, the final version of the House Committee's Bill, published in August, differed in some important respects

5. Press release, House Committee on Ways and Means, May 27, 1969.
6. See *Foundations and the Tax Bill, op. cit.*

from the tentative version announced in May. Most of the differences, including the elimination of the absolute prohibition of grants to individuals, were in the direction of common sense.

Before the Senate Finance Committee had completed its work, Senator Albert Gore succeeded in attaching an amendment that would have limited foundations to a forty-year life span. When the Bill with this amendment came to the Senate floor, the Coordinated Testimony Group with the help of other foundations and various organizations of foundation recipients worked successfully to defeat it.[7]

Thereafter the Conference Committee hammered out compromises between the House and Senate versions, and Mr. Nixon signed the Act the day before New Year's Eve. It could have been much worse, and the foundations helped to sidetrack some of the more extreme proposals that had been suggested en route.

B. BENEFITS OF THE ACT

The sections of the Tax Reform Act that applied to foundations were, therefore, jerry-built. Representative Mills and his Ways and Means Committee had one batch of fish to fry, Senator Long and his Finance Committee another. The Bill that was passed in each house was of course a considerable compromise, and the final version that got through the Conference Committee was even more so. Many have complained about the unclear language, the lapses in logic and other faults. Surely this is to be expected, however, when the final Act was necessarily the outcome of a complicated process of accommodation to the widely diverse points of view of both proponents and opponents of foundations. In any event, and with the beginning of the new year, the job was done, and foundations began to look at the results.

The initial thing to be said is that the Bill, on balance, is strong and useful legislation, embodying requirements for the behavior of foundations that are needed and long overdue.

The first benefit is the series of firm prohibitions against self-

7. See *Congressional Record:* Senate, Dec. 4, 1969, pp. S15729–S15737; Dec. 5, 1969, pp. S15755–S15760.

dealing interlocking directorates, speculative investments, excess business holdings and similar organizational or personal relationships for the sake of private advantage. As was noted in Chapter II above, it used to be possible for foundations to be manipulated to the advantage of individuals, families or companies. But the Tax Reform Act tried to put a stop to all that, and came remarkably close to doing so. In section after section the problems that the Treasury Report had noted five years previously were made the subject of firm and helpful legislation, and the sections against various types of self-dealing are to be thoroughly applauded.[8]

Another important provision of the Bill is the requirement for full disclosure. The old Form 990-A has now been revised so that henceforth all foundations will have to report fuller information than was necessary in the past. Moreover, each foundation must provide opportunity for the public to see its annual report, either by publication or by availability for inspection at the foundation's office. Foundations simply will not be able to hide as was once possible.[9]

The requirements of the Act, however, are not as complete in this area as is desirable for the good of the foundation field itself. Other steps beyond what the law requires must be taken before the public will have been given a full chance to understand the work of foundations. For example, there is no requirement for uniform standards of financial reporting, whereas this is an area of great need. At the present time, any comparison of statistics for foundations is risky business, for there is no consistent basis used by them for determining assets, income, grants, programs and administrative expenses. Moreover, though the new law will require a mountain of information from each foundation and thus will increase greatly the amount of time and energy that a foundation must give to the preparation of its return, it may still be that the information will be incomplete and that more should be required. For example, the Peterson Commission feels that there should be "more detailed reporting of investment activities . . . a fuller description of grant purposes

8. TRA, *op. cit.*, Code Sections 4941, 4943, 4944, 4946.
9. *Ibid.*, Act Sections 101(d) and 101(e).

[and] procedures for awarding grants [and] for determining that the funds have been used for grant purposes."[10] In the main, however, the Act's requirement for full reporting is on the right track.

Two other benefits that must be credited to the Bill are, strangely, omissions. That is, in one or another of its earlier versions the Act included restrictions or provisions that would have been highly disadvantageous to foundations. Thus the fact that the final version of the Act as signed by Mr. Nixon omitted these negative items can be looked upon by foundations as an immensely helpful development. These two happy omissions, referred to above, are the House Committee's early provision that would have prohibited all grants to individuals and the Senate Committee's proposal to impose a forty-year limitation on the life of foundations. The plight of foundations would be a great deal worse if these provisions had not been defeated.

Here again, at least one of these benefits-by-absence is less than complete. The law does indeed allow the making of grants to individuals, and it is altogether proper that the government be concerned that such grants be made on an "objective and non-discriminatory basis," as the law requires. But the further requirement that the Internal Revenue Service give advance approval of each foundation's program or programs suggests a methodology that could cause both foundations and governmental agencies a great deal of unnecessary trouble.[11]

This matter of grants to individuals is a major concern for the Danforth Foundation, because of its several programs of fellowships and awards involving thousands of people each year. Congress made it clear that they wanted to put an end to the practice of bestowing arbitrary and even whimsical grants on individuals on a person-by-person basis. It has already been noted that, because a few grants of this sort by other foundations had been widely criticized, there was danger for a while that all grants to individuals would be prohibited. But when the final Bill was put together the threat had been removed, and grants

10. Report of Peterson Commission, *op. cit.,* p. 154.
11. TRA, *op. cit.,* Code Section 4945(d)(3) and (g). See also Troyer, *op. cit.,* pp. 1926–1937.

196

to individuals of the sort that the Danforth Foundation has long practiced still seemed to be approvable.

But the words "seem" and "approvable" suggest a measure of uncertainty. The explanation rests on a matter of timing. The Bill makes it possible for programs of grants to individuals, carefully defined, publicly announced and impartially adminis- tered, to be approved by the Internal Revenue Service, on the basis of Regulations and guidelines to be issued by the Treasury Department. At the moment of writing, however, final Regula- tions on this point have not yet been announced. But a "tem- porary regulation" of Treasury, thoughtfully issued in January, 1970, so as not to embarrass either donors or recipients by a long delay, advised that existing well-framed programs of grants to individuals should be considered "approvable" until the final Regulations were to come out.[12]

The Danforth Foundation, therefore, has proceeded with its programs of fellowships and awards, in the confidence that when final Regulations are issued approval will be forthcoming in due course. Since we long ago abandoned the practice of making grants to individuals one by one, or on the basis of any one person's say-so, we expect that this feature of the Bill will pose no difficulty for the continuation of our present programs. The way the Act leaves this matter, therefore, is in the main an asset, and most foundations sponsoring programs of grants to individuals, including Danforth, are moving ahead as if there is no uncertainty in respect to what the law is or how it will be enforced. Yet it will be helpful when the question of grants to individuals is finally cleared up and uniformly understood.

Another feature of the Act that, on balance, is probably beneficial is the institution of an audit fee. Many foundation people, to be sure, opposed the establishment of such a fee on the ground that it was an invasion of the principle of tax ex- emption. Other foundation people, however, indicated in the Congressional hearings that such a fee seemed proper. The justi- fication for a tax of any sort is that foundations ought to be expected to defray the costs of regular Government audits of

12. Temporary Regulation para. 143.1(c), adopted by Treasury De- partment 7022, January 19, 1970.

their books; and many were strongly in favor of the establishment of regular auditing procedures.

But the largest amount estimated by Treasury officials or by others outside government as needed for the cost of periodically auditing all foundations was roughly 2 percent of their annual income. The Bill, however, requires a payment of 4 percent, and since this amount is considerably more than is required for such a purpose, the institution of the audit fee or excise tax takes on punitive overtones. The tip-off that punishment was at least partly intentional is in the Bill's failure to earmark the proceeds of this tax for auditing activities. The money will go straight into the general revenues of the Government.[13]

A second reason for deploring what otherwise could have been a sound move is that the tax is to be figured on annual income rather than on market value of a foundation's holdings. The less its endowment produces, the less it will have to pay—which puts a premium on depressed earnings, and thus penalizes in comparison those foundations that seek a larger income for the ultimate benefit of their recipients. Foundation representatives tried to make this case, to no avail. The fact of the matter is that it isn't properly described as either audit or excise. It is an income tax, the first ever placed on a charitable organization.

The outcome, therefore, is that all foundations are now having to pay the 4 percent tax, and thus have that much less to use on behalf of the interests, institutions and programs they seek to serve. Ironically, the ultimate penalty will fall on recipients, not on the foundations themselves.[14] The deleterious effects are so serious as almost to wipe out the benefit of the basic idea.

Another bittersweet feature, barely on the credit side of the ledger, is "expenditure responsibility," as inadequately defined by the Bill. Nobody should object to the requirement that a foundation must see that grants are spent for the purposes for which they are made, must get "full and complete reports"

13. TRA, *op. cit.*, Code Section 4940.
14. For opinions and facts on the 4 percent excise tax, see Report of Peterson Commission, *op. cit.*, p. 167; *Foundations and the Tax Bill, op. cit.*, chaps. II & III; *Foundations and the Tax Reform Act of 1969, op. cit.*, pp. 7–8, 40; and "Foundation Excise Payments," *Non-Profit Report*, July, 1971, pp. 1–2, and further listings in succeeding issues.

from most grantees, and must make "full and detailed reports" to the I.R.S. But these three worthy duties are hamstrung by uncertainties: When, and when not, must the grantor exercise "expenditure responsibility"? Why the differences? What is a "full and complete report"? When is one sufficiently "detailed"? How much kibitzing must be performed? And suffered? If enforcement gets picayune, who will want to receive or to make a grant?[15]

Finally, the pay-out requirement that the Act imposes on foundations should generally be accounted a boon, but again, one with flaws in it.[16] This question of pay-out was perhaps the most unexpected and radical feature of the new legislation on foundations. As explained earlier, it will have almost no effect on the Danforth Foundation, for we are already spending at a rate higher than the 6 percent of market value of assets that the Act requires be attained by 1975, after a phase-in. But only a handful of foundations are in this happy situation. The overwhelming majority will find that this requirement will force a sharp change in their expenditure policy. Some foundations are already complaining about it and at least two, Kellogg and Pew, have tried to get legislative relief.[17] The actual figure is bound to be arbitrary and 5 percent, say, or even less, might be sounder, all things considered. Yet six percent does not seem to some foundation people to be too high, granting the legitimacy of encouraging foundations to make appropriate contributions to the charitable causes they were established to serve. ·

The Peterson Commission bears considerable responsibility for the inclusion of this item in the Act. Mr. Peterson himself testified before the Senate Finance Committee in October, 1969, to the effect that foundations should "be required to

15. TRA, *op. cit.*, Code Section 4945(d)(4) and (h)(1)(2)(3). For comment see Troyer, *op. cit.*, pp. 1937–1958.
16. TRA, *op. cit.*, Code Section, 4942.
17. See Eileen Shanahan, "House Tax Panel Eases Rule on Foundation Spending," *New York Times*, Oct. 14, 1971. For recent changes in pay-out percentages, as allowed by TRA Code Section 4942(e)(3) and fixed by the Secretary of the Treasury, see footnote no. 36, chap. II, above, p. 64.

make annual distributions to charity in the range of 6 to 8% of their asset market values." The Commission's reasoning was: "The annual total return of a wide variety of balanced investment funds over the previous ten years was about 9 to 10%. Allowing for an annual rate of inflation of 2 to 3%, we felt that a pay-out of 6 to 8% would permit a reasonably managed foundation to maintain its size in *real* dollars."[18]

Yet the final result did not altogether please the Commission, for there are flaws in the way in which Congress set up this provision. For example, the actual pay-out requirement is an either-or proposition: A foundation must spend 6 percent of its market value assets or all of its annual net income, excluding long-term capital gains, whichever is higher. A definition of income that excludes long-term capital gains represents a distortion of the central intent of this provision, for "the income test will tend to cause foundations to invest in gross stocks or other appreciating assets in order to receive return in a form which is not 'income.' "[19]

It was the Peterson Commission's position, therefore, that "the only correct yardstick for measuring investment performance is the *total rate of return*—the measure used by practically all mutual funds, profit-sharing funds, pension funds and other endowments. It includes interest, dividends, realized and unrealized capital gains. .. A distribution requirement based solely on asset size ... would put the emphasis where it belongs: on the overall investment performance of the foundation, not on the form of the return it receives."[20]

Other aspects of the pay-out requirement as required by the law are subject to question: How and on what criteria should the 6 percent standard be changed from time to time? Does the Bill allow the Treasury Department sufficient latitude in setting an annual pay-out percentage that will achieve the objective of insuring substantial philanthropic distributions? Do older foundations have enough time to solve problems of divestiture

18. Report of Peterson Commission, *op. cit.*, p. 147. (Italics are the Commission's.) One member of the Commission dissented from these pay-out recommendations; for his views see pp. 158–159.

19. *Ibid.*, p. 149.

20. *Ibid.* (Italics are the Commission's.)

200

or diversification of assets which the pay-out requirement forces upon them? Should not new foundations also be given some phase-in? Questions remain, and further legislation may be necessary in order to put this new feature of the tax laws on a thoroughly sound and defensible basis.[21] But in the eyes of this writer the institution of a pay-out requirement is on the right track.

C. HANDICAPS AND PROBLEMS

The benefits that the legislation has brought are only one side of the matter. The other side is the body of handicaps that the Act has thrown in the way not merely of a few wrongdoers but of the great company of reputable foundations. Some of these have already been mentioned, as flaws that keep helpful sections of the Bill from being as constructive as they might have been. Some of the faults are minor, some of the problems raised can undoubtedly be solved, and some of the objections that foundations make have only secondary significance. But a few of the difficulties are of major proportions.

First is the not-so-simple matter of language. The Bill is hard to understand; its various provisions and requirements are difficult to fathom; and one can readily appreciate that many a large foundation's staff of professionals and many a small foundation's donor and lawyer will simply throw up their hands in despair. Not even a tax bill, whose broth must inevitably be prepared by too many cooks, need be as ill-phrased and illogical as this one is in parts.

The very definition is beclouded. The Bill sets up various categories of "public" and "private" foundations, the specifications for which do not conform to the normal uses of language. Most but not all of the foundations we are discussing fall into the "private non-operating" classification, and most but not all of those in that pigeonhole are of the type we are considering. Read that sentence again, please. It really does make sense, more so than Section 509 in which the "private foundation" is

---

21. See *ibid.*, pp. 147–151; Williams in *Foundations and the Tax Reform Act of 1969, op. cit.*, pp. 8–12.

"defined." In any event, it is as far as we need to go in commenting on this unnecessary complexity.[22]

Besides faults already noted, many other objections can be raised. For example, the Bill includes a catch-all prohibition against expenditures that are not in furtherance of the exempt purposes for a charitable organization. The intent is to permit only genuine and proper administrative expenditures, and compensation for foundation managers is limited to "reasonable amounts." Though the intent is impeccable, the whole business is so fuzzy that sound enforcement is undoubtedly going to be difficult.

As the Bill now stands, it would seem quite possible that unjustified administrative expenses could often get by, whereas justified ones might very well be called up short. It is highly desirable, of course, for all foundations to practice economy of administration, but an unsympathetic or simply ignorant enforcement of the imprecise regulations of the Act might very well prove to be a serious handicap to the wise administration of many a reputable foundation. This could be especially true if the foundation, as is the case with Danforth, is an operating as well as a grant-making agency, with programs of its own administered by members of its professional staff. Such foundations will necessarily spend more for administration of substantial in-house activities than would be the case if their sole activities consisted in grant-making. The Bill seems to be deficient in allowing for a mature definition and enforcement of standards of administrative expense.[23]

In many sections of the Bill sanctions against errors and mistakes seem to be unusually severe. In defining penalties to be imposed on those guilty of misbehavior, the Bill gives the impression of being a highly punitive document, and some have suggested that the level of fines and other penalties is so high

22. TRA, *op. cit.,* Code Section 509. Consider, for example, this deathless piece of prose: "For purposes of paragraph (3), an organization described in paragraph (2) shall be deemed to include an organization described in section 501(c)(4),(5), or (6) which would be described in paragraph (2) if it were an organization described in section 501(c)(3)." See also Williams, *op. cit.,* pp. 4–7.

23. See Report of Peterson Commission, *op. cit.,* pp. 156–157.

as to make it difficult for foundations to attract able trustees and staff members. For example, the tax on improper grants, or on what the Act calls "taxable expenditures," is 10 percent of the expenditure for the foundation, plus 2½ percent for each manager who had a part in the decision. The second time around it jumps to 100 percent and 50 percent respectively; and the foundation is not allowed to pay any manager's tax for him. Managers may be both trustees and staff. Though hedged about with various limitations as to how wilful the culprit and how heavy the fine, the sanctions still wear a harsh and unfriendly countenance.[24]

Of a piece with these and other obstacles thrown in the way of existing foundations is the inhibiting effect of the Bill in regard to the establishment of new ones and to the practice of philanthropy in general. As for the so-called "birth control" effect, many commentators have agreed with the Peterson Commission's judgment: "Contributions to grant-making foundations in the future will be discouraged by provisions in the tax law—this because the provisions make contributions to a grant-making foundation a less attractive prospect for a wealthy individual than it has been in the past."[25]

The audit fee or excise tax, noted above, is one evidence. Two other signs are the treatment accorded to gifts of long-term capital gain property, which is the way most foundations are set up, and donations of control stock in a corporation, which is also a common practice. For the first, the Bill provides less tax incentive for contributions of appreciated property to foundations than to other charitable organizations. For the second, the limitation on foundation ownership of corporate control stock seems to be greater than needed in order to guarantee that the donor will not use his foundation to protect his control of the corporation. In the time since the Act was passed, the rate of establishment of new foundations seems to have decreased sharply and the rate of dissolution of old founda-

24. TRA, *op. cit.*, Code Section 4945(a)(b). See also Troyer, *op. cit.*, pp. 1963–1967.
25. Report of Peterson Commission, *op. cit.*, p. 165; see also pp. 166–168, 176.

tions has increased at perhaps an even greater ratio.[26] Whatever Congress intended, the result of the passage of the new legislation is that philanthropy through foundations has been greatly discouraged.

The most serious issue raised for foundations by any part of the Tax Reform Act is the prohibition against "any attempt to influence any legislation . . ." If the sentence stopped there, no one would have legitimate ground for objection, for surely a foundation ought to stay out of politics. Furthermore, a prohibition against a foundation's substantial direct political activity was already on the books.

But the sentence continues: ". . . any attempt to influence any legislation through an attempt to affect the opinion of the general public or any segment thereof."[27] The latter part of that sentence raises problems as dangerous for the work of philanthropic agencies as have ever been posed in this country.

In other words, the language of the Bill seems to suggest that "an attempt to affect [public] opinion" is an improper activity for foundations, unless it is in some field that conceivably would never need be subject to legislation. If it were related to legislation, it would be a "taxable expenditure" incurring heavy penalties.

But what would be left for foundations to do? What fields could a foundation work in safely? They might well believe that they must eschew working in any field of the social sciences, perhaps also the humanities, and even the natural sciences, at least in their applicability to human problems. Conservation of national resources? Air and water pollution? Beautification of highways? Such innocent-sounding activities would be too dangerous, for they would sooner or later touch on legislation.

This is admittedly an extreme reading of the danger. The point being made, however, is that the specific language of the Bill is most harsh, and if the outcome proves to be less restric-

26. See, for example, F. Emerson Andrews' judgment that "under the restrictions newly imposed by the Tax Reform Act of 1969, it is probable that the formation of new foundations is being slowed and many existing foundations will be terminated or combined." (FD-4, "Introduction," p. viii).

27. TRA, *op. cit.,* Code Section 4945(e)(1).

tive than here suggested, it will turn on a lenient interpretation, not on what the words actually say. If the words are construed quite narrowly, foundations might as well close up shop.

If similar phrases were to be enacted to apply to other tax-exempt agencies such as universities, churches and community agencies, they too would have to shut down. All such non-profit institutions, including foundations, are dedicated to change and improvement in some aspect of the social order; and sooner or later, therefore, nearly every facet of their work will inevitably touch upon a topic that could be expected to show up on the agenda of some legislative body, local, state or national. The prohibition against "an attempt to affect [public] opinion," narrowly construed, would allow literally no room for the continuance of the constructive work of foundations or, by implication and possible extension, of other tax-exempt organizations.

Take the grants of the Danforth Foundation as a case in point. We work, by choice, in the fields of education and urban affairs, because we believe that problems in these fields are crucial for our time, and that even though our efforts are bound to be minuscule in comparison with those of Government, it is important that private as well as public energies and resources be brought to bear.

In our work we have in mind the molding of public opinion, local or national, not merely on behalf of the project itself but also on behalf of the purposes or goals that that project seeks to serve. To support a socially purposeless project would be wasteful and thus preposterous. (An endowed home for indigent cats has sometimes been the suggestion of the cynic.) The pursuit of worthy purposes could and often does lead to a recognition that changes are needed in regional or national life, and thus eventually to new legislation. To disavow "an attempt to affect the opinion of the general public" would mean, for us, to withdraw from the fields of education and urban affairs, at the very time that private as well as public efforts in these fields are most needed.

This point of view was presented in my testimony before the Senate Finance Committee in October, 1969, as part of the total testimony by foundation representatives on various parts

205

of the proposed Tax Reform Act. A similar position in respect to the "effect of program limitations" on foundations was presented by Homer C. Wadsworth, President of the Kansas City Association of Trusts and Foundations, and the total group of twenty-one witnesses present on behalf of the Foundations' Coordinated Testimony Group concurred in our position. Wadsworth and I gave a number of illustrations of recent grants, of the Kansas City Association and the Danforth Foundation respectively, as being representative of those of other foundations that would be called in question by a rigid interpretation of the Bill's restrictive language.[28]

Illustrations could as readily be furnished by countless other foundations from many fields of social concern and human endeavor—population, quality of environment, the arts, public broadcasting, regional planning, the administration of justice and on and on. Rare would be the foundation, small as well as large, that could not give a multitude of examples—not the support of politically partisan efforts but of rational, impartial studies and projects. Such grants are not aimless but are directed toward making a difference. Differences are brought about in our society in many ways, to be sure, but one of the important ways which any foundation would be loath to forego is through the changed attitudes and opinions of the public, which ought to, and eventually do, get incorporated in legislative changes, locally or nationally. It would be tragic for America if this kind of activity by foundations were to have to be discontinued.

For all our efforts, however, the language of the Bill was not substantially changed. Yet the wording of the explanation that accompanied the Bill seemed to presage a less rigid position or foreshadow a non-punitive interpretation by the Treasury Department and the Internal Revenue Service. Referring to the offending passage, Section 4945 (e), the Joint Committee stated that "this provision ... does not prevent the examination of broad social, economic, and similar problems of the type the

28. *Foundations and the Tax Bill, op. cit.,* pp. 72–88. See also Troyer, *op. cit.,* pp. 1914–1921; "Notes Regulating the Political Activity of Foundations," *Harvard Law Review,* June, 1970, pp. 1843–1869.

government could be expected to deal with ultimately, even though this does not permit lobbying on matters which have been proposed for legislative action."[29]

For many months no Regulations or guidelines were issued for this section of the Act. This left foundations quite uncertain what to do. Some responded to the situation nervously, even fearfully, trying to make sure they did nothing that could incur the displeasure of the Internal Revenue Service when it came to enforce this strange and ugly provision. Other foundations proceeded with their normal work, in the confidence that the regulations of the Internal Revenue Service, when finally issued, would be considerably less harsh and more enabling than the bare words of the Act might suggest. This latter was the response of the Danforth Foundation, as we announced in our *Annual Report* for 1969–1970. That Report says, ". . . we propose to continue the general direction of our efforts, in full compliance with what we take to be the spirit of the Bill," even though the language of the Bill may seem contradictory.[30]

Now at long last the proposed Regulations on this part of the Bill have been issued. In respect to "attempts to affect the opinion of the general public," the Regulations read: ". . . any expenditure paid or incurred by a private foundation in an attempt to influence any legislation through an attempt to affect the opinion of the general public or any segment thereof is a taxable expenditure."[31] There is no way to get the nasty language completely out of the Bill.

But from that point on, the Regulations try to soften the blow: "For purposes of this paragraph, expenditures for examinations and discussions of broad social, economic, and similar problems are not taxable even if the problems are of the type with which government would be expected to deal ultimately." This humane loophole enables the Regulations to go on to say:

29. *General Explanation of the Tax Reform Act of 1969,* H.R. 13270, 91st Congress, Public Law 91–172, Washington, D.C., Government Printing Office, 1970, p. 49.

30. *The Danforth Foundation Annual Report, 1969–70,* p. 13.

31. See "Foundation Excise Taxes: Taxes on Taxable Expenditures," para. 53.4945, *Federal Register,* Vol. 36, No. 55, March 20, 1971, pp. 5357–5367. Quotation is from p. 5360.

"Thus, the term 'any attempt to influence any legislation' does not include public discussion, the general subject of which is also the subject of legislation before a legislative body, so long as such discussion does not address itself to the merits of a specific legislative proposal."[32]

That the Regulations are indeed trying to find a way around the harshness of the Act's provision is indicated by the example given. The Regulations say: "For example, a private foundation may, without incurring tax under section 4945, present a discussion of environmental pollution, a problem being considered by Congress and various State legislatures, provided the discussion is not directly addressed to specific legislation being considered."[33]

Further chipping off the sharp edges of the provisions is achieved by the exceptions which the Regulations allow. The lead sentence about the "taxable expenditure" of "an attempt to influence any legislation ..." begins with the comment that all this taxing for misbehavior is to take effect "except as provided in paragraph (d)(1) of this section [relating to the making available of nonpartisans analysis, study or research]." Section (d)(1) says, "Engaging in nonpartisan analysis, study, or research and making available to the public or to governmental bodies the results of such work do not constitute carrying on propaganda, or otherwise attempting, to influence legislation."[34]

In the next paragraph "nonpartisan analysis, study, or research" is defined to mean "an independent and objective exposition of a particular subject matter, including any activity which is 'educational' within the meaning of ... this chapter. The analysis, study, or research may contain recommendations, findings, or conclusions, if there is a sufficiently full and fair exposition of the pertinent facts to enable the public or an individual to form an independent opinion or conclusion."[35]

All of this is meant to be helpful. And all of the ensuing

32. *Ibid.*
33. *Ibid.*
34. *Ibid.*
35. *Ibid.*

208

i-dotting and t-crossing does indeed humanize and liberalize
the wording of the law, for any foundation staff members or
trustees who have the time, wit and patience to plow through it.

But there is no way to escape the fact that the exceptions as
allowed by the Regulations are themselves subject to nerve-
racking imprecisions of definition and judgment. A study of an
important social issue that might otherwise be thought to have
fallen under the proscription of the law, because it contains
"recommendations, findings, or conclusions," can still escape
the law's penalty if it appears to be "a sufficiently full and fair
exposition"—but there is no way to make those judgmental
words, "sufficiently," "full" and "fair," more precise than they
in fact are. Though the Regulations try hard, they cannot fully
resolve the awkward issue that the base position of the Act in
respect to influencing public opinion is ill-conceived, surpass-
ingly negative and impossible either to interpret or enforce.

A good example is furnished in the section advising how to
put out a "nonpartisan analysis" in sections, say, on a TV
series. This is approvable, the Regulations state, even if one
part is not quite as non-partisan as the whole package—in
which case, however, one must let folks know ahead of time.
Otherwise there will be trouble. "A determination that a broadcast or publication is part of a series will ordinarily not be
made on the basis of after-the-fact representations, but will
ordinarily require: a) A public announcement before each
broadcast or publication that it is a part of a series; and b)
The existence of plans, scripts, working outlines, or similar
documents for such a series that predate the actual presenta-
tions. If a private foundation times or channels a part of a series
which is described in this subdivision in a manner designed to
influence the general public or the action of a legislative body
with respect to a specific legislative proposal in violation of
section 4945 (d)(1), the expense of preparing and distributing
such part of the analysis, study, or research will be a taxable
expenditure under this section."[36]

Helpful? Not quite. So what does one do? He tries to make
sure that no part of any series is going to be less non-partisan

36. *Ibid*

than any other part, and if this is tricky, then he gives up the idea of treating the matter in a series. To be on the safe side, he probably gives up the idea altogether. When it takes this much minute attention, why bother?

There are long sections, with numerous and lengthy examples, on "making available results of analysis, study or research," "technical advice or assistance," and "decisions affecting the powers, duties, etc., of a private foundation."[37] When one has pushed through to the end of the regulations that deal simply with this one matter alone, he realizes that even though the Internal Revenue Service does indeed make a laudable effort to enable the legitimate activities of foundations to continue, the small-minded meanness and suspicion that went into the framing of the original prohibitory phrases in the Act still prevail.

D. RESULTS OF THE ACT:

So where does it all come out?

In a strange sense it seems that many of the benefits which the Bill provides are flawed by being less wise or less sound than they should have been, and many of the handicaps are diluted by humane aspects that make them less serious than they might otherwise have been. The benefits are not very good, the handicaps are not too bad. Strike a balance, and the whole thing is at least bearable. If some people are highly critical of its seriously negative provisions, other people have been equally highly critical that the Act simply does not go far enough in regulating and thus in changing the behavior of foundations.

The fact of the matter is, the majority of the large foundations are not complaining about the deleterious effects of the Bill in as audible a way as they and others had first expected they might. Not only is it the case that knowledgeable people have judged the Bill to be bearable; it is further the case that foundations are in fact living with it quite well.[38]

37. *Ibid.,* pp. 5360–5361.
38. See, for example, *op. cit.:* ". . . most experienced foundation people, trustees as well as managers, are inclined to the view that

210

It is here, however, that there seems to be a considerable discrepancy in attitude. Many foundation executives are indeed making their peace with the provisions of the Bill but are still deeply annoyed with Congress. Take for example the point of view of Alan Pifer, President of the Carnegie Corporation, who played a leading part in the testimony of foundation people before Congress and who on several occasions has pointed out that the Bill "did address itself to some real problems" and that the outcome is going to be beneficial in some regards for all foundations. Certainly it is true that, during his presidency, Carnegie itself has continued to exercise a role of major leadership in the field of organized philanthropy and has not allowed the restrictive aspects of the Bill to reduce the effectiveness and imaginativeness of its own work.

Yet in a speech to the Conference of the Council on Foundations, in San Francisco, May 29, 1970, he referred to "events of the past year" in language that was sharp and even a little bitter. "It was a period during which foundations were kicked in the shins and had their noses bloodied, and consequently we who work for them tend now to harbor an understandable sense of injustice."[39]

He then gives chapter and verse: "We resent the unfairness and shortsightedness of some features of the legislation and the extra administrative burden these will cause us. We resent the irrational emphasis placed by the Congress on a few uncharacteristic instances of administrative caprice in foundations and the excessive attention given to a few egregious cases of real abuse, while the overall positive record of foundations in American life was ignored. We resent the impression left with the public as the result of the legislation, that foundations were simply indicted, tried, found guilty and punished—just like that. We resent the tax on foundations, which will drain some 50 million dollars from charity each year.

"We recall our surprise and disappointment at the failure of a Republican Administration to recognize that the attack on

the 1969 Act can be lived with comfortably ... the application of the 1969 Act to date has created less difficulty than was expected." (p. 3)

39. Pifer, "Foundations on Trial," *op. cit.*, pp. 12–13.

private foundations was at bottom an attack on the private sector. And finally, we remember our distress at the unsympathetic tone of the President's comments on foundations in his statement at the signing of the Tax Reform Act."[40]

Many a foundation executive says a hearty Amen. Take Mr. Nixon's comments, for example: Noting that "tax-free foundations were brought under much closer Federal scrutiny," the President praised the result by saying that "Congressional consideration of this matter reflected a deep and wholly legitimate concern about the role of foundations in our national life."[41] "Deep" is neutral enough, but "wholly legitimate" was resented because it sounded as if Mr. Nixon condoned all the excessive expressions of "concern" that Congress had produced.

The real harm that the Act has done is psychological, not substantive. This is the explanation for such a statement as Pifer's, and for the resentment among foundation people in larger measure than seemingly the negative features of the Act could justify.

Chief among the results of the Act, then, must be noted not so much what foundations have done or have had done to them, but what they feel. They have been made to look upon themselves, as the Peterson Commission suggested, as " 'second class' charitable organizations."[42] Because they are at a relative disadvantage in comparison with other charitable organizations, by virtue of the 4 percent excise tax and other provisions of the law, they have sometimes taken on the look of apologetic, hang-dog agencies that are either not sure of the way the public feels toward them or *are* sure that the public doesn't like them. More serious than all the actual hobbles and handicaps of the new law is the inferiority complex that it seems to have given many foundations.

Another psychological result of the Act, paralleling the self-doubt among foundations, is the feeling of confidence it has given to their critics. Whereas once upon a time it was possible

40. *Ibid.*, p. 13.
41. "Nixon's Statement on Signing Tax Bill," *New York Times,* December 31, 1969.
42. Report of Peterson Commission, *op. cit.,* p. 45.

to pooh-pooh the critics because they were nearly always strange, hare-brained characters, the events of the last few years in Congress, culminating in the passage of the Tax Reform Act, have made criticism of foundations respectable.

It is those who would defend foundations who are now looked upon as somewhat strange. Castigating foundations is the latest fad, and anybody searching around for bandwagons is sure to climb on. For example, Governor Wallace has discovered the political hay to be made with his admirers out of scold-the-rich rhetoric; and when he discusses taxes, as he often does, he takes dead aim on those well-known tax evaders, the foundations. He is sometimes so bold as to name four: Ford, Rockefeller, Carnegie and "Mellon."[43] He seems not to know there is more than one Mellon to cut up. Wallace is not doing anything original here; rather, he is simply following a safe path that the Tax Reform Act blazed. Criticizing foundations is now an easy and popular indoor sport.

Apart from these psychological results of the Act, more substantial outcomes are already evident. Obviously the requirements of the Act itself will change the way of life of foundations: an excise tax to be paid, an audit by IRS to be undergone, a report to be published and through everything else the content and methodology of activities to be carefully examined. Hardly any of this is bad.

For the central result of the Act that foundations will themselves experience and are already aware of is that it encourages and even requires a level and an intensity of self-examination that heretofore only a very few foundations have attempted. The one most widespread and impressive effect of the Tax Reform Bill on foundations of all sorts and sizes has been that it has persuaded them to rethink their central purposes and functions. Some would have it that the Bill has forced foundations to clean house, but such a pejorative is patently unfair because seldom necessary. The self-examination now going on consists in a reordering of their affairs and redirection of their energies, all within the framework of their being philanthropies dedicated to the public service. For the first time in many years

43. See Lesher, *op. cit.;* Fitzgerald, *op. cit.*

annual reports of foundations have begun to be interesting to read, for the evidence of their self-examination is spread large in the various statements they have given to the public.[44]

Has this increasing amount of self-analysis led to change, innovation, bold action? Or has it led, rather, to marking time or even retreat? The record is not clear. No counting of entries on one and the other side of the ledger has yet been attempted, nor would the criteria for such a count be generally agreed upon. There is at least minimal gain, however, in simply the fact of self-examination by foundations, some of whom have never before undertaken such a task.

Yet though the results are not subject to proof, and though some observers have felt that the chief result has been the slowing down of foundation activity, it may be well to register a contrary point of view. The Tax Reform Act, together with all the criticism of foundations that surrounded it, seems not to have deterred most of the large ones in their support of change. Taking note of the charges brought against them, foundations have continued and increased their efforts to address themselves to the crucial problems of our society. Cautious counsel has advised placating the disturbed members of Congress and going slow for a season, and some foundations have indeed taken this tack. But in the main, statements by foundations, issued in greater numbers than ever before, show their determination to contribute to the public welfare at points of greatest need.

It is almost as if foundations, taking note that they have sometimes been criticized for being too blatant about their social concerns, have concluded that they have not been relevant enough, or sufficiently diligent in informing the general public. In my view, the weight of the self-examination that has taken place to date is on the side of making the foundations more active, more concerned about the quality of life around

44. See, for example, Birnbaum, *op. cit.;* "Reviewing the President's Reviews," *Non-Profit Report,* July, 1971, p. 2; annual reports for almost any recent year from such foundations as Carnegie, Danforth, Ford, Kellogg, Rockefeller, Sloan and many others; Caryl P. Haskins, "A Foundation Board Looks at Itself," *Foundation News,* March–April, 1972, pp. 9–14.

them, more courageous in addressing themselves to social problems.

Another development strongly influenced by the passage of the Tax Reform Act is the growing cooperation among foundations. Collusion has never been the danger, nor is it now. On the contrary, foundations customarily lived in isolation from one another. Now, however, they know more about one another than ever before, they work together in increasing numbers of ways and their cooperative organizations are being progessively strengthened.

The most inclusive trade association in the field is the Council on Foundations. Up to the time of the Tax Reform Bill only one or two of the larger foundations had ever bothered to join, though a few had supported the budget of the Council with occasional grants. Most of the large foundations are now members, and thus the Council itself has taken on a much stronger and more representative role.[45]

Cooperation is also represented by other groups and services. As an informal association, the Foundation Executives' Group serves as an effective instrument for cooperation among a dozen of the large foundations. The National Council on Philanthropy brings foundations together with recipients and others interested in giving. The Foundation Center (formerly called the Foundation Library Center) specializes in making reliable information available to foundations themselves and to the general public, through the main office in New York City, a branch office in Washington and regional depositories in eight other cities.

Coordination of effort has been especially encouraged locally and regionally through a variety of associations, conferences and workshops. Meetings of foundations and about foundation problems have never been better attended than in the last few years, and some of the regional associations are especially effective in fostering cooperative programs among foundations in their parts of the country. Details on the present state and large promise of cooperative work will be given in the final chapter; it is

45. See Council on Foundations, *Annual Report 1971,* which lists 499 members as of December 31, 1971.

enough now to note that much of this cooperation was in process of happening even if there had been no Tax Reform Bill. That it is taking place, whatever the causes, increases the pertinence and breadth of philanthropic work.

Parallel to the growing cooperation among foundations is the developing sense of common cause among recipients of foundation support. It should never have been necessary that foundations blow their own horn, though they ought always to have been willing to keep the public informed about their activities. When the worst features of the proposed Tax Reform Act were being discussed in Congress and around the country during 1969, foundations severally and together discarded their usual reticence and began to tell their story in concert. This was good, but even better was the telling of the story by those who knew it from the receiving end. Groups of grantees in a wide variety of fields, e.g., hospitals, museums, colleges and universities, realizing that restrictive legislation on foundations would ultimately hit them even harder, spoke up to list the benefits they had received from foundations and to praise the record of foundations' accomplishments through the years.[46] If recent times have brought more criticism of foundations than formerly, they have also brought greater awareness of the value of foundations to American life, and more willingness to speak to this point on the part of some of the recipients themselves.

Then what of the results of the Bill? It is not a disaster. It is not a boon. Its results have been good, bad and uncertain. On balance they tend toward the side of being good.

But it is really too soon to say. The answer, ultimately, will turn on what the foundations themselves make of the Bill, and of the criticism that produced it. The real test is still to take place.

46. See, for example, *Foundations and the Tax Bill, op. cit., passim;* "Consequences of the Tax Reform Act of 1969," Memorandum to Members of Congress from American Association of Presidents of Independent Colleges and Universities, February 2, 1971, MSS; Press release, Presbyterian College Union, January 11, 1972.

VI

The Task Ahead

A. Introduction

THERE is much to be done.

The ground we have covered shows how badly in need of repair is the public image of the philanthropic foundation. No longer left alone as they once were, foundations must learn how to fend off *unjustified* attacks to which they have recently been subject. They must learn how to respond constructively to the *legitimate* attacks. And they must learn to tell the difference between the two.

They must say their piece more persuasively, in respect both to the kind of organization they are and to the contributions they are making. They must figure out how to live with the Tax Reform Act and other restraints and restrictions. They must develop standards of good behavior, and learn how to apply them fairly and evenly.

But not all the learning and doing should be that of the foundations. Since the chief part of this chapter is to be spent in discussing what should be the foundations' own agenda for action, it may not be amiss to begin with the recognition as to what others should do—recipients of foundation beneficence, the general public and Government on its various levels. Not only can foundations not repair their image all by themselves, they ought not to be expected to do so. Other agencies, entities and groups of people have an obligation to see to it that the record is set straight, that the wild-swinging attacks against

217

foundations do not go unanswered, and that the accomplishments of foundations are properly appreciated.

It has been noted earlier that, on the one hand, recipients have seldom spoken up on behalf of foundations, and that, on the other, some of them did try to do so helpfully in the Congressional hearings during 1969. Foundations need to pay more attention to their recipients as sources of friendly and informed support. This is something other than following up on grants with individual recipients one by one. This is the cultivation of associations and groups of recipients, so that they may be aware of what foundations have done for them as a group or class and may say a supportive word in season.

It is not being suggested that foundations should develop their claques. The public generally and various agencies of Government would be quickly suspicious of any orchestrated applause or the use of cue cards. Foundations need real friends, not artificial ones, and those who testify on their behalf ought not to be, or to need to be, subpoenaed.

To get such genuine friends in abundance, all it takes is for the foundations to let others know that they are in need of objective testimony and impartial support.

One can almost hear the confirmed critic chortle in glee at such phrases. "Objective testimony" on behalf of foundations, when the foundations themselves are hoping for such a word, listening intently, perhaps even encouraging its being made? "Impartial support"? That phrase is a contradiction in terms! So might easily run the reaction of those who attack foundations; and their disbelief that benefactees could ever say an honest word about benefactors would undoubtedly be accompanied by raucous laughter.

But I don't believe it. On the contrary, I believe that "objective testimony" by grantees on behalf of grantors is possible, and that there *is* such a thing as "impartial support." This is not to say, of course, that there is no such thing as boot-licking, hand-kissing and general kowtowing. Such demeaning behavior does indeed take place, and some few foundations are probably fooled by it.

By and large, however, when people in a particular field

218

praise one or more foundations for activity in that field, they are both informed and sincere. Those who have benefited from the Salk vaccine, for example, can point out its value—and who is better able to know that it was a great scientific accomplishment growing out of an imaginative foundation action? Colleges kept alive or made more vigorous by judicious foundation grants can join with one another in saying an informed word of thanks and praise. City folks who suffered some urban sore that Government couldn't or wouldn't touch but that some foundation dared to alleviate, can say as much.

Suspicion of the gratitude and admiration that a recipient may have for a donor is an easy thing to arouse, but it simply does not fit the facts of human experience. Appreciation is a genuine and honest emotion, and forthright expression of it is an exercise in integrity, not in its opposite. Recipients have sometimes been slow to voice their thanks lest they be thought to be currying further favor. Foundations must find the tactful, yet candid, way of enlisting the support and appreciation of those who have come to know their activities most intimately.

If recipients need to speak up, the general public needs to listen. This presupposes the requirement that the media give the general public a full and fair chance to hear. The mythical John Q's ignorance about foundations is appalling. We have noted this fact earlier; now we take note that this ignorance is costly not alone to foundations but also to citizens themselves. Good causes go unsupported because their protagonists don't know where to go for support. Worthy institutions and agencies solicit indiscriminately because they have never learned to focus their entreaties. Except when some foundations seem to be in trouble, the media have seldom looked upon organized philanthropy as newsworthy. Thus the newspapers, radio and television have seldom reported to the public basic information about the activities of foundations, whether local, regional or national.

The need of the public to be better informed is well illustrated by the experience of the Danforth Foundation in St. Louis. Prior to becoming its employee, I knew the Foundation as a national educational fund, and I assumed, of course, that it was so known and respected in its own hometown. The fact of

219

the matter, however, is that old-time St. Louisans, especially those who happen to be friends of the Danforth family, are quite regularly ones who know least about the Foundation. They think it is connected with the Ralston Purina Company, or is a Danforth family charity, or (being confused with Danforth family charities) runs a summer camping program or conducts city-wide Christmas caroling. Every now and then it comes as a shock to some intelligent St. Louisan when he learns that the Danforth Foundation is none of these things.

Part of the misunderstanding is, of course, inevitable. All of us pigeonhole the information we collect through the years, and we like our data to stay in the slots to which they were first assigned. Thus misunderstandings about any foundation are always likely to be more prevalent in its hometown than anywhere else.

But this does not excuse the way in which the media often perpetuate the myths. St. Louis newspapers are a considerable cut above the average, yet even they are more likely to fall into errors of interpretation about the Danforth Foundation than are newspapers in other parts of the country. They don't need to take the trouble to find out, because they think they already know.

The point of this comment is not to make picayunish protest about the way in which one foundation is treated by the media —for in point of fact the Danforth Foundation is quite well off in this regard, in comparison with the treatment received by many other foundations in other cities around the country. Rather, the point is simply that the media as a whole don't do a very good job in giving the public a clear and dependable account of the functioning of foundations in American life. The public are poorly informed, and the media need badly to improve their coverage.

As for the Federal Government, the Tax Reform Act itself prescribes much that must be done. There is, first of all, the audit, and it is to be hoped that henceforth audits of foundations will be systematic, thorough, frequent and impartial. Since the excuse for imposing the 4 percent excise tax was that it could defray the costs of regular audits, the Internal Revenue Service

220

will now be expected to do its duty without fear or favor.

For the Government to fulfill this requirement will not be easy, for the IRS does not have a sufficiently large number of trained operatives to undertake this job for the thousands of foundations to which the legal requirement applies. There is reason to believe, however, that the IRS is going about this enlarged assignment with intelligence and vigor. Using some carefully selected foundations as guinea pigs, the IRS is spending large periods of time in their offices, not because those foundations are suspect but because the IRS can learn much about the auditing task in general by a careful inspection of the ways in which some well-managed foundations keep records, arrive at decisions concerning programs and grants, ask for and receive the advice of competent consultants, follow up with recipients and evalute their work. In this process the IRS is itself learning how to perform its auditing task most efficiently, what questions need to be asked and what others are none of its business.

For example, the Danforth Foundation has recently had a seven-month visitation by the IRS, and it turned out to be a pleasant and profitable experience for all concerned. After certain obvious matters were looked into, the frank approach of one IRS officer was "What other questions ought we to ask?" We tried to be helpful.

Another IRS man, however, got off base: he asked, "Since the Danforth Foundation has lots of fellowship programs, can you give assurance that none of the students receiving one of your fellowships has taken part in any campus protest?" To this kind of question we had to say, "That is not the Internal Revenue's proper business." It is a question in which there is, properly, a lot of legitimate interest these days, in the colleges and universities, in the foundations that support the work of their students in any way, and in the general public. But nothing in the mandate that the IRS has been given by Congress can justify its asking that kind of question as part of its audit.

Let it be quickly added that the IRS people themselves understood the answer we made to that question posed by an inexperienced agent. The feeling bears repetition, that on the basis of the Danforth Foundation's experience the IRS audits

221

will be done carefully and conscientiously. Any legitimate foundation has nothing to fear from the way in which the Internal Revenue Service is approaching its new statutory task.

As a result of the auditing exercise, however, the Government will have several other chores to perform. First, if the audits do not turn up any substantial record of misbehavior, then by all rights the Government ought to set the record straight in respect to the charges and innuendoes that have been so widely circulated about foundations. Public announcement of the results of the audits is not required by law, but it would be a very fair and useful thing to do. Some such report could well be part of the publication of a list of organizations that qualify as private foundations under the definitions of the Act; and the publication of such a list would itself be a public service in light of the wide uncertainty that now exists as to what a foundation is and how many there are.

It is to be expected that the audits will ferret out at least a few signs of mischief. When and as this occurs, in whatever amount or degree, even in the smallest measure, IRS and other branches of Government will be called upon to enforce the provisions of the Act having to do with sanctions and penalties. Again, this task will not be easy, and much will turn on whether the IRS assumes ignorance and inadvertence, on the one hand, or malice, self-serving and impure motive on the other. The Act itself often sounds harsh and punitive. It will be important, therefore, for the IRS in its task of enforcement to be assiduous and firm, but not to assume, as the Act itself sometimes seems to do, that all foundations are guilty until proved innocent.

As was indicated in the preceding chapter, whether or not a foundation is in violation of some of the puzzling and unclear sections of the Act will turn not so much on what the Act itself says as on the way in which the Treasury Department draws up the Regulations for its interpretation. It goes without saying that Treasury officials must do so with a great deal more sensitivity, common sense and attention to the nuances of language, than was accomplished by the framers of the Act. The record thus far is good. Sheep can still get taken for goats, and maybe a few goats will be able to masquerade as sheep; but on the whole, the Regulations will separate one group from the other on defensible grounds. Various agencies of the Government will need to continue to be as successful in the shaping of Regulations bearing on the supervision of foundations as they have been in the past.

Government at various levels could and should do much else. It is expected that one result of the heightened interest in foundations will be the introduction of regulatory or taxing legislation in various states, and such steps have already been taken in a number of them.[1] Lest cities also get into the act, some foundations have begun to make annual donations to the budgets of city Governments, either to forestall the possible imposition of a tax or simply to take grateful notice of the benefits received from public services. However foundations themselves respond to the possibility of city or state action, these lesser levels of Government need to be as well-grounded and well-ordered in their actions toward organized philanthropy as the Federal Government should be.

Among suggestions as to what Government at various levels should do, the most important is that a hard look be taken at the national policy on tax incentives for charitable giving. It is widely held that the Tax Reform Act on the national level and certain threats of action on the state level are seriously endangering the will to give and/or the capacity to give of a considerable portion of the American public.[2] Singling out foundations for peculiar treatment, the Tax Reform Act indirectly, and

1. See Marion R. Fremont-Smith, "Impact of the Tax Reform Act of 1969 on State Supervision of Charities," *Harvard Journal on Legislation,* Vol. 8: 537, pp. 537–569; A. A. Heckman and Robert W. Bonine, "Private Foundations and State Legislation: A Case Study" (on Minnesota), paper presented to National Conference of National Council on Philanthropy, New York City, April 14, 1971, MSS; "California—1% Tax on Foundations," *Non-Profit Report,* June, 1971, p. 5.

2. See, for example, Report of Peterson Commission, *op. cit.,* chaps. 4, 16, & pp. 165–168; Wadsworth, *op. cit.,* p. 4; Charles H. Percy, "The Role of Private Philanthropy in a Free Society," an address to the American Bar Association, St. Louis, August 9, 1970, MSS; Alan Pifer, "The Jeopardy of Private Institutions," reprint from *Annual Report, Carnegie Corporation of New York, 1970.* For a pre-TRA 69 discussion of tax incentives, see T. Willard Hunter, *The Tax Climate for Philanthropy,* Washington, D.C., American College Public Relations Association, 1968.

perhaps inadvertently, raises questions about the nature and scope of tax exemption in general. Inequities in tax incentives and inequalities in tax exemptions combine to force us to debate on a national level, the pros and cons of public charity, its practice by both public and private groups, and the appropriate recognitions that Government should give to its practice.

The Report of the Peterson Commission is a significant contribution to the beginning of this national discussion, and its suggestion that the Federal Government establish an "independent" governmental agency to serve as an "Advisory Board on Philanthropic Policy" is one that bears careful study.[3] But this is only the beginning of the public debate about tax incentive and exemption that is long overdue in this country, and to lead the American people in the consideration of these important matters is the chief responsibility of Government in this area in the immediate future.

B. What Foundations Must Do

No matter what others must do—recipients, the general public, the media and Government—the main job of creating a sound understanding of foundations by American society must be accomplished by the foundations themselves. The task of overcoming the present disrepute into which foundations have fallen and of replacing it with more positive and appreciative attitudes must be an effort of multiple hands, to be sure, but those who will have to bear the major burden are the people connected with foundations.

Henceforth in this discussion let us make it "we," not "they" —for I speak as one who shares responsibility for the nature and quality of foundation programs. We who serve foundations in any major way—as original donors or trustees or professional staff or formal consultants—have got to repair the damage; we cannot look to others to take the lead. We have got a difficult, crucially important job to be done, now, and nobody else is going to do it for us.

Before enumerating the various things that foundations must

3. Report of Peterson Commission, *op. cit.,* chap. 20.

do, however, I need to make two or three personal and professional disclaimers. First, to refer to damage is to imply agency, and I want the reader to know clearly the position I hold. The good reputation of foundations has been hurt neither by insiders alone nor by outsiders alone but by both. Critics have criticized unduly, but they have often had something to criticize. Donors, trustees and staff people of foundations have complained justifiably about unfair criticism—but have sometimes given cause for it. My comments hereafter will be directed largely to foundation people, but let it not be forgot that they are not solely responsible.

For one of our own number to tell us what we need to do is an act of temerity. Let me enter, then, a personal disclaimer as to having all the answers and as to calling my colleagues to repentance. No such thing, of course. On the contrary, the situation isn't so bad as to require setting up a sawdust trail, and in any event I'm in no position to do the preaching. All I hope to do is to call upon my own experience, limited yet still considerable, in a brief discussion of five areas for improvement. These five areas are (1) definition of purpose, (2) structure and finance, (3) program and operating policy, (4) communication, and (5) cooperation. Out of a better record that we must and shall write in these five areas foundations will develop, I believe, a basic rationale to undergird their own work and philanthropy in general. To this task we shall turn our attention in the final section.

1. *In Definition of Purpose:*

By and large the purposes of foundations are poorly conceived and sloppily explained. By saying as much, I do not mean to give comfort to the congenital critic who is prepared to quote out of context any supposedly damaging admission on the part of a foundation supporter. There is no way to keep him from doing so, and in any event the position must be stated.

The position is simply this: the generous reflexes of philanthropists have often outrun their powers of conceiving and/or expressing their reasons for such generosity. Donors have usu-

225

ally been men of action, and to whatever extent they had a philosophy for their giving it was usually learned in shorthand at some such homely place as mother's knee.

Part of the problem is a love of the grandiose; another part is simply a lack of sophistication. Many a foundation states in its charter that it is out to build a better world. The Danforth Foundation used to display a torch on its published materials with the motto "Hold High The Torch." The W. Clement and Jessie V. Stone Foundation uses on its letterhead the comment "Dedicated to help make this a better world in which to live." Excelsior is the motto of every foundation, and through its efforts the world is going to be a better place.

The chief trouble, however, is neither high-flown nor fuzzy language. It is, rather, that those responsible for the foundation's work have seldom paused to consider with meticulous care the primary reasons for the existence of the foundation and the chief ends to which its work should be directed. Action, yes; philosophy, no. Programs, yes; policies, no. Most of the statements about the purposes of foundations—and there have been a number of unusual thoughtfulness in recent days—have been composed for an annual report or a state occasion by some one foundation official and seldom represent the considered judgment of the personnel of that foundation as a whole. Take me as an example: when I've written such an essay it has always been in the hope and the desire that it would express correctly and adequately the points of view of my associates on board and staff, but never in the pretense that they had in fact voted approval or even with the full assurance that they would. The point is, foundation managers, whether of board or of staff, have seldom taken the time or trouble to define precisely the purposes of the organization for which they are responsible.

The point, further, is that there must be some improvement in this matter of defining the purpose of a foundation. We do not need a spate of freshly minted statements of goals, full of clichés that will reassure Congressmen and other gullible types. Trouble is, Congressmen aren't as gullible as they were once thought to be. And we have enough such statements already.

What we need, instead, is a larger willingness on the part of all foundation people, whether engaged in policy-setting or management, to think deeply about what the foundation should be and do. As was noted in a previous chapter, some of this desirable self-analysis has already been undertaken by many foundations, as a happy outcome of the Tax Reform Act. We need much more of this self-examination, both by each foundation of itself and by the whole field in as much concert as possible, to the end that there develop first among the foundations and finally in the public at large a clean, rational, persuasive case for philanthropy. Is it really true, as some critics contend, that foundations not only do not know what they are doing but have no chance of ever knowing? Are there no decent purposes for them to lay hold of? If such notions are not to be countenanced, then foundations have got to get hard at work in defining their purposes more explicitly and cogently than they have ever done to date.

2. *In Structure and Finance:*

Here, the first job for foundations is to make sure that they are in full compliance with the provisions of the Tax Reform Act of 1969. It is not likely that any of the large foundations will be caught short in this regard, unless it wants to be in order to institute some kind of protest or test case. The professional staffs of large foundations will be alert to ways in which their work would be seriously handicapped if they have not observed the law meticulously. Moreover, lawyers retained by the large foundations will be at pains to put their employers in the clear. Finally, the Internal Revenue Service itself can be expected to take a special interest in the large foundations, and to see to it that they cut no corners in the observance of the law.

This may not be so true, however, for small foundations that have little or no professional staff and only limited, unspecialized legal advice. Unaware that the Tax Reform Act has imposed new obligations, they can easily fail to comply with some small-type requirement in structure or finance. One of the heartening developments in the foundation field in the last few years, however, is the growth in seminars and workshops for

227

foundation officers, at which not only the Tax Reform Act but other matters having to do with sound foundation practice are discussed. The day when foundations were content to be ignorant about accepted standards of management or even about details of Federal regulations is fast drawing to a close; and foundations of all sizes, large, medium and small, are prepared to observe the law.

But compliance with the Act is only a bare beginning, and foundations should and will receive no credit for doing what in any event they must do. We who are in foundation work must encourage our respective organizations to take seriously some of the recommended changes in structure and in handling finances that were made during the debates in Congress and recently in other public discussions of foundation behavior. The Act did not succeed in regulating everything, and some of the concerns on which the Act touched only peripherally must be given most serious attention by us who work in the field.

For example, foundations have got to diversify their boards. Many foundations that don't even have a board, except on paper, must establish one. Moreover, these boards must be occupied by other persons than simply the alter egos of the original donor. Granting the limitations of effective size, they must be as broadly representative as possible, so as to function impartially in the areas of the foundation's choice. To be broadly representative while still effective in size is to run the risk of adopting tokenism, and this foundations must strive to eschew. Yet it is better to have one woman than none at all, one black, one Jew, perhaps even one redhead and one southpaw, than none at all. Both tokenism and the effort to escape tokenism can get pretty silly. The point is that foundations must set themselves up to be governed by a group rather than just by one or two, where a variety of points of view will have a chance to be heard and considered.

Another example: All that foundations ought to do in respect to responsible administration of its program was not legislated by the Act, nor can it be. Take the simple matter of administrative salaries: nobody ought to be on the payroll of a foun-

228

dation who is not contributing substantively to its work. This means in most instances that trustees ought not to be paid; and further, that when they do perform some service, their pay be modest, and commensurate with a fair price for the time and effort they expend. Fat salaries to members of an inner circle and subsidies to old family retainers have got to come to an end.

As for the employed staff of the foundation, the appropriate standard to be set for their salaries is not that of the corporation or business world, but is the practice of other tax-exempt agencies of comparable scope and significance. Most large foundations pay their professional staff members at rates comparable to those of leading universities. The only foundation executives who receive huge, business-style salaries are those whose foundations continue to possess some awkward, overly intimate relationship with a business corporation. Other administrative expenses besides salaries need also to be looked at critically, for it is not enough that most foundations never practiced the bestowing of special favors or the padding of operational accounts. The time has come when all foundations must cease any remaining vestiges of management laxity or luxury.

In still another area improvement beyond what the Act requires must be made. In one sense the Act is ambivalent: whereas the excise tax discourages a higher investment performance, the pay-out requirement puts a premium on getting larger returns from the foundation's endowment. Less income, less tax, versus more income to meet imposed pay-out. Apart from the Act, however, and its somewhat illogical requirements for the management of a foundation's resources, it behooves a foundation to show to the public a heightened desire to use its resources for the general welfare.

Just as hoarding was never an appropriate part of a foundation's expenditure policy, so investing in low-yield securities can no longer be considered a proper investment policy for a charitable agency devoted to the public good. Even if the Government should repeal the pay-out provisions of the Act tomorrow, foundations must strive to do better than the present law requires. This means, for most of them, a major overhaul in both invest-

229

ment and expenditure policy. As traumatic as this experience will be for some foundations, nothing less is ever likely to repair their image in the public mind.

Is it important that foundations begin to pay attention to the kinds of corporations in which they hold stock? In recent days sensitivity has risen among some foundations in respect to the corporations represented in their portfolios whose allegedly anti-social policies and activities have become visible and may all along have been reprehensible. Egged on by Ralph Nader, a conscientious few foundations as stockholders have remonstrated with corporation management, and have even voted against management in one or two proxy fights. All foundations except a disreputable few can be expected, of course, to refrain from investing in illegal, fly-by-night enterprises, but whether foundations should forswear investing in armament manufactories, distilleries or traders with South Africa is a matter of intense difference of opinion. It is my personal view that no plumbline for the guidance of all foundations in this regard can be laid down, though individual foundations will undoubtedly want to, and should, follow their individual paths of conscience. It should be added, however, that more than an alert but untutored conscience is needed. Competent analysis of the social performance of companies, often not available except on an amateur basis, should be sought before foundations adopt judgmental postures.[4]

Somewhat related to this concern is the relatively new practice of a few but growing number of foundations, of making what are called "program-related" or "socially motivated" investments. This policy can be defended, it seems to me, and heartily applauded if it is part of a foundation's program rather than an aspect of its fiscal management. In any event, it is to be expected that challenges as to where foundations invest their

4. See John G. Simon, "Foundations as Stockholders: Corporate Responsibility," in NYU Proceedings, *op. cit.*, Tenth Biennial Conference, pp. 39–61; articles on "Campaign GM" and "Shareholder Responsibility" in *Non-Profit Report*, December, 1970, April, May, and June, 1971; Burton G. Malkiel and Richard E. Quandt, "Moral Issues in Investment Policy," *Harvard Business Review*, March–April, 1971; Henry C. Suhrke, "Investment Without Injury," *Non-Profit Report*, March, 1972.

money will grow. Whether or not they welcome this development, they will have to learn to say something besides, "It's none of your business."

The most important thing to note in respect to what foundations must do about structure and finance is a matter of spirit or atmosphere rather than a matter of compliance with the law or with accepted standards of good behavior. The greatest single dereliction in this area today is not some one form of abominable behavior but some several forms of self-serving attitudes. The sorry fact is, a great many people who or whose forebears have established a foundation look upon it as their own and thus slip, probably unconsciously, into asking, How can I use it for my own satisfaction, pleasure or profit? These are not evil people, except very rarely; they are simply ordinary people of extraordinary substance, normally selfish, predictably limited in their own outlook and understanding, accustomed to having their own way. It probably took such people, once upon a time, to be willing to establish foundations in the first place; and that many of those who manage foundations today, especially small family foundations, are of this general sort should come as no surprise. It is this same kind of upright, hard-driving, self-centered person who has been responsible for building major businesses, and labor unions and for making the American brand of capitalism and democracy work.

Trouble is, this isn't enough. Foundation managers have got to rise above their normal ego drives and reverse the cut of the question they unconsciously ask. The new direction must be: How can "my" foundation be made most useful to others? To raise such a question, to be sure, has to do with more foundation matters than just structure and finance; but it is at the point of structure and finance that the posing of such a question would begin to make a major difference. Foundations have narrow or irresponsible boards, engage in poor administrative practices, and rest content with low investment yields because the prevailing concern has been, What can this outfit do for me? rather than, What can it do for others? When such a redirection in the prevailing trend of thought in many foundations takes place, the present inadequate handling of matters of structure and finance will automatically undergo first scrutiny and then improvement.

To ask as much is not to raise one's expectations too high. The temper of foundation management need not be so unselfish as to be unreal or unattainable. Rather, what is to be expected is the same kind of other-directed impulses and energies that inform the occupations devoted by definition to the welfare of society. A doctor or a lawyer can be as selfish as the next fellow; a minister can seek his own ends; even a priest can want to get married. But though practitioners of these and other socially beneficial vocations may fall short of the high ideals of their order, the vocations themselves profess as their primary concern a life and work of service, and most of their members follow through pretty well in practice.

Agencies given tax exemption because of their non-profit nature fall in this category. Foundation personnel, therefore, like school and college people, and employees of church, museum and hospital, are service-oriented by definition of the organization with which they are related. If they see their own role rightly, there is no ground for debate in respect to the temper of the structural and financial affairs of their respective foundations: they must so order those affairs as to serve the public first, and to be of as large service as the size and condition of the foundation's resources allow.

3. *In Program and Operating Policy:*

Much of what has just been said about the spirit that must prevail in foundation work applies to the area of program and operating policy as much as to the area of structure and finance. Moreover, in this area the Tax Reform Act gives less incentive to be virtuous. In fact, it can be argued that the Act is a detriment rather than an aid to improved foundation performance.

The thrust of the Act is toward caution. Until the full meaning of the prohibition against "an attempt to affect the opinion of the general public," as discussed in the preceding chapter, is revealed by the Treasury Department's Regulations and the IRS's enforcement of them, foundations are going to be tempted to walk softly and carry no stick at all.

The burden of the Act's advice to foundations is, "Watch out! You can get into trouble." Little in the Act seems to say, "You are doing a fine work. Keep it up!" Most of the large foundations have not noticeably shifted their sail, but the prior set of their sail was not on an unusually aggressive course. Some of the large foundations and a considerable number of the small ones have grown at least cautious, if not cowardly, in the presence of the Act's provisions, buttressed by a generally critical attitude in the public. Sit tight. Keep cool. Play it safe.

But this simply will not do. The support of the status quo is not a sufficient justification for foundation activity, for money set aside for special charitable purposes is to make things better, not merely leave them the same. Charity has received recognition at the hands of Government, through tax deductions and tax incentives, presumably because it will work some improvement in the lot of men and things that are its legitimate objects.

Thus charity is not a form of a society's protection of its past or present. It is not an element of stand-pattism. Personal contributions that you and I may make to agencies that have won our confidence cannot possibly be guaranteed to be bets on the future, for many a non-profit tax-exempt agency to which our gifts might go may have reached such a status by developing some skill in fending off the future rather than welcoming it. But if the individual charity may seldom be gauged to the improvement of mankind in general or even some modest segment, we have a right to expect more of corporate or organized philanthropy—institutionalized, chartered, given formal recognition as an agency devoted to the benefit of the society.

What it is we have a right to expect is innovation and experimentation. Foundations must take with utmost seriousness their responsibility to explore and to initiate. It is a strange thing that, in an America supposedly in love with the frontier in both geographical fact and spirit, the profit sector has indeed developed an appreciation of inventiveness whereas often the non-profit sector looks at it askance. Not that it ought to be

233

the other way around. Let business and industry continue to treasure the dash and verve of innovation and experimentation. But let us bring to the same level of public acceptance such exploratory and wide-searching behavior by educational, scientific, welfare, charitable and other tax-exempt institutions. Foundations, along with the rest, have got to feel free to, and then have got to develop the nerve to, experiment.

Innovation, moreover, must come to be not only a matter of the style but also of the content of a foundation's work. In other words, foundations must plunge into new areas, take up topics that are not yet popular or that indeed are already unpopular, address themselves to subjects that are not simply predictable and safe. This means marching into the jaws of controversy, and every foundation had better face this question head on. If any foundation adopts the aim of staying out of controversy at all costs, it deserves little credit for whatever good it may still manage to do. For the areas of greatest need are almost inevitably the areas of controversy; and if a foundation knows its own nature well enough to know that it exists to improve the lot of man and society, then sooner or later it must also come to the knowledge that ways of improvement are subject to continual public debate, often bitter, and that controversy is inevitable.

A few caveats, however, are in order. Foundations have no business mounting soapboxes and waving red flags. If they know their proper role, they don't fight causes at the barricades. Certainly they don't pick a fight, or go out of their way to get in one. Their stance vis-à-vis controversy is simply to accept it when it comes, not to go searching for it. If the foundations are doing their job—seeking solutions for the difficult problems of our time—then controversy is a price that must be paid.

Let us be more specific. To be on the growing, cutting edge of life is to deal with the new, the unfamiliar, the strange, and thus inevitably for some people, the worrisome, the fearful, the outrageous. Foundations must look into the byways, and try to speak to the needs that others are neglecting. Wounds are sometimes so deep that band-aids are not enough; foundations must be prepared to use surgery when necessary.

234

Choosing a course, they must see it through to the point of making a difference. Every one of the trouble spots of our society is within their proper purview: urban decay, war, poverty, civil rights, hunger, bad housing, overpopulation, unemployment, race and class prejudice and what have you. This doesn't mean that every foundation ought to get embroiled in every controversial issue, for such a strategy would be obviously self-defeating. But it does mean that, in whatever field the foundation decides to work, it should find out what the real problems are and go to the heart of them. Tippy-toe and patty-cake are games only for children.

The limitations to which all foundations, even the largest, are subject mean that they can never pretend to be self-sufficient in the solution of any major problem. For example, not even Ford can clean up those public schools that are jungles. Ford can't even clean them up in New York City by itself. Whatever the problem, therefore, if it is general, sizeable and urgent, any foundation must realize that it will have to have help, from governmental agencies or from other private sources or both.

If the foundation's efforts are not to be defeated by dilution, it will likely come to feel that its support must be focussed on some segment of the total problem, some identifiable and isolatable part, some specialized program. To bite off more than one can chew is an exercise not in bravery but in waste, and the warrior who marches off in all directions at once never arrives anywhere.

To support specialized programs may very well mean that foundations will seldom direct the overall grand strategy. Let it then be consciously recognized and accepted: A foundation's role is not to solve the pressing problems of society. It is the much more modest one of working on such problems, but always in conjunction with other and perhaps more powerful agencies. It does the supportive jobs here, there and yonder; seldom can it perform the huge, central task. It fills the nooks and crannies; and it won't do its job really well unless it can believe that nooks and crannies are also important.

These two bits of programmatic advice are not as contradictory as they sound at first hearing. The resolution is simply

235

that, though a foundation should choose an important problem and hit it hard, it should also concentrate on some manageable part of the problem, leaving to others the more synoptic task.

Four specific comments remain to be made in this section, two having to do with program and two with operating policy. As for program, a foundation should never forget that one of its priceless assets is its independence. Even though it may have to limit its work to a small segment of some overriding social concern, a judicious use of its own freedom in the design and performance of the self-chosen task can often give the work far-reaching significance.

This independence or freedom makes some particular kinds of work especially attractive to foundations and especially useful to the general welfare. I refer to the sponsorship of analytical and evaluative studies of major institutions and movements in American life. Analysis in depth, leading to dependable, impartial evaluation is indeed a tricky business, but for all the difficulties it poses, it is a *sine qua non* if a society wants to understand and improve itself. All the institutions of our society, public and private, need periodic appraisal, and the movements and causes that sweep across the land need impartial examination.

Since neither the institutions nor the movements can be expected to appraise and examine themselves, this is where the foundations come in. They possess the necessary independence to turn a searching, sympathetic, critical eye on almost any organization or issue, or to see that competent observers do so; and they have the necessary finances to pay what it would cost. In Chapter IV we saw that many of the most useful activities of foundations in recent years have been studies of various sorts and sizes. Because foundations have often done this kind of thing well, it has sometimes been suggested that this is their chief role or their safe path of escape from controversy.

Such notions, however, do not square with the facts of foundation behavior, for support of projects of analysis and evaluation is still a minor part of foundation activity, yet when it has taken place, it has often been fed by, and in turn fed, some controversial social concern. But the point here is not to say how brave and useful certain studies have been; it is to call attention to the large opportunity that foundations possess, by virtue of their freedom, to provide for careful analysis and evaluation of various agencies and features of American life, an opportunity that thus far foundations have not sufficiently seized.

Related to this program emphasis is another to which foundations have given insufficient attention. This one is closer home. When foundations come to describe their portfolio of activities, seldom if ever do they refer to their own follow-up procedures. This is true for two reasons: First, monitoring, if thought of at all, is considered not as part of a foundation's program but as part of its internal administration; and secondly, most foundations do very little of it. Like many another fault, this one will be repaired in part by the Tax Reform Act, for its insistence on "expenditure responsibility" will force foundations to keep closer tabs on recipients of grants. Much of this will be to the good, in spite of the bureaucratic red tape with which the Act's provisions are entangled, for it never did make sound philanthropic sense for a foundation to send off a check and then forget about it.

But though the Tax Reform Act may have gone too far in the paper work required and the penalties to be exacted, in one respect it does not go far enough. The Act approaches the problem negatively, in order to make sure that grantees don't take advantage of grantors and/or that grantors don't toss money around cavalierly. The aim is to prevent abuse. But in their own programs of follow-up, foundations must do better than this; they must take an affirmative attitude toward surveillance, so that first the foundation, and later the larger society, may learn something useful from the grants for other institutions and other occasions.

This calls, therefore, for something more than gumshoe tactics, and the kind of grant-monitoring that foundations ought to practice is a much more demanding activity than they have been wont to recognize. What is really needed is something correctly described not as monitoring but as evaluation, for a considerable part of every foundation's activity should be the gathering for itself and the disseminating to the concerned public reliable analyses of the effect of its grants and programs.

The last two comments in this section will have to do with operating style. Each is often a defense that the foundation world uses against outside criticism, or a boasted virtue that foundations proclaim. It is not a happy thing for me to say that each, however, is more professed than practiced.

First of these two modes of operation is flexibility. Here is supposed to lie one of our major differences from Government: We in the foundation field are flexible, whereas Government is you-know-what. The trouble with this contorted self-back-pat is that it is so seldom true. Not that Government is very often flexible—that part is surely the case. But foundations are often inflexible too. To have made firm decisions about fields of work and procedures to be followed is a great advantage to all concerned, not only to the foundations themselves but to outsiders who need to know clearly what is possible. But to apply those decisions with a kind of rigidity that prevents questioning or reconsideration is a handicap that most foundations often impose upon themselves unnecessarily. Flexible doesn't mean wishy-washy, but it does mean adjustable; and foundations need more of this temper.

Partner to flexibility is speed. Foundations sometimes claim a superiority to other institutions because they can come to decisions more quickly. They can, but often they don't. As is the case with flexibility, the potential is there but the performance is often lacking.

This is not to say that delays in the decisions of foundations are caused simply by bullheadedness or insensitivity. On the contrary, speed is sometimes difficult to provide; and if practiced as an end in itself, would almost certainly lead to unsound procedures and unwise decisions. The effort to get foundations away from unilateral action—spur-of-the-moment one-man judgments—is one that almost automatically prolongs the decision-making process. It is still the case, however, that a foundation can take thought in advance as to how it wishes to behave when a crisis arises or when a quick action should be taken; and then it can put that procedure into effect when conditions warrant. Foundations, by nature, have the chance to be both

238

flexible and speedy, and they need to begin to make good on their oft-stated claim.

4. *In Communication with the Public*

Because of the long-time myth that philanthropy is a personal and private thing, many foundations grew up practicing silence rather than communication. To go around telling the public what you were doing was looked upon as bad form, and only the show-offs and blow-hards, it was thought, sent slick-paper Annual Reports to massive mailing lists.

Times have changed. Before the Tax Reform Act specified that foundations must begin to practice full disclosure of their holdings and activities, leading foundations had begun to be accountable, even forthright, in what they told the public about themselves. We have noted earlier that communication with the public is a problem area, but that foundations as a group are already beginning to do a bettter job.

So what now remains to be said? Five things.

First, improved communication with the public means making available clearer, more understandable information. Whether a foundation's report is the mimeographed statement of somebody's little back-pocket fund or the stiff-backed three-color picture-spattered production of a giant, the literate citizen ought to be able to figure it out, to know what that foundation is doing, and how, where, when and why. In some cases the reader can't tell whether it was the decision or the payment, or both, that was made in the year under review. The lack of uniform standards for reporting on finances and programs, and for classication of grants, has been remarked by many critics. Since this problem in communications must be solved cooperatively—for no one foundation will be able to impose its style and standard of reporting on all others—we will return to it in the next section.

Secondly, good communication means not only preparing understandable prose but also shipping it out to those who ought to read it. Foundations need to give more attention to dissemination. The impression one gets now is that the mailing lists of most foundations are Rube Goldberg inventions that obviously don't hang together. The President of the university (more likely the emeritus than the incumbent), the nice lady who sent that complimentary letter, the man who ran for Congress ten years ago and my Aunt Susie—they are all there, and are likely still to be there when they are all dead. Immortality is being on a foundation's mailing list. Which may be all right, for there is no harm in letting Aunt Susie know. But what isn't all right is the lack of attention that foundations give to the problem of getting reliable information about their work into the hands of the people who should have it.

It is in this connection that foundations must give thought to in-depth communication with specific publics. "The remarkable success of American agriculture is due not so much to superior invention as to superior dissemination and implementation of research results, largely through the work of field agents who showed individual farmers what new inventions and practices could mean to them."[5] What is true for agriculture is true for other fields as well. The third thing to note, then, is that as long as foundations work in specialized fields—which will be as long as foundations exist—it will be much more important for people in those fields, rather than just the vague, general public, to be kept fully informed.

Fourth, this in-depth communication must therefore be more intensive, more targeted, more productive of changed ideas than we in the foundation field have usually thought was necessary. Reporting was an obligation, and when we had laid forth some bare facts for all to see, we felt a bit virtuous about it. But that stance must now be superseded by one that looks on reporting as an opportunity, and not so much as an extraneous addendum to our activity as an integral part of the activity itself. Communication must proceed to the point of becoming education. A foundation has got to look upon its job of informing the public as the chance to share with others the concerns and dimensions of its own program and of its ramifications near and far.

Finally, communication that is clear and uniform, is widely and wisely disseminated, possesses depth for specific publics

5. Report of Peterson Commission, *op. cit.,* p. 136.

and is intensive enough to be truly educative is the kind that individual foundations working unilaterally cannot furnish in sufficient measure for the field of philanthropy as a whole. Each foundation can tell its own story, but no more. To paint the larger canvas will require service agencies more numerous and effective than what the field has supported in the past. Which leads us directly into the next section, concerned with what foundations must do—

5. In Cooperation with Each Other:

To cooperate in order to communicate better with the public is only one of the five prevailing reasons and types, all of which we shall note in a moment. Cooperation now comes in all sorts and sizes, but there needs to be more of it in every category. But first, a comment or two on the organizational forms that cooperation has begun to take and should develop further:

We noted in the preceding chapter that one of the effects of the 1969 Tax Reform Act was the encouragement it gave to foundations to work more closely with one another, and that this increase had already started before the Act was passed. Now we need to specify the levels on which cooperation has taken place, and/or should.

The lowest level is local, and the instruments come in various forms. Community foundations could be looked on as a form of cooperation, so pronounced as to result in the loss of identity of any one trust that enters into the common pool. It would be well, therefore, to distinguish them as an exercise in conglomeration from those associations of independent entities that simply agree to work together. The local cooperative associations as well as the community funds are growing in number and strength, to the point that a recent survey asks whether they may be "the way of the future."[6]

The first organ of local cooperation (as distinct from community fund) was the highly regarded Kansas City Association of Trusts and Foundations, established in 1949. Though it had

6. Bertram G. Waters III, "Are Cooperative Associations the Way of the Future?" *Foundation News*, January–February, 1972, pp. 19–24.

no imitators until the 1960s, there are now upwards of twelve or fifteen similar associations, some of them informal, in various cities from Boston to Honolulu. Occasionally a national foundation will help to establish such an association in its hometown, so that local needs to which the national foundation finds it difficult to respond may get a better hearing from local family funds and corporation charitable trusts, working together. This is the explanation for the 1970 origin in St. Louis of the Metropolitan Association for Philanthropy, sponsored by the Danforth Foundation. The Babcock Foundation has helped with an informal association in Winston-Salem, the Falk Medical Fund with one in Pittsburgh, and the Florence and John Schumann Foundation with one in Essex County, New Jersey.[7]

The highest degree of cooperation attained by local associations is in those whose member foundations agree not merely to share information but to make grants together, often in the name of their central office. The Kansas City Association followed this practice from the first; other grant-making associations are the Foundation Services, Inc., of Minneapolis, the New Hampshire Charitable Fund, and the Inner City Fund of Chicago.[8] Grant-making and other joint programs' efforts constitute the way the local associations will need to go, if cooperation is ever to get beyond pleasant talk and recipient agencies are ever to be effectively served.

Foundations that are separated geographically find it harder to make grants together, but a systematic program of sharing experiences can be generally helpful. The progenitor of regional associations for mutual encouragement is the Conference of Southwest Foundations, whose twenty-fourth annual meeting took place in April, 1972. The Southeastern Council of Foundations was formed in October, 1970, and bids to become a similarly useful group in its part of the country.[9] Meetings from

7. *Ibid.;* "St. Louis Metropolitan Association for Philanthropy, Inc.," *Danforth News and Notes,* September, 1970, p. 7.

8. See Waters, *op. cit.*

9. See notes on the Conference of Southwest Foundations in *Foundation News,* July–August, 1970, p. 138 and July–August, 1971, p. 145, and on the Southeastern Council of Foundations, *ibid.,* January–Febru-

time to time, sponsored by less formally organized associations, have been held in nearly every section of the country. Periodic luncheon groups, such as the New York Foundation Round Table, and gatherings of foundation people under other auspices, such as the Brookings Institution's Conferences on Public Policy for Foundation Officials and New York University's biennial Conferences on Charitable Foundations, do not themselves represent cooperation so much as help to make cooperation more likely.

Meetings for mutual encouragement, often leading to cooperative efforts, occur for specialized groupings of various sorts. In recent days foundation representatives have gravitated together because they were interested in Southeast Asia or were black or were concerned about citizenship education or were puzzled by IRS regulations or hoped to cooperate with the Office of Education, just to mention a few that this writer heard about. Nearly every time we meet, something happens beyond what the foundations represented at the session were already doing. This kind of ad hoc gathering, composed of special groups or based on common interests, can be greatly expanded, with profit to the world of philanthropy and the general welfare.

Cooperation on the national level is best represented by those groups already mentioned, the Council on Foundations, the Foundation Center and the National Council on Philanthropy, in which all who so desire may participate. All the reasons for and types of cooperation to be mentioned below are fostered by these agencies, and it may be that for the first time in the history of American philanthropy the field is now sufficiently organized; the next step must be that those organizations themselves gain sufficient strength to perform their functions well, to win confidence and to give leadership.

To lay the ground work for such a development the Council on Foundations, the Foundation Center and the National Council on Philanthropy moved together in early 1970 to set up a special Committee on the Foundation Field, of which John

ary, 1971, p. 708; "Philanthropy in the Southwest," The Hogg Foundation for Mental Health, University of Texas, Austin, n.d.

Gardner was Chairman, and on which I had the honor of serving with A. A. Heckman of the Hill Foundation, James A. Norton of the Cleveland Foundation and Don K. Price, Dean of Harvard's Kennedy School of Government. Our assignment was to "delineate and examine, in the light of present circumstances, those services that need to be provided to, and functions performed in behalf of, the foundation field; and to recommend an organizational structure for the field most appropriate thereto."[10] The chief structural recommendation of the Committee, that there be a consolidation of the Council on Foundations and the Foundation Center, has been achieved in spirit though not quite fully in fact. The Council and the Center now share offices and have coordinated their work closely, and together they are undertaking the cooperative tasks that the Committee outlined.[11]

Before proceeding to a discussion of those tasks, three further matters in regard to the organizational forms of cooperation need to be quickly noted. First, cooperation with foreign foundations has begun, though just barely, and can be expected to grow modestly in the years ahead. This is being encouraged by the Foundation Center, the International Standing Conference on Philanthropy (INTERPHIL), and the Ditchley Foundation, which sponsored a British-American conference on "The Role of Philanthropy in the 1970s" at Ditchley Park, England, in April, 1972.[12]

Secondly, the most complete form of cooperation imaginable

10. Report, Committee on the Foundation Field, April 15, 1970, submitted to the Council on Foundations, the Foundation Center, and the National Council on Philanthropy, MSS (Hereafter referred to as Report of Gardner Committee). See also "The Gardner Report," *Non-Profit Report*, September, 1971, p. 14.
11. See The Foundation Center, *Annual Report 1971*, p. 10; Council on Foundations, *Annual Report 1971*, p. 4.
12. See H. V. Hodson, "Proposal—A World Foundation Center," *Non-Profit Report*, May 1971, pp. 1–4; "INTERPHIL," brochure of International Standing Conference on Philanthropy, Geneva, Switzerland, n.d.; *Directory of European Foundations*, Torino, Fondazione Giovanni Agnelli, 1969; Nathanial Spear III, a series of seven articles "on foundations abroad," *Foundation News,* from September–October, 1970 to November–December, 1971.

is surely merger. This is indeed being practiced by a few—the joining of Avalon and Old Dominion in the A. W. Mellon Foundation is the most spectacular recent example—and explored by many others—it is rumored that the two Edna McC. Clark Foundations are in process of becoming one. Especially sensible are those mergers in which family funds, too small to employ staff, form or join with community foundations for the better performance of the charitable function.

Third of these brief comments has to do with the suggestion that there be created either a Federal Commission on Foundations as a regulatory agency or a quasi-governmental Advisory Board on Philanthropic Policy, or both. The merits and demerits of these ideas are being widely debated, but neither is likely to be in existence in the immediate future.[13] In any event, each would be an example of the Government's keeping in touch with or tabs on the foundation field, but not an example of cooperation within the field itself. Whatever Government sets up will not substitute for the large and increasing amount of cooperation that foundations themselves must undertake.

The reasons for cooperation are, stated differently, the cooperative tasks. Stretch them out or slice them up, you could have two or ten, or any number you wanted. I have chosen to mention five: The point to remember is that these are not merely the duties of foundations severally, for we have already noted a number of them. These are the tasks that, however much an individual foundation may pursue one or more of them, must be tackled primarily by foundations in concert.[14]

a. As already noted, the first reason and task of cooperation is to communicate better with the public. Present communication, including dissemination of information, is still distressingly unsystematic, even though it is light years removed from the impressionistic, whimsical and often reluctant reporting of only a short while ago. Foundations working together must give

13. See Report of Peterson Commission, *op. cit.*, chaps. 19 & 20; NYU Proceedings, *op. cit.*, Tenth Biennial Conference, pp. 11–12, 22–24.

14. See Report of Gardner Committee, *op. cit.*; Report of Peterson Commission, *op. cit.*, pp. 139–144.

prime attention to the development of various ways of informing the public in toto, and special segments of the public in particular. The development of standards and uniform categories of reporting is not a job for individual foundations, but for the broadly based service agencies, primarily the Foundation Center and the Council on Foundations, and also such groups as the American Association of Fund-Raising Counsel, the National Council on Philanthropy, the Council for Financial Aid to Education, and, not least, the Interal Revenue Service. The foundations themselves can work with these organizations, especially the first two, and this is what must take place if the story is to get fully told and heard.

b. Cooperation must look inward as well as outward. The next major duty is that of exchanging information inside the field. Again, a lone foundation can do very little. It is the service agencies and the publications, *Foundation News* and *Non-Profit Report,* that do and increasingly must spread the word, bad as well as good; but their task can be considerably lightened if the foundations themselves want to have it spread and cooperate to that end.

c. Exchanging information is only the beginning of the inside job. The next level is the discussion of, leading to the assumption of, tasks in common. That such work is already being undertaken, as we have had occasion to note here and there, is harbinger of an even richer future of joint planning and joint action in the sponsorship of broad programs or specific projects or grant series on particular topics. The fear by some foundations of being guilty of collusion was nearly always a bugaboo, and only those who were motivated by political aims such as Patman and Wallace were ever moved to raise the imaginary specter of foundation conspiracy. If it makes increasing sense that hospitals or museums or colleges work together when circumstances permit, foundations are discovering, but not yet fast and fully enough, that it makes sense for them too.

d. A further step beyond cooperating on program is the striking of common cause on the overall determination of philanthropic policy. Each foundation makes, and should make,

246

its own decision in respect to the fields in which it means to work and the methods it intends to employ. But this does not make each foundation *sui generis,* for though its decision on fields and methods may be unique in its details, the basis for its decision, and for its very existence as a foundation, lies in propositions and strategies that apply to other foundations as well, and perhaps to the field of philanthropy as a whole. Later on in this chapter I will elaborate on this position; let me say now that to the extent to which foundations recognize that they follow similar policies and strategies, they are also beginning to recognize the advantage that would accrue from discussing them with one another, hammering them out together, and speaking to the world at large, especially to Government, in the language of common purpose.

This is the primary reason that the Council on Foundations, acting on a suggestion of the Committee on the Foundation Field, added Robert Goheen to its administrative lineup. Forsaking the presidency at Princeton, he is the full-time employed Chairman of the Council, complementing David Freeman as the Council's President, and giving added strength to the effort to state before the public the foundations' philosophical case. There are those, both critics and admirers of foundations, who would have it that this particular task of cooperation boils down simply to lobbying, but this is to cheapen the idea unjustly. Some lobbying is involved, to be sure, and especially with the Federal Government; and it should be recognized that lobbying on its own behalf is an altogether legitimate exercise for the foundation field to take. But lobbying is only a small part of this aspect of cooperation. The main task, now beginning and needing great elaboration, is the joint approach to the defining of the nature and role of philanthropy.[15]

e. Those types and reasons for cooperation mentioned thus far have to do, one way and another, with the content of foundations' work. There remains to be noted one important

15. See Report of Gardner Committee, *op. cit.;* Richard Fitzgerald, "A Conversation with Robert Goheen," *Non-Profit Report,* April, 1972, pp. 9–15; "Chairman-Elect Goheen Emphasizes the Public Interest Role of Foundations", *Newsletter,* Council on Foundations, December, 1971.

cooperative task that is concerned with methodology, namely, the setting and observance of high standards of behavior for the foundation field.

Everybody praises righteousness and feels the other fellow should comply. But once questions of definition of standards, accreditation and policing are raised, the consensus breaks up. Some conscientious foundation people, such as F. Emerson Andrews, Orville Brim, John Gardner (in 1964), Manning Pattillo and Murray Rossant, have called at one time or another for setting up a code of conduct or adopting and seeking to enforce some basic principles of good management. Other equally conscientious philanthropoids, such as John Gardner's Committee on the Foundation Field (in 1970), and Alan Pifer, Warren Weaver and Donald Young, question whether a specific code, especially as it would probably entail accrediting and policing activities, is either wise or possible.[16]

But the differences are not as great as they appear to be at first. Serious students of foundation behavior, including foundation executives without exception, so far as I am aware, feel it crucially important that a set of standards be persuasively enunciated and increasingly observed. The differences are on what the standards should specify, though there is a large consensus here, and on how regulation or self-regulation in light of the standards should be achieved. A growing number of foundation people both hope and expect that the Council on Foundations will assert leadership in this regard commensurate

16. For various points of view on self-regulation, codes of conduct, accreditation and related topics, see: Eleanor K. Taylor, *Public Accountability of Foundations and Charitable Trusts*, New York, Russell Sage Foundation, 1953, chap. 6; John Gardner, *Annual Report, Carnegie Corporation of New York, 1964;* Mortimer M. Caplin, "A Code of Practice Is Needed," Donald R. Young, "A Foundation Code of Practice: A Negative View," and John W. Riehm, Jr., "More Is Needed Than a Code of Practice," NYU Proceedings, *op. cit.*, Seventh Biennial Conference; Weaver, *op. cit.*, pp. 204–205; Manning M. Pattillo, Jr., "Principles of Foundation Management," *Foundation News*, May–June, 1968; Yorke Allen, Jr., "Self-Regulation by Foundations," unpublished monograph, September 23, 1969, MSS; Richard H. Sullivan, in The Foundation Center, *Annual Report 1970;* Report of Gardner Committee, *op. cit.*, Alan Cranston, "Foundations on Trial," *op. cit.;* Richard Fitzgerald, "Foundation Standards and Accrediting," *Non-Profit Report*, January, 1972, pp. 1–14.

with its new stature as the most representative body that the field has ever had. Unless foundations are willing to turn over completely to Government the defining and enforcing of acceptable philanthropic behavior, the setting of standards and the encouragement of their observance may prove to be the most important single form of cooperation, and reason for cooperation, among foundations.

C. A Basic Rationale

Each foundation bears responsibility for putting its own house in order. That is to say, each foundation should clarify its own purpose and function, strengthen its own organizational and financial structure, plan carefully its program and operating policy and engage in communication with the public and fruitful cooperation with other foundations. But the most important task of all is one that no single foundation can do even for itself. A great many foundations are going to have to work on it, in conjunction with a lot of other thoughtful people outside the foundation field. This task is the development of a basic rationale.

The implication is intentional. Though there may be exceptions here and there, foundations as a class do not possess a basic rationale on which all, or the great majority, agree and which informs all their work. We are not talking now about performance, the grounds on which foundations have usually been criticized, whether justly or no. We are talking, rather, about the fundamental justification for the existence of foundations, the philosophy that defends their being even when and if, on occasion, they perform poorly. As a foundation man, I am forced to take the outrageous position that, as a class, foundations do not have a basic rationale and do not know what it ought to be.

But we have made some good beginnings. By virtue of the thoughtful philosophizing of philanthropists and observers in recent years we who are concerned about such a subject today do not have to start from scratch. Perhaps the person most responsible for initiating the broad and serious discussion of foundation philosophy is F. Emerson Andrews, once on the staff of the Russell Sage Foundation and known most widely for his leadership of the Foundation Center and for his authorship of various books and treatises. Others have contributed much to the philosophical discussion: Dean Rusk, Albert Sacks, Milton Katz, Warren Weaver, Donald Young and Alan Pifer.[17] These and other leaders have brought us to the threshold of finding a central, persuasive justification for the existence and continuing activity of foundations in American life.

The available rudiments of a rationale begin with the assertion that foundations are essential to the free society. Most of those who think about foundations affirmatively base their position in one or another version of this seminal thought.

Such an essentially simple position encapsulates some profound observations. What "society"? How and why "free"? And in what sense "essential"? To proclaim the position, as many of us in foundation work like to do, involves us in a philosophical justification for foundation activity far beyond what we normally have the time or inclination to recognize.

The "society" is, of course, the whole society, not some one arbitrary segment of it. Individual foundations may indeed limit their activities by choice, necessity or both to some one group or segment of the society, and this is altogether understandable and defensible. What is not defensible, however, is

17. See Andrews, op. cits.; Dean Rusk, The Role of the Foundation in American Life, Claremont, California, Claremont University College, 1961; Albert M. Sacks, "The Role of Philanthropy: An Institutional View," Virginia Law Review, April, 1960 (excerpts in Reeves, op. cit., pp. 63–75); Milton Katz, The Modern Foundation: Its Dual Character, Public and Private, New York, The Foundation Library Center, 1968, "Occasional Papers: Number Two"; Weaver, op. cits.; Young, op. cits.; Pifer, op. cits., and The Foundation in the Year 2000, New York, The Foundation Library Center, 1968, "Occasional Papers: Number One."

For other useful "think" pieces see: Cranston, op. cit.; Calkins, op. cit.; Fosdick, op. cit.; Douglas Dillon, "The Role of Private Philanthropy in Modern American Society," Rockefeller Foundation, 1971; Kenneth E. Boulding, "Towards a Pure Theory of Foundations," Non-Profit Report, Special Insert, March, 1972; Martha R. Wallace, "The Foundation Meets the Fund Raiser," Foundation News, January–February, 1971, pp. 1–5; Kenneth W. Thompson, "The Future and the Foundations," Foundation News, September–October, 1970, pp. 183–187; Fritz F. Heimann, "Developing a Contemporary Rationale for Foundations," Foundation News, January–February, 1972, pp. 7–13.

for that foundation to argue that only one or another segment of society is worthy of foundation activity or philanthropic concern. Activity has to be limited; basic justification must not be. Foundations as a class must be concerned about the national interest as a whole.

This society or nation is thought of as "free." A multitude of meanings can be given to the word, but when we use the term to characterize a society in which foundations are justified and needed, we usually have reference to a form of democratic Government, with place in it for both consent and dissent.

We have reference, further, to the fact that our kind of Government is not all-embracing, and though it addresses itself to the national interest, it does not pretend to accomplish all needed actions on behalf of the general welfare. In our kind of society, Government or the so-called public sector will indeed be big—too big for some, not big enough for others—but it does not commandeer the total range of human interest and need. Whether more or less than it has been and/or ought to be—arguments can always be raised about those various possibilities—the so-called private sector does exist and foundations are part of it.

"Essential" means, then, that we must have both public and private institutions, and both public and private concern for the general welfare. We noted in Chapter I that "private" is a slippery word, and we must be careful when we use it to disavow any anti-governmental or anti-social overtones. We mean for it to carry the connotations of non-governmental and public-spirited. Surely a sound, defensible philosophy for foundations must put great store upon the fact that they are *private* institutions in this sense, and that in our type of free society such institutions are immensely useful.

To a political extremist of any hue a justifiable philosophy might well seem to be contributory to the opposite extreme. Far left would probably look on a sound charter for philanthropy as a sell-out to the right wing; far right would see it as a support for left-leaning subversion. In truth of course it would be neither; rather, it should be middle-of-the-road, and thus capable of being interpreted as supportive for any political

251

position that was itself toward the middle of the road. Never either-or; always both-and.

In other words, foundations must take the two-fold position that Government ought not to be the whole show and that Government has an immensely important part to play. The foundations' stance in respect to the importance of the private sector, therefore, consists in feeling that they neither should nor could substitute for Government but that justification for them requires finding ways to complement and supplement Government. This free society as a totality possesses all sorts of interests, needs and problems. Government cannot, and cannot be expected to, solve them all. Foundations find their primary excuse for being in their joining with Government, private and public together, in addressing the condition of the life around.

All kinds of complementarity and supplementation, even active cooperation, are possible, and many that are either practiced already or recommended can be used as prospectus for the basic rationale. Government can do some things better than foundations: then let foundations stay away from those activities. Foundations can undoubtedly do some things better than Government: then let foundations do so, not only for much of their activity but also for their excuse for being in those areas.

Foundations can or should be able to experiment more widely and freely than Government; they can innovate, play around with new ideas, take risks, even show partiality for one or another group on occasion. Increasingly accountable in general, foundations are not subject to the ballot box as the personnel and organs of Government inevitably are. Pluralism in general is probably a good thing. Ours is a pluralistic society, and foundations can encourage its tendencies to remain so. All these and similar insights are used to buttress the position that foundations are essential to a free society and that we must have a strong, imaginative private sector to match the vigor of the public domain.

So much for what we usually say. This is where our justification often stops, and this is exactly where it is imperative that we try to keep going. Foundations should take risks, remember?

If the proper role of foundations is to complement and supplement the role of Government in the service of the total society, then the ideals of foundations, even as also the ideals of Government, must take full cognizance of, and possess basic congruence with, society's ideals and goals. Notice what we are saying: no foundation's proper goal is the protection or enhancement of any one person's bias or whim, a donor's, a manager's or anyone else's. Foundations exist by the grace of the public; that is, we receive exemption and other status at the hands of the law, in order to serve the general welfare or some acceptable portion of it. So does Government. And the society, through the electorate, is continuingly informing the Government as to the elements of the general welfare that are in need of its attention.

By virtue of the fact that foundations are in the private, not the public, sector, they possess a measure of freedom in respect to the needs of the society and the definition of the general welfare which the Government often cannot exercise. But neither a foundation nor any other class of agencies in the private sector is free to ignore, scorn or treat frivolously society's own understanding of its needs and problems.

Consider the difference between a person and a foundation on this point. Any individual can waste his substance in riotous living if he so chooses, and though the moralists may inveigh against him, he has not overstepped the bounds of what his society allows even if it does not always approve. But if a foundation is to be true to the only proposition that can serve as a sound rationale for its existence, it simply does not have the liberty to waste its resources. No matter that foundations may not always live up to what they should stand for, the philosophy that undergirds them must maintain that they exist, along with Government, to tackle and try to solve the major problems of the society.

The problems themselves are defined, at least in part, by the ideals. Segregation is no problem unless an integrated community is the ideal. Discrimination is no problem unless equal

253

opportunity is the ideal. Disease and pollution are no problems unless health and a clean environment are the ideals. Injustice and the miscarriage of justice are no problems unless an even-handed treatment for all persons is the ideal. War and conflict among nations are not really problems—why get worked up about killing strangers?—unless peace and brotherhood are ideals.

Pushed by the logic of society's demands on both public and private sectors, one arrives at the surprising proposition that foundations cannot justify their existence unless they accept as their own the virtues and values espoused by the social order of which they are a part. To the cynic this could say very little. To the institution determined to protect some selfish interest, this could say something quite threatening. But to the overwhelming number of foundations in this country wanting to find a philosophy that can justify their continued philan-thropic activity, this may be the most important insight for them to examine and eventually affirm.

The central ideals of America constitute and define the much-maligned American Dream, or the even more cliché-ridden American Way of Life. Declaration of Independence, Gettys-burg Address, Pledge of Allegiance to the Flag, "America the Beautiful,"—these and scores of other shorthand ways of saying what we as people believe and want to see our nation increas-ingly become, are useful ingredients for a summary of founda-tions' purposes.

Let us not hesitate, then, to draw the conclusion: A founda-tion is not a-moral. It is not a secular institution, in the sense of being morally neutral. On the contrary, it is an ethical enterprise. And it will never understand itself accurately until it understands itself in this fashion and confesses as much.

The preposterous truth is, foundations have got to want to go around doing good. Since they do not constitute a religion, or even the institutions of a religion, they don't pretend to define the good. They let the society do that—the democratic heritage, the Hebrew-Christian tradition, or what have you. Moreover, they need not be blatantly righteous about doing good. In fact, to protest as much is to make the performance suspect. Like some other non-profit agencies that desire to be effective, foundations may sometimes wish to assume publicly a toughness of temper that they dare not possess.

Such a pose may be provoked by the knowledge that doing good is a thankless task and the do-gooder a term of reproach. But the immoral ones according to any ethical standard have always jeered at the moral, and foundations cannot escape the penalty of their own essential nature if they are true to it. Foundations are square. There is hardly a swinger in the lot. The point, however, is not that this is their actual state; the point, rather, is that they are normatively square and simply cannot get around it.

A moral quality, then, resides in the very nature of the foundation as an institution. Lest this seem pretentious, however, let it be noted that this is no less so than is true for almost any other non-profit, public-service institution, for the hospital or the university or the church. This is true even when individual members of the institutional group violate the moral quality which they ought to embody. A hospital can turn away a very ill person who is unable to prove he can pay the bill, but that doesn't make it a guardian of the community's health. A university can be a gouging slum landlord, but that doesn't demonstrate its academic excellence. A church can sponsor a segregated private school, but that doesn't help it spread the gospel. Individual foundations can be as unethical as individual anything-else, but this does not contradict—in fact, it may simply underline—the prevailing and inescapable moral dimension that characterizes the field as a whole.

But unless some specific moral qualities can be named that apply or ought to apply to foundations as a species, then the general position that organized philanthropy is an ethical enterprise ends up by being nothing more than sweet sentiment. What *is* the good that foundations by nature must serve? What are the values and virtues they must believe in?

Perhaps it needs to be said at this point, though parenthetically, that to raise such questions is not to open up new ground. The answers I am about to suggest are present in nearly every discussion of desirable foundation behavior. The only difference—and the only excuse for saying such things

255

here—is that these values are usually mentioned descriptively, whereas they deserve to be recognized definitively. To illustrate what I mean, let me take a value that doesn't apply, even though in the hierarchy of values it is said to be next to godliness. But suppose it did apply: my complaint is that most commentators say that a foundation should be clean, whereas my position is that it should go deeper than simply the practice of bathing—it should *believe* in it.

Out of what could be a lengthy list I will mention four values that serve to shape the peculiar character of foundations. It is my view, further, that if and when foundations become fully aware of their need to possess these four, they will thereby develop certain sensitivities to their role in society—we shall take note of three—that can make their philanthropy more fruitful.

The first represents a confession that I spoke too soon, in one sense, in denigration of cleanliness. Like everybody else, a foundation needs to have clean hands; and more, to possess integrity in its inner being. Only then will it have integrity in its dealings.

The second value in which foundations need to believe is universality of outlook. All foundations work under diverse limits all the time, but such particularity is a strategy they must pursue, not a philosophy they can afford to adopt. Particularity is justifiable because limitations of size or geography cannot be overcome, or because setting boundaries of subject and project makes achievement more likely. But universality must be the mood even when the action has to be focussed. The Pocket-change Fund may be capable of doing no more than helping the Chicano kindergarten on the south side of town, but its reason for doing so needs to be that it believes in education for all youngsters everywhere.

Which leads to the third value, a concern for humanity both in general and in particular. Foundations are in the business of benefitting people, nothing less, ultimately nothing else. To fund an art museum or cancer research, dinosaur study or plant exploration, is to have found a proximate task for the service of an ultimate goal—unless, of course, the funding agency

256

doesn't want anyone to appreciate the art or be helped by the research or develop new understandings of time and space.

The concern for humanity may be no more than embryonic. Likely, many a foundation goes through the motions of its regular round without ever bringing to conscious attention the love of mankind that alone could justify those motions. But this is not to suppose that it has some other, certainly not some better, motivation. This is simply to say that, for a foundation, the performance of the daily task is apt to be largely reflex, even as would be the case for any other outfit. When thought does accompany deed—that is, if a foundation is ever forced to say why—either it roots its efforts in a belief in the importance of persons, and thus the importance of benevolence on their behalf, or it discovers its efforts have no rootage at all.

Make no mistake about why a foundation exists. Give no half-way answer. It exists on the basis of a belief in the primary worth of human beings, as shaky a proposition as the rational mind ever encountered and as indispensable. Its *raison d'être* is to serve them.

We are not in the habit of calling the fourth a virtue or a value. Yet it is indeed a recognition that a foundation needs to make about itself, a belief having ethical significance that is basic to its self-understanding. This is the recognition of frailty, the belief in sin. As it applies to a foundation it is the realization—the consciously accepted value, if you will—that giving is potentially an immoral act. Jesus is supposed to have said that it is more blessed to give than to receive, though it was Paul, who wasn't there, who attributed it to him. When Jesus summed up his own list of blesseds, benevolence was absent, yet he believed in it—viz., the story of the Good Samaritan. But on more than one occasion he took pains to point out that giving was ethically dangerous.

Its danger lies in its assumption of virtue by the agent, of the virtue of agentry, with an accompanying train of other unvirtuous assumptions. The relatively innocent desire to help is so thinly distinguished from wanting to be the helper. But the latter is capable of all sorts of distortions: wanting to be

257

widely known as the helper, wanting to make some decisions for the helpee, wanting to dictate, to paternalize, to manipulate. It is not likely that a foundation, any more than a person, will escape these faults by thoughtlessness or accident. Only by being conscious of the danger is there chance to escape. In other words, a foundation must believe in the potential immorality of giving.

So much, then, for four essential values out of the many it might be useful for a foundation to possess: integrity, universality of outlook, concern for humanity and recognition of the potentially immoral character of giving. No foundation, in fact, is ever likely to possess these in full and sufficient measure, is ever likely to operate consistently in their light with nary a slip. These are what a foundation needs to believe even though it doesn't always emulate them. They are the value baggage of the archetype, the prototypical foundation.

Believing them even when not always practicing them, a foundation will develop some insights into its station and role, some sensitivities as to its natural condition, that will see it through its times of stress and fend off its bent toward self-deception. Maybe a foundation can squeeze into the Beatitudes after all: "Blessed are those who hunger and thirst after righteousness . . . blessed are ye when [Congress]men shall revile you and persecute you and say all manner of evil against you falsely."

The first sensitivity is to the limited effect of a foundation, no matter the size and oomph of its effort. It is always the catalyst, almost never the decisive agent. As Albert M. Sacks has written, "The inadequacies of philanthropy overshadow its virtues, and it must in the end rest content with 'capillary' action."[18] We noted this matter in Chapter IV, as a comment on the actual achievements of foundations. Now we note it not merely as a fact of their behavior, but as an important attitude they need to possess toward their activity. Any foundation must be prepared to recognize that it should inevitably play a dependent role, not only with government because it has to, but also with its own recipients because it is right to. The

18. Quoted by Reeves, *op. cit.,* p. 72.

258

respect that a foundation must have for a recipient, in order for the foundation to have felt the recipient to be worthy of a grant, should be of such an order as to spare the foundation from delusions of grandeur.

A second insight has to do with that favorite form of self-justification, the innovative function that foundations should perform. As I've made clear earlier on, I have no quarrel with the "venture capital" line of thought, for surely foundations ought to be alert to the new idea, the fresh approach, the different and perhaps better strategy. The only trouble with this philosophy is that it often reads as if innovation should be an end in itself, the great, overarching excuse of a foundation's existence.

As I see it, this is not the case. Innovation is derivative; it is a tactic responsive to the presumed non-innovative behavior of Government. Well and good; let us then use it when the situation calls for it. But let us also be prepared to be conservative at times. The values we have been thinking about do not command innovation alone. They direct us to examine the situation as dispassionately as possible, and then they fortify us for responding to that situation as best we can, with the old or with the new. Our values tell us that innovation is fine if it isn't a fetish.

Finally, we note how fragile is a foundation. Just about the time it seems to have set its course, a change in mood in Congress or the media or the public generally or among its own donors, trustees and staff, can make it into something completely different from what it was. Changes can be for both the better and the worse, of course, and in any event one does not deplore change per se. But that they can occur so quickly and so thoroughly suggests that when a foundation sees to do good it must do it forthwith; otherwise, it may lose its chance.

In this regard the difference between foundations and other non-profit ameliorative institutions may be considerable. The urgency of time may not be quite as great on the others. Next week if not this may be time enough for those institutions with a firmer continuity to accomplish their aim.

But foundations rest on a disposition which tends to be

259

evanescent in nature. The philanthropic urge is seldom as compelling as hunger or sex or the need for sleep. Earning and saving, we noted at the start, receive more sanction than giving. Foundations are part of the fragile, ephemeral world of philanthropy.

This is why when they are attacked unjustly it is a serious matter. Critics need to be set straight, less irreparable harm be done. This is also why when they are attacked justly it is similarly serious. The foundations themselves need to set things straight, lest the harm done be deserved. Finally, this is why their accomplishments should be understood and appreciated. Selfishness needs no encouragement, but whenever the seed of genuine regard and service for one's fellowmen begins to grow, it needs watering.

For all their fragility, however, it would not be true to the nature of foundations if we were to end on a note of weakness. As part of the activity of philanthropy in general, and as evidence of a belief in the value of benevolence, foundations are as strong as love is strong. To earn and to save seem somehow dated, caught in a Puritan ethic, but to give is a universal imperative.

Index